Jewish Legal Theories

THE TAUBER INSTITUTE SERIES FOR
THE STUDY OF EUROPEAN JEWRY
    Jehuda Reinharz, General Editor
    ChaeRan Freeze, Associate Editor
    Sylvia Fuks Fried, Associate Editor
    Eugene R. Sheppard, Associate Editor

THE BRANDEIS LIBRARY OF MODERN JEWISH THOUGHT
    Eugene R. Sheppard and Samuel Moyn, Editors

This library aims to redefine the canon of modern Jewish thought by publishing primary source readings from individual Jewish thinkers or groups of thinkers in reliable English translations. Designed for courses in modern Jewish philosophy, thought, and intellectual history, each volume features a general introduction and annotations to each source with the instructor and student in mind.

Jewish Legal Theories: Writings on State, Religion, and Morality
    Leora Batnitzky and Yonatan Y. Brafman, editors
Sabbatian Heresy: Writings on Mysticism, Messianism, and the Origins of Jewish Modernity
    Pawel Maciejko, editor
Modern Middle Eastern Jewish Thought: Writings on Identity, Politics, and Culture, 1893–1958
    Moshe Behar and Zvi Ben-Dor Benite, editors
Jews and Diaspora Nationalism: Writings on Jewish Peoplehood in Europe and the United States
    Simon Rabinovitch, editor
Moses Mendelssohn: Writings on Judaism, Christianity, and the Bible
    Michah Gottlieb, editor
Jews and Race: Writings on Identity and Difference, 1880–1940
    Mitchell B. Hart, editor

FOR THE COMPLETE LIST OF BOOKS THAT ARE FORTHCOMING IN
THE SERIES, PLEASE SEE HTTP://WWW.BRANDEIS.EDU/TAUBER

Jewish Legal Theories

Edited by
Leora Batnitzky and
Yonatan Y. Brafman

WRITINGS ON

STATE, RELIGION,

AND MORALITY

Brandeis University Press

Waltham, Massachusetts

BRANDEIS UNIVERSITY PRESS

An imprint of University Press of New England

www.upne.com

© 2018 Brandeis University

All rights reserved

Manufactured in the United States of America

Designed by Eric M. Brooks

Typeset in Albertina and Verlag by Passumpsic Publishing

For permission to reproduce any of the material in this book, contact Permissions, University Press of New England, One Court Street, Suite 250, Lebanon NH 03766; or visit www.upne.com

Library of Congress Cataloging-in-Publication Data

NAMES: Batnitzky, Leora, 1956– editor.

TITLE: Jewish legal theories : writings on state, religion, and morality / edited by Leora Batnitzky and Yonatan Y. Brafman.

DESCRIPTION: Waltham: Brandeis University Press, 2017. | Series: The Tauber Institute series for the study of European Jewry | Series: The Brandeis library of modern Jewish thought | Includes bibliographical references and index.

IDENTIFIERS: LCCN 2017018673 (print) | LCCN 2017031963 (ebook) | ISBN 9781512601350 (epub, mobi, & pdf) | ISBN 9781584657439 (cloth: alk. paper) | ISBN 9781584657446 (pbk.: alk. paper)

SUBJECTS: LCSH: Jewish law. | Judaism and state. | Judaism and politics.

CLASSIFICATION: LCC BM520.2 (ebook) | LCC BM520.2 .J49 2017 (print) | DDC 296.1/801—dc23

LC record available at https://lccn.loc.gov/2017018673

5 4 3 2 1

Contents

Foreword

It is a privilege to welcome this volume on Jewish legal theories into the Brandeis Library of Modern Jewish Thought. To both its exponents and enemies, ancient and modern, Judaism places law, law following, and law interpretation at its core. Debates over how to make sense of the law continued for millennia, and the approaches to interpretation that Jews developed have long invited comparison with parallel theories of law in other traditions and in modern secular thought. But since the eighteenth century, it has not been just the interpretation of Jewish law that continued to change, for Jews gained entry to the circle of state citizenship, eventually on equal terms with their hosts. As a result, Jews had to abandon or reconfigure the separate legal authority they had struggled to maintain over their communities previously, making Judaism a religion like others, with faith a private affair. In their pioneering collection of sources, Leora Batnitzky and Yonatan Brafman have given readers unique insights into these transformations, at a time when the study of Jewish law is burgeoning as a topic of interest in the secular university, coming to match its centrality to traditional Jewish education. For readers in both settings, Batnitzky and Brafman have provided an exciting set of materials that track the modernization of the Jewish people and their struggles to resolve the relationship of their ancestral law to the nation-state and secular citizenship. The volume concludes with sections on how these dynamics changed when Jews turned to found their own state in the twentieth century and on Jewish feminism's understanding of law and legal interpretation. The volume is unprecedented and furnishes the best starting point to revisit the ancient theme of the Jews and their law in a new era.

Samuel Moyn and Eugene R. Sheppard, Editors
The Brandeis Library of Modern Jewish Thought

Acknowledgments

We would like to thank Samuel Moyn and Eugene Sheppard, the editors of this series; Sylvia Fuks Fried, the executive director of the Tauber Institute for the Study of European Jewry at Brandeis University; and Phyllis Deutsch, editor in chief of the University Press of New England, for their support, patience, and very helpful feedback throughout the process of putting this volume together. We are extremely grateful to the many translators for their excellent work on the selections translated into English for the first time in this volume. The work of the translators would not have been possible without the financial support of Brandeis University's Tauber Institute and Princeton University's Center for Human Values, Council of the Humanities, Committee on Research in the Humanities and the Social Sciences, and Program in Judaic Studies. We thank all of these organizations for their generosity. We thank Shira Billet, Simeon Cohen, and Mark Lettney for research and administrative assistance and Sally Freedman for her help in the final stages of editing this manuscript. We are also grateful to Daniel Brafman, Benjamin Brown, Menachem Butler, Yakir Englander, Adam Ferziger, Lawrence Kaplan, Ysoscher Katz, Yehudah Mirsky, Chaim Saiman, Marc B. Shapiro, Michael K. Silber, Norman Solomon, and Elli Stern for their important help as we conceived and worked on this volume. Finally, a special note of thanks to Suzanne Last Stone, who has supported and encouraged us both, along with many others, as we have thought about Jewish law and legal theory.

Introduction
Leora Batnitzky and Yonatan Y. Brafman

The readings included in this volume all attempt, explicitly or implicitly, to characterize what Jewish law is—hence, the title of the volume, *Jewish Legal Theories*, by which we simply mean theories of what Jewish law is. As the reader will see, there is not just one modern Jewish legal theory, but rather many diverse and often competing ones. The volume focuses on modern Jewish legal theories from 1670 to 2010. This introductory essay describes continuities between modern Jewish legal theories and their premodern predecessors, as well as affinities between modern Jewish legal theories and modern legal theories more generally. The first part of the essay introduces the different kinds of sources, practical legal questions, and recurring premodern interpretative themes that appear throughout this volume. The second and third parts of the essay consider the development of modern Jewish legal theories in the broader context of the development of modern legal theories. We argue that modern Jewish legal theories, like their secular counterparts, emerged only in the framework of the rise of the sovereign nation-state. For this reason, we point out that while arguments about Jewish law are often used to claim continuity between the Jewish present and past, modern Jewish legal theories also represent a break between modern and premodern Judaism. Against the background of this argument, the third part of this essay also describes the different parts of this volume and how they fit together.

Themes and Continuities in Modern Jewish Legal Theories

In this volume we have included material from philosophical and theological treatises, *responsa* (practical decisions offered by a rabbinic decisor in response to a specific question), and both public and private debates between scholars and rabbis. Some of the texts, whether philosophical or more rabbinic in style, explicitly offer a theory of Jewish law. Others, in contrast, display a theory of law only in their argumentation. We hope that the variety of sources will give the reader some sense of the different forms in which modern debates about Jewish law have taken place. We have tried to complement the theoretical material with debates about practical legal problems. At the same time, we have tried to make the implicit theoretical assumptions undergirding practical arguments more explicit. Given constraints of space, we have included shorter excerpts from material that has been previously published in English and have reserved more space for selections that are translated here for the first time from Hebrew and German. We also chose not to include any living thinkers in the first four parts of this volume. We made this choice since many arguments made by contemporary Jewish legal theorists echo the sources included in this volume. We hope this volume will provide readers with a framework through which to explore the arguments of living Jewish legal theorists. It was not possible to apply the same distinction between living and deceased authors to the selections included in part 5, on feminist approaches to Jewish law. These approaches are much more recent, and there simply are not earlier sources on which to draw.

A number of practical legal problems recur throughout the volume, along with different proposed solutions. Arguments about practical matters bring with them assumptions about what Jewish law is, who the Jews are, and who has the authority to answer these first two questions. For instance, the question of whether Jewish women should be permitted to vote in national elections comes up in different parts of this volume. Different opinions about whether Jewish law can change—which include assumptions about whether a later court can undermine the decision of an earlier court, whether underlying principles guide Jewish law, whether Jewish law can conform to state law, whether Zionism presents a new egalitarian framework for Jewish law, and whether it is necessary to clarify the distinction between law and custom—lead to different answers to the question. Arguments across ideological perspectives about whether it is permissible to sell land in Israel to non-Jews or whether in vitro fertilization is permissible are similarly based on presumed answers to many questions about the scope of Jewish law (should rabbinic authorities worry about nonobservant Jews?) and basic questions of identity (does Jewish law posit an essential difference between Jews and non-Jews?). Arguments about whether there is a tension between Jewish law and democracy ought to be of interest to many people today. Is it possible to have a theocracy that is also democratic? And is it possible in a democratic society to live in a self-enclosed religious community governed by religious law?

A number of central premodern themes and figures persist in modern arguments about the nature of Jewish law. The most basic theoretical issue with which modern Jewish legal theories must grapple is central to any consideration of Jewish law: the relationship between what is called the oral and the written law. The Hebrew terms for what are often translated (generally into German and English) as the oral and written law are actually the Oral Torah (*Torah she-be'al peh*) and the Written Torah (*Torah she-bikhtav*). It is perhaps easiest to define the Oral Torah by what it is not: the Written Torah—that is, the Pentateuch. Yet even this definition is complicated since the Oral Torah is also written down in the form of the Talmud, which is composed of two parts: the Mishnah and the Gemara. The Mishnah, canonized in the second century CE, reflects the oral commentary (written down) on the Hebrew Bible of a group of rabbis known as the Tannaim (Aramaic for "repeaters"). The Gemara is the oral commentary (also written down) on the Mishnah by a later group of rabbis known as the Amoraim (Aramaic for "sayers"). There are actually two Talmuds, the Palestinian and the Babylonian, which reflect the oral commentary on the Mishnah of rabbis in Palestine and Babylonia, respectively. Scholars tend to date the canonization of the Palestinian Talmud to the fifth century CE and the Babylonian Talmud to the sixth century. Almost all of the thinkers included in this volume refer to the Babylonian Talmud, which remains the authoritative text of rabbinic Judaism. Subsequent oral traditions were also written down. Nonetheless, all of these texts—unlike the Pentateuch—constitute the Oral Torah. Arguably, any oral teaching, written down or not, could constitute Oral Torah.[1]

On the one hand, the idea that there is a relation between the Written and the Oral Torah and that the rabbis are the gatekeepers of the Oral Torah constitutes rabbinic Judaism. But on the other hand, the Talmud does not offer a clear-cut answer to what exactly constitutes the relation between the Oral and the Written Torah. The issues here are simultaneously theological and legal. Was the Oral Torah given to Moses at Sinai along with the Written Torah? If so, why is there a continual need for interpretation? If not, what kind of authoritative status does the Oral Torah have? Do the rabbis merely channel the Oral Torah, or is the Oral Torah itself a creative human act? In the Oral Torah's more minimalist form, the rabbis play no active role in formulating it. In its more maximalist form, the activity of the rabbis itself can be understood as Oral Torah. Both perspectives can be found in rabbinic sources. Yet either viewpoint raises problematic questions about the nature of revelation and about whether it is possible to separate human authority from divine authority. Can the Oral Torah directly contradict the Written Torah? And how can different aspects of the Oral Torah seem to contradict each other? The Talmud offers many answers to these questions, as do subsequent rabbinic thinkers. In the modern period, arguments about the relation between the Oral and Written Torah become the contested arena of rabbinic authority. The reader will see that in some times and places in the modern period, making a direct claim to rabbinic authority in determining the Oral Torah actually undermines rabbinic authority, while at other times it has the opposite effect.

Like any legal theory, modern Jewish legal theories must answer the question of whether and how law might change. This is both a theoretical issue pertaining to different understandings of the Oral Torah's relation to the Written Torah and very much a practical issue. Throughout the volume, different rabbinic scholars deal with this problem by focusing on the question of whether a later rabbinical court has the authority to overturn an earlier court's decision. This question is the central location for discussions of legal change, which become important for all these modern figures. The question is also ripe for theorizing about how the "system" of Jewish law works. Many modern Jewish legal thinkers turn to the great medieval Jewish philosopher and jurist, Maimonides (Moses ben Maimon [1135 or 1138–1204], also known as Rambam) to make their arguments. Maimonides is important to a wide variety of modern Jewish legal theorists largely because he is one of the few premodern Jewish thinkers to offer explicit political and legal theories. Yet Maimonides' writing has been used both by those who wish to forestall change in Jewish law and by those who wish to advance change. Maimonides interprets Deuteronomy 13:1 ("All this that I command you, you shall observe, you should not add or subtract anything from it") as prohibiting the amendment of biblical law.[2] And he interprets Deuteronomy 17:11 ("You shall act in accordance with the instruction given you and ruling handed down to you; you must not deviate from the verdict that they announce to you either to the right or to the left") as endowing rabbinic commandments with biblical authority.[3] Eighteenth- and nineteenth-century proponents of what we call today Ultra-Orthodoxy infer that even rabbinic law cannot be changed. Yet Maimonides' views on this issue are complex and can be interpreted in a number of ways. In fact, in the twentieth century, his views were used to argue for the possibility of adapting Jewish law to the new Zionist reality. On the one hand, he explicitly allows a court to reject the interpretations of biblical law of previous courts that it believes are in error.[4] While this seems to allow a great deal of freedom to change Jewish law, interpreters were quick to point out that it is inconsistent with the authority of the Mishnah and Talmud and thus devised explanations for why contemporary courts lack this power. On the other hand, Maimonides directly bars a court from overturning even the rabbinic enactments and decrees of an earlier court unless certain circumstances are met.

It is disagreement over what these circumstances are that lead some rabbinic scholars to argue that even rabbinic law can change in some circumstances and others to argue that it cannot.[5]

Any legal theory must not only answer the question of whether law can change but also consider the basis on which particular laws might change. Different readings throughout the volume turn to another medieval rabbinical sage, Naḥmanides (Moses ben Naḥman [1194–1270], also known as Ramban), in answering this question. Following Maimonides, Naḥmanides sought to articulate particular principles by which law changes. These principles are not external to the Oral Torah but internal and implicit within it. Naḥmanides argues that since particular laws cannot account for every possible human situation, rabbinic sages must turn to these principles to decide what must be done in a particular situation. These general principles are found in scripture in verses such as "Do not curse the deaf or put a stumbling block before the blind" (Lev. 19:14). In implementing the underlying principles of law, rabbinic scholars might appear to be changing laws. Yet what appears to be change is actually a product of the law's own internal principles.

In the history of modern legal theory, the American legal philosopher Ronald Dworkin (1931–2013) famously employs an argument about principles to criticize legal positivism, which we can broadly define as the distinctly modern claim that law constitutes a sphere of its own and as such ought to be understood as distinct from political and moral values. Dworkin argues that legal positivism cannot account for legal change because the positivist attempt to describe law as devoid of underlying values misses the fact that principles, as distinct from rules, are internal to law. A principle, for Dworkin, is "a standard that is to be observed."[6] While Dworkin employs his claim about principles to further particular liberal and progressive rights-oriented ideals in the English-speaking world of the late twentieth century, modern Jewish legal theories use Naḥmanides' argument about principles to advance a large variety of ideological positions. In the nineteenth century Abraham Geiger (1810–74), the intellectual founder of Reform Judaism, draws on Naḥmanides to argue that Jewish law is no longer relevant in the modern era. Geiger believes that his argument does not undermine Jewish law but actually is consistent with the underlying principles that have guided the ways in which Jewish law has changed over time. (Geiger also draws on Maimonides' historical account of the development of Jewish law to make this argument).[7] But Naḥmanides is also used to defend the ongoing vitality of Jewish law. For instance, in the late twentieth century, the religious

Zionist Eliezer Berkovits (1908–92) interprets Naḥmanides much as Geiger does, yet he uses Naḥmanides to argue not only for the binding nature of Jewish law but also for Zionism.[8] Indeed, in the twentieth century, Conservative, Orthodox, Zionist, and even Ultra-Orthodox rabbis turn to Naḥmanides in making arguments about principles that are inherent in Jewish law. Some argue that these principles invite significant change to Jewish law, while others maintain that the principles actually confirm that change is not possible.

As we will discuss in the next section of this introduction, the attempt to delineate a category of law as distinct from other categories is central to the development of modern legal theory. This issue plays out in modern Jewish legal theories in two different debates, the first about whether law can be separated from moral and theological reasoning, and the second about whether law can be separated from custom. The first debate concerns rabbinic deliberation about the possibility of offering reasons for biblical commandments. This debate in rabbinic literature is known as *ta'amei ha-mitzvot* (reasons for the commandments). The source of the debate is a distinction found in scripture between two seemingly different categories of law: *mishpatim* (ordinances) and *ḥukkim* (statutes). In classical rabbinic literature, mishpatim are those laws—such as laws prohibiting murder and robbery—that are readily discernible by human reason. In contrast, ḥukkim are laws such as the prohibition on wearing clothes that are made from a mixture of wool and flax, which are understood as decrees from God that have no obvious explanation from the perspective of human reason. Modern Jewish legal theorists turn, once again, to Maimonides to make their claims.[9] Maimonides argues that there are indeed reasons for all the commandments, but he also maintains that the reasons are only general and do not apply to all particular commandments. For instance, Maimonides suggests that the biblical laws of animal sacrifice must be understood in their specific historical context. These particular commandments were for the general purpose of warding off idolatry and were not made for reasons distinct from this general function.[10]

Maimonides focuses on ta'amei ha-mitzvot in the context of his concern with the relationship between divine wisdom and the commandments. In contrast, modern Jewish legal theorists focus on ta'amei ha-mitzvot as part of an exploration of possible reasons why individuals should follow the commandments. In this volume, some Ultra-Orthodox rabbis use ta'amei ha-mitzvot to link Jewish law to a more holistic vision of Torah. However, the theme of ta'amei ha-mitzvot is most often connected to Jewish positivist arguments about law and therefore to attempts to separate adherence to Jewish law from moral or other justifications. One reason that modern rabbinic scholars can use Maimonides to make this argument is that they focus only on his legal code, the *Mishneh Torah*, and ignore his philosophical treatise, *The Guide of the Perplexed*, in which he elucidates his view of ta'amei ha-mitzvot. The choice of reference is significant because it represents the modern narrowing of conceptions of Jewish law that parts ways with Maimonides' holistic understanding of Torah, discussed in more detail in the third part of this introduction.

A second recurring debate concerns whether law is distinct from custom. In fact, asking this question involves already taking a stand on whether they can be separated. This is of course a perennial topic in legal theory, and the two major directions that this issue takes parallel two major directions in modern legal theory and in constitutional theory in particular. The first direction insists on an organic dialectic between law and custom. The second insists on an absolute distinction between the two. As Haym Soloveitchik (b. 1937) has remarked in a seminal essay, "it is no exaggeration to say that the [medieval and early modern] Ashkenazic[11] community saw the law as manifesting itself in two forms: in the canonized written corpus (the Talmud and codes), and in the regnant practices of the people. Custom was a correlative datum of the halakhic system. And, on frequent occasions, the written word was reread in light of traditional behavior."[12]

As we will discuss in the third part of this introduction, it became increasingly difficult for modern Jewish legal theorists to maintain an emphasis on both written codes and customs. The debate about custom crosses ideological lines. Because they seek to understand Judaism in holistic terms, some Ultra-Orthodox as well as some Zionist thinkers insist on a connection between, and even a blurring of the distinction between, law and custom. Similarly, nineteenth-century historians of Jewish law and twentieth-century feminist thinkers contend that Jewish law and custom together reflect the evolving self-consciousness of the Jewish people over time. Other thinkers across Liberal, Orthodox, Ultra-Orthodox, Zionist, and anti-Zionist groups contend that it is necessary to clarify what is and is not Jewish law to maintain the law's unchanging integrity.

The Modern Nation-State and the Emergence of Modern Legal Theory

This brief discussion of some of the recurring themes in modern Jewish legal theories might prompt the reader to wonder whether anything unites these diverse conceptions of Jewish law. Our suggestion is that modern Jewish legal theories, as different from each other as they may be, are united in their shared attempt to answer a distinctly modern question: Is it possible or desirable analytically and practically to separate the spheres of law, politics, and religion from one another? To begin to appreciate why this question is particularly modern as well as its implications for thinking about modern Jewish legal theories, it is necessary to consider briefly the emergence of modern legal theory and its relationship to both the idea and the development of the sovereign nation-state.

The French philosopher Jean Bodin (1530–96) is largely credited with articulating the outlines of what would come to be a particularly modern conception of sovereignty, defined minimally as an independent and supreme political authority governing a particular territory.[13] Bodin's theory of sovereignty was a direct response to sectarian violence, and central to his theory was the subordination of religion to the state.[14] Like medieval constitutional thinkers, Bodin insisted that the king ruled by virtue of divine and natural law.[15] Yet he also argued that sovereignty as "absolute power only implies freedom in relation to positive laws, and not in relation to the law of God. God has declared explicitly in His Law that it is not just to take, or even to covet, the goods of another. Those who defend such opinions are even more dangerous than those who act on them."[16] In defining sovereignty in this way, Bodin rejected the notion that papal authority could extend to temporal matters.

As would Thomas Hobbes (1588–1639) after him,[17] Bodin maintained that the sovereign ruler created law but was not subject to or limited by his own law. In this way, the sovereign is both an ultimate and a wholly independent authority. As Bodin put it in his 1576 *Six Books of the Commonwealth*, "the only ruler who is sovereign in an absolute sense is one who holds nothing of any other prince, for the vassal, even if he is the Pope or the Emperor himself."[18] And law, for Bodin, "is nothing else than the command of the sovereign in the exercise of his sovereign power."[19] Modern political theorists disagree about whether the monarch is the best sovereign or the people themselves in the form of a democratic order best constitute sovereignty.[20] They also disagree about whether the sovereign's own law limits the sovereign. But modern European political thinkers agree in conceiving of territorial sovereignty as the centralization of political power and authority and in defining the modern nation-state in terms of sovereignty.

With the rise of the modern nation-state, law and modern legal institutions became the key vehicles through which sovereignty was exercised.[21] Early modern political jurisprudence—in particular. the philosophies of law articulated by Hugo Grotius (1584–1654), Samuel Pufendorf (1632–94), and Christian Thomasius (1655–1728)—attempted to provide theoretical frameworks for thinking about and implementing state and international law as distinct from empire, churches, and cstatcs.[22] A fully adequate account of these early modern jurists is of course far beyond the scope of this introduction, but for our purposes three general points are important. First, Grotius, Pufendorf, and Thomasius each attempted to defend a particularly modern (as distinct from Scholastic) conception of natural law rooted in the individual's—and, analogously, the sovereign state's—right to self-defense. Each emphasized a natural right of sovereign states to govern their citizens and to defend themselves as well as a kind of natural justice that governed the relations between sovereign states. Second, while each of these jurists wrote from within a Christian context, a cornerstone of each of their arguments was what we might call, somewhat anachronistically, a distinction between the private and public spheres, with religion belonging to the former and the pursuit of social harmony and political security to the latter. And third, while Grotius and Pufendorf insisted on an overlap between natural and civil law, Thomasius held that although natural law may influence civil law, the two were fundamentally distinct from one another.[23] The insistence on a distinction between civil or state law and natural law would become a founding assumption of modern legal theory until the mid-twentieth century.[24]

As scholars from many different perspectives have noted, these early modern natural law theories, whether intentionally or not, undermined traditional notions of natural law from within.[25] Conceptually, early modern natural law theories left two fundamental tensions unresolved. First, before the seventeenth century, most philosophers and theologians who advocated a notion of natural law of some kind ascribed some sort of purpose—often a moral one—to human nature, the natural world, or both. Early modern jurists rejected the metaphysical and moral assumptions of Scholastic and other premodern conceptions of natural law by defining human nature largely in terms of self-preservation. In this way, early modern natural law theories internalized the scientific worldview of their age in viewing nature and human nature in terms of mechanical laws, not moral purpose. Second, early modern jurists turned to the history of law, especially to Roman law, to construct a conception of law that was both historical and transcended history. These two tensions intrinsic to early modern jurists' notions of natural law would be decisive for what remain basic debates within modern legal theory about whether it is possible to articulate a concept of law independent from morality or politics and whether law as such has any meaning outside of its particular historical contexts and articulations.

Another founding assumption of modern legal theory was that law, as a distinct subject, must be understood "scientifically." Gottfried Wilhelm Leibniz (1646–1716) was the first to articulate a theory of law in scientific terms. Like the early modern jurists mentioned above, Leibniz sought to articulate a modern conception of natural law. Legal science, for Leibniz, would bridge the gap between positive law and the broader principles of justice by providing reasons for laws.[26] Already in the eighteenth century, opposition to natural law theory was fueling the development of modern legal theory. Still, modern legal theory would follow Leibniz in understanding the study of law as a science.

In Britain, Jeremy Bentham (1748–1832) offered the first systematic utilitarian account of law. Seeking to maximize pleasure and reduce pain, Bentham's utilitarianism translated Leibniz's conceptions of justice and perfection into principles of law for achieving peace and security.[27] In Germany, Immanuel Kant (1724–1804) made both metaphysical and moral arguments against the possibility of natural law by severing human subjectivity from nature (what Kant called "things in themselves") and also by insisting on a radical distinction between the way things are and the way they ought to be.[28] Kant famously and negatively contrasted the heteronomy of positive law with the autonomy of the moral law, a contrast that finds a parallel in his distinction between Jewish law and Christian religion.[29] Nevertheless, Kant's emphasis on duty, as opposed to consequence, as the only criterion of morality would become, in perhaps surprising ways, an important cornerstone of a number of nineteenth- and twentieth-century Jewish legal theories across the Liberal, Orthodox, and even Ultra-Orthodox spectrum.

In the nineteenth century, John Austin (1790–1859) in Britain and Friedrich Carl von Savigny (1779–1861) in Germany introduced two opposing schools of legal thought. Despite their deep differences, both insist on the importance of legal science, and both acknowledge a debt to Leibniz in so doing.[30] So too, while they differ greatly in their respective conclusions about what law is, Austin and Savigny both begin by rejecting natural law. Scholars and theorists of law consider Austin's philosophy of law the first articulation of legal positivism, defined most basically as a systematic attempt to conceptualize law in morally and politically neutral terms. In Austin's words, "the existence of law is one thing; its merit or demerit is another. Whether it be or be not is one enquiry; whether it be or be not conformable to an assumed standard, is a different enquiry. A law, which actually exists, is a law, though we happen to dislike it, or though it vary from the text, by which we regulate our approbation and disapprobation."[31]

Like Hobbes before him, Austin tied his notion of law to sovereign command

and the threat of punishment. For this reason, Austin's positivism poses a problem for modern Jewish legal theories since Jewish law in the modern period, as will be discussed in the next part of this introduction, has no sovereign authority. Yet twentieth-century legal positivists, most notably H. L. A. Hart (1907–92) in Britain and the legal theorist Hans Kelsen (1881–1973) in Austria, would reject the command aspect of Austin's theory.[32] They would, however, retain Austin's fundamental claim that law is morally and politically neutral. This aspect of legal positivism finds its expression in many different modern Jewish legal theories. A narrower form of legal positivism, known as legal formalism or conceptualism, can also be found in many modern Jewish legal theories. Legal formalism or conceptualism is largely concerned with how judges make decisions and can be defined most simply as the view that law is internally coherent and self-generating. As the reader will see throughout this volume, different forms of legal positivism and formalism would allow various modern Jewish legal theorists to claim that Jewish law is a sphere unto itself that is immune to moral and political influences or judgment.

Like other German historians of the nineteenth century, Savigny understood historical method as a science, and it was through historical method that he sought to articulate a legal science. In so doing, he rejected not just natural law theory but also the attempts by legal positivists and others to reduce law to rules and rule making. Savigny rejected the ideas that law is a subject that can be detached from other spheres of human life and that law can be sharply distinguished from folkways and customs. As he put it, "law has no self-dependent existence; on the contrary, its essence is the life of man itself, viewed on one particular side."[33] Scientifically understood, law lives in the common consciousness of a people. Law both binds a people to its past and, as something living, is always changing. Savigny's arguments would strongly influence different forms of German nationalism. They would also appeal to some nineteenth-century historians of Jewish law and find expression in their works, as well as in some Zionist legal theories and some Jewish feminist arguments about Jewish law in the late twentieth century.

We have seen that, despite the significant differences between the modern legal theories discussed in this section, they all emerged from the arguments initiated by early modern jurists, whose claims remain decisive for recognizing that modern law and its institutions became the agents of the sovereign nation-state.

The brief account of the coterminous developments of modern claims about the sovereign state and modern law offered here is not meant to reduce law to power or even to enter normative debates in contemporary legal theory. Rather, this account is meant to suggest that by their very structure, nature, and history, modern legal theories are intimately tied to arguments about the sovereignty of the modern nation-state. For this reason, modern legal theories always carry with them political perspectives on the modern nation-state, whether these perspectives are explicitly articulated or not. Since modern Jewish thinkers are faced with the challenge of articulating conceptions of Jewish law that do not quite fit into modern characterizations of law, we will see in the next section of the introduction that modern Jewish legal theories present a fascinating case for thinking about modern conceptions of law as they relate to the modern nation-state. Modern Jewish legal theories are the creative result of thinking through this challenge. As such, they provide an opportunity to think not only about what Jewish law is but also about the possibilities and limitations of our modern concepts of law.

Modern Jewish Legal Theories

This volume begins with well-known but essential excerpts from the *Theological-Political Treatise* published anonymously in 1670 by Benedict de Spinoza (1632–77). We begin with Spinoza for two reasons. First, he offers an account of law that denies Jewish law the status of law. As will be suggested below, in doing so Spinoza, despite his intentions to the contrary, helped created the modern category of religious law for modern Jews. Second, Spinoza lived just as the modern nation-state was beginning to be conceptualized, and his life, again despite his own self-understanding, offers a way to understand what would become the modern Jewish experience and predicament. Let us begin with a brief account of Jewish political and legal life before the advent of the modern nation-state and then turn to Spinoza more specifically.

Many modern Jewish thinkers and historians have defined politics in terms of state law. This has led them to argue that Judaism and particularly Jewish law are not political. Based on this claim, these thinkers maintain that there is no tension between being Jewish and feeling allegiance to a particular sovereign state, since the latter is political and the former is not.[34] Many Zionist thinkers and historians also equate politics with state law and contend that in contrast to the premodern era, in which Judaism and Jews were not political, Judaism and Jews become political with the establishment of a Jewish state.[35] But this equation of politics with state law obscures the historical reality and Jewish theological justification of premodern Jewish political life, as well as the modern political implications of the claim that Jewish law is not and never was political.[36]

Historical scholarship continues to uncover and describe the political authority and power exercised by premodern Jewish communities. In the premodern era, a Jewish individual was defined legally, politically, and theologically as a member of the Jewish community.[37] While premodern Jewish communities were answerable to and existed only by permission of external authorities, premodern Jews governed themselves, and individual Jews were subject to the Jewish laws of their local communities—which often varied greatly from one another. Jewish communities from the rabbinic period on were not fully sovereign, but neither were their external political authorities. This meant that Jewish communal leaders all had to negotiate their relationship to external authorities not just from the perspective of the Jewish community's relationship to an outside power, but also from the perspective of the Jewish community itself. While the extent of the rabbis' political power in the rabbinic period remains unclear, what cannot be doubted is that rhetorically the rabbis claimed political authority for themselves.[38] Nor can it be doubted that Jewish leaders increasingly exercised a significant amount of political power over the members of their communities.

Salo Baron's (1895–1989) 1928 description of the political structure of medieval Jewish communities remains the most concise summary of premodern Judaism's political status:

> Complex, isolated, in a sense of foreign, it [the Jewish community] was left more severely alone by the State than most other corporations. Thus the Jewish community of pre-Revolutionary days had more competence over its members than the modern Federal, State, and Municipal governments combined. Education, administration of justice between Jew and Jew, taxation for communal and State purposes, health, markets, public order, were all within the jurisdiction of the community-corporation. . . . Statute was reinforced by religious, supernatural sanctions as well as by coercive public opinions within the group. For example, a Jew put in *Cherem* [excommunication] by a Jewish court was practically a lost man, and the *Cherem* was a fairly common means of imposing the will of the community on the individual. All this self-governing apparatus disappeared, of course, when the Revolution brought "equal rights" to European Jewry.[39]

The political functions of the premodern Jewish community—which included, as Baron notes, the administration of justice between Jew and Jew and the enforcement of sanctions on its members—were the province of Jewish law and were often practically executed and theoretically justified by rabbinic authorities.

Spinoza's life captures the beginnings of the stripping away of Jewish political authority and power from the Jewish collectivity. Spinoza was excommunicated from the Amsterdam Jewish community in 1656.[40] His excommunication testifies to the political power of the premodern Jewish community as just described, while his ability to live an independent life free of any religious community anticipates Jewish modernity, in which the Jewish community does not exercise political or legal power over individual Jews. Spinoza's account of Jewish law also set the conceptual challenge for modern theories of Jewish law. Spinoza defines law as universal and maintains that as the perfect being, God, by definition cannot be a lawgiver, just as God cannot be said to have created the word. To understand God as a lawgiver and a creator is, according to Spinoza, to ascribe human qualities and especially human need and desire to God. In these ways, Spinoza denies philosophical and theological validity to the very notion of divinely revealed law. He famously contends that what he calls the laws of the Hebrews are pertinent only in the context of their original, political meaning: "ceremonies . . . do not belong to the divine law and hence contribute nothing to happiness and virtue. They are relevant only to the election of the Hebrews, that is . . . to the temporary and material prosperity of their state, and therefore could have relevance only insofar as that state survived."[41] Because the ceremonial law no longer corresponds to a political kingdom, Spinoza concludes that Jewish law is not the divine law.

As Spinoza knew full well, and as his excommunication shows, Jewish law did not disappear in the postbiblical period. In fact, what we call "Judaism" and "Jewish law" today developed after that period. But Spinoza, influenced by Hobbes, adopts a view of sovereign authority as supreme and undivided. This means that particular laws, as opposed to the divine law—which, again, is universal and timeless—can be only laws of a sovereign state. Spinoza thus distinguishes law that is by definition tied to the sovereign state and true religion that demands only knowledge and love of God. For him, Jewish law therefore qualifies neither as law nor as religion. More generally, the category of religious law is one that Spinoza would reject precisely because something that is a law cannot be religious, and something that is religious cannot be a law.

Spinoza's formulations are instructive because modern Jewish legal theories evolved in the context of the sovereign nation-state, and in this context Jewish law fits uneasily into the categories of either law or religion. This led Jewish thinkers to theorize a category of Jewish law as something religious and not political. We must underscore that while there are conceptual problems at play here, modern Jewish legal theories had to grapple not just with theoretical questions of Jewish law but also with a fundamental challenge to the authoritative status of Jewish law for Jews. The very fact that Jewish thinkers begin in the eighteenth century to offer theoretical accounts of what Jewish law is suggests that something is not working. As Jacob Katz (1904–98) has put it, the political predicament for Jewish traditionalists was stark: "The observance of the Jewish tradition could and would be enforced by the organs of the Jewish community. The authority to do so was conferred on the Jewish community by the state, and constituted a part of communal autonomy. There was also a measure of control over the ideas. . . . The post-traditional Jewish community was denied the right to impose its will concerning thought and action on the individual."[42] Modern Jewish legal theories arose because the scope and authority of Jewish law narrowed with the emergence of the modern nation-state. Jewish thinkers and religious leaders had to answer the question of what Jewish law was to adapt to these changing circumstances. Like early modern jurists, some Jewish legal theorists constructed theories of Jewish law to change that law for the modern age. In contrast, other Jewish legal theorists constructed theories of Jewish law to preserve Jewish laws in the modern age.

This is not to deny that there were premodern theoretical accounts of Jewish law. But they were not the norm. As mentioned above, Maimonides offered the most fully articulated theoretical account of Jewish law. His philosophy exercised little influence on and in fact was rejected by his contemporaries and many later thinkers. Yet Maimonides' work is essential for modern Jewish legal theories (which offer a wide array of interpretations of that work) because he is unusual in articulating a theory of Jewish law. It is also helpful to consider Maimonides' philosophy of law briefly to appreciate the difference between the historical circumstances and theoretical framework that guided Maimonides and those that guide modern Jewish legal theorists.

To begin with, the political framework of Maimonides' concept of law is absolutely explicit.[43] As he puts it in the *Guide of the Perplexed*, "the Law as a whole aims at two things: the welfare of the soul and the welfare of the body. As for the welfare of the soul, it consists in the multitude's acquiring correct opinions. . . . As for the welfare of the body, it comes about by the improvement of their ways of living with one another. . . . This cannot be achieved in any way by one isolated individual. For an individual can only attain all this through a political association, it being already known that man is political by nature."[44] For Maimonides, the political nature of law includes the divine law: "although it [the divine law] is not natural, [it] enters into what is natural."[45]

The political nature of Maimonides' conception of law is not only abstract but also practical. We see this clearly from an example in the *Mishneh Torah*. For instance, Maimonides justifies using physical force to get a husband to "consent" to a divorce: "With regard to this person who [outwardly] refuses to divorce [his wife]—he wants to be part of the Jewish people, and he wants to perform all the [commandments] and eschew all the transgressions; it is only his evil inclination that presses him. Therefore, when he is beaten until his [evil] inclination has been weakened, and he consents, he is considered to have performed the divorce willfully."[46] Maimonides offers a theological explanation for his notion of "consent," which is that a Jew cannot freely choose not to follow the commandments. Therefore, when a man consents after being beaten so that he will follow them, his consent is real. Maimonides' justification that a man "wants" to be part of the Jewish people is of a piece with his view that the evil inclination to not follow the commandments is not a free choice. For Maimonides it is not a choice for a Jew to be part of the Jewish people, just as it is not a choice for a Jew not to follow the law. Put another way, being part of the Jewish people and following the commandments are choices that admit of only one option. It is important to note that Maimonides' justification of coercion is not merely instrumental, just as his view of politics is not instrumental. Both are at the core fundamentally pedagogical because they are in the service of furthering a life devoted to goodness and truth.[47] And, as we saw above, Maimonides' account of the authority of the Jewish community to exercise its power over its individual members accords with the historical and political situation of premodern Jewry.

The very modern notions of "ceremonial law," "Jewish law," or even *halakhah* as distinct categories are instructive because they reflect the circumscribed scope of what could be considered Jewish law. Throughout the *Guide* and in the quotations above, Maimonides does not use the term "halakhah" but rather the term "Torah" to refer to the law, and when he refers to what is translated as the "divine law" he uses the term *Torat Moshe Rabbeinu* (the Torah of Moses our teacher).[48] In the original Judeo-Arabic, Maimonides uses the term *sharia*, as opposed to *fiqh*, the former corresponding to Torah and the latter to halakhah.[49] Similarly, in the *Guide* Maimonides does not use the term "halakhah" as a free-standing category; instead, in the *Mishneh Torah*, written originally in Hebrew, he uses the term *hilkhot*, meaning "laws of," as in laws of divorce. Law (as halakhah) is not an autonomous category but rather a subcategory of the larger category of the political (as Torah). For Maimonides and premodern Jewish thinkers generally,

Torah is a comprehensive category, referring not only to politics and law, but also to all Jewish teachings and human knowledge, broadly conceived.

Modern political circumstances challenged the holism of Maimonides' account of Jewish law. The readings collected in part 1, "Jewish Law and the Rise of the Modern Nation-State," offer different answers to the question of what Jewish law is in direct response to the development of the European modern nation-state. While part 1 presents an array of conceptions of Jewish law from the seventeenth to the twentieth centuries, most of the thinkers included in this part agree that Jewish law is different in kind from state law. To varying degrees, these thinkers characterize Jewish law as both religious and private while also describing Jewish law in terms similar to those used in different strands of modern legal theory. Our introductions to specific readings point to some of the parallels between debates about what Jewish law is and modern legal theory. For instance, Moses Mendelssohn's (1729–86) argument that changes to Jewish burial practices may be permitted and Samson Raphael Hirsch's (1808–88) argument that Jewish law never changes both find parallels in the legal reasoning of positivists. The arguments of the Jewish historian Zacharias Frankel (1801–75) draw on the German historical school of law articulated by Savigny, while the Israeli legal scholar and jurist Menachem Elon (1923–2013) relies explicitly on Kelsen's legal positivism.

Part 2, "Eastern European Views of Law: Dissolution of Jewish Communal Power," includes readings from the eighteenth to twentieth centuries that emerged without Jewish emancipation in Eastern Europe. The Jewish legal theories articulated in this part of the volume do not initially respond directly to the development of the modern nation-state, but they do emerge in the context of the dissolution of Jewish communal power in Eastern Europe, beginning with the Polish government's 1764 dissolution of the Council of the Four Lands—a centralized body that had governed Polish Jewry for two centuries.[50] As the structure of Jewish autonomy continued to fall apart over the next century, rabbinic scholars reconceptualized Jewish law in terms of both intellectual study and ethical formation. The legal theories included in part 2 differ in style, language, and substance from those presented in part 1. Nevertheless, the two sets of readings are similar in that they both offer privatized conceptions of Jewish law. These privatized notions find expression either in the form of study and direct engagement with early rabbinic sources or in the understanding of law as a spiritual and ethical exercise. Both of these new conceptions of Jewish law stood in opposition to the monumental medieval legal codes developed by Yosef

Karo (1488–1575) and Moshe Isserles (Poland, 1520–72), known respectively as the *Shulḥan Arukh* (The set table) and *Ha-Mapah* (The tablecloth), which present Jewish law as mainly concerned with the practicalities of everyday life. Both the intellectualist and ethical interpretations of what Jewish law is can be understood as responses to the collapse of what had been the political function of Jewish law.

Our introductions to specific readings draw parallels between some of these legal theories and legal formalism and conceptualism as well as modern debates about law, virtue, and supererogation. Part 2 also includes some practical rabbinic negotiations with state authority in different times and places, showing, as is the case with Mendelssohn and Hirsch in part 1, that similar philosophies of law can lead to different legal conclusions in different historical contexts. For instance, writing from the Russian Empire in the nineteenth century, Yisrael Meir Kagan (1838–1933; also known as the Ḥafetz Ḥayim) argues that Jewish soldiers must take every opportunity to leave the Russian army to avoid violating Jewish law. And in twentieth-century America, Joseph Soloveitchik (1903–93) maintains that in becoming US military chaplains, Orthodox rabbis are permitted to place themselves in situations where they may violate Jewish law.

Whereas parts 1 and 2 focus on Jewish legal theories that in effect privatize Jewish law by defining it as something religious (as opposed to political), the readings included in part 3, "Ultra-Orthodoxy and the Rejection of the Modern Nation-State," and part 4, "Jewish Law and the State of Israel," stress the simultaneously national and religious characters of Jewish law. The ideological positions and practical consequences of many of the readings included in parts 3 and 4 are diametrically opposed to one another, but both sets of readings may be understood as sharing features of political theology. In the context of modern legal theory, "political theology" is a term made famous by the Nazi jurist Carl Schmitt (1888–1985), who argues that the modern state—and especially the modern ideas of sovereignty and law that define the modern nation-state—has its unacknowledged origins in theology: "all significant concepts of the modern theory of the state are secularized theological concepts."[51] For Schmitt, recognition of the modern state's theological origins points to the weakness and ultimate unsustainability of the liberal state. The selections included in parts 3 and 4 can be understood as falling under the rubric of political theology because their shared basis is a rejection of the liberal nation-state coupled with a claim to return to law's theological and political unity. This is not to equate any of these readings with Schmitt's legal and political conclusions. As we will see, opposition to the liberal nation-state in these political theologies takes different forms whose practical political implications diverge not only from those of Schmitt's work but also from each other. Nevertheless, like Schmitt's arguments about political theology, their opposition to the European nation-state draws heavily on the reality and some of the ideals of the modern nation-state.

Part 3's readings focus not on the private engagement of elites with defining Jewish law conceptually but rather on attempts to rethink the scope and meaning of Jewish law as part of a struggle to reconstitute the Jewish community and rabbinic authority after the evolution of the modern-state. These theories of Jewish law are part of a larger strategy of self-segregation on the part of Ultra-Orthodox communities. At a time when Jews are no longer segregated from non-Jews in Europe, arguments about Jewish law become a vehicle for separating Jews from non-Jewish society as well as from other Jews who do not adhere to the Ultra-Orthodox conception of Jewish law. Strikingly, the legal theories included in part 3, in sharp distinction to those included in parts 1 and 2, emphasize the complementary national and religious characters of Jewish law. They do so in opposition to the modern nation-state, while recognizing nonetheless that the modern nation-state makes such self-segregation both necessary and possible in the first place.

Part 4's Zionist legal theories address, both before and after the establishment of the State of Israel in 1948, questions about what kind of public, political role Jewish law might play in a Jewish state. The selections all grapple with how the history of Jewish law in the diaspora relates to the new reality of a Jewish nation-state. Many of the thinkers represented maintain that Zionism requires a complete rethinking of the concept of Jewish law, while also insisting on the continuity between rabbinic authority and Zionist legal theories. Many of the selections also consider whether Jewish law and egalitarian values can or should be reconciled. Zionist legal theories reiterate and transform several trends in modern Jewish legal theories that are introduced in the volume's first three parts, such as legal positivism, the historical school of law, the privatization of Jewish law, and Jewish political theology.

The last section of the book, part 5, "Jewish Feminist Views of Law," brings together the focus on the individual stressed in the selections of the first two parts of the book with the focus on the collective foregrounded in the third and fourth parts. Like virtually all of the selections in this reader, feminist accounts of Jewish law grapple with the questions of whether or how Jewish law can or should change. While a number of important Jewish feminists reject Jewish law outright as discriminatory and patriarchal, the Jewish feminist accounts chosen for this section each assume—in different ways—the continued legitimacy of Jewish law for Jewish women and men. Our introductions to the selections in part 5 underline the continuity of themes in Jewish feminist and modern Jewish legal theories more generally as encountered in the first four parts of the book, as well as the differences in feminist Jewish legal theories. An interesting contrast here is between Rachel Adler (b. 1957), who wants to reinstitute halakhah as a holistic *nomos* in a way that is both feminist and premodern, and Tova Hartman (b. 1943), who insists that we can distinguish between true halakhah (which contains resources for egalitarian ideals) and patriarchal ideology (which is not actually halakhic). The volume concludes with Jewish feminist views of law because the encounter between feminism and Jewish law in many ways epitomizes the encounter between premodern conceptions of Jewish law and the modern nation-state. It is, after all, the very modern idea of the rule of law, whose ideal is to treat all individual members of a community equally, that at least in theory links the modern nation-state with egalitarian ideals. Indeed, one of our selections, by Isaac Breuer (1883–1946), makes precisely this point to distinguish Jewish law from modern law as such.

The categories that constitute the different parts of this volume are offered as heuristic devices for beginning to appreciate not only the diversity of modern Jewish legal theories, but also some of the common questions that guide them. Indeed, a number of thinkers could have been included in different parts than the ones in which they appear in. For instance, Isaac Breuer is included in part 3, "Ultra-Orthodoxy and the Rejection of the Modern Nation-State," but he could have been included in part 4, "Jewish Law and the State of Israel." And Naḥman Krochmal (1785–1840) is included in part 2, "Eastern European Views of Law: Dissolution of Jewish Communal Power," but he could have been included in part 1, "Jewish Law and the Rise of the Modern Nation-State." In addition, all of the selections in part 5, "Jewish Feminist Views of Law," could have been included in part 1. As editors, we have used the five rubrics that make up the structure of this volume as hypothetical constructs to help us think critically about both the historical circumstances that produced particular Jewish legal theories and the theoretical challenges to which they respond. We hope that presenting these legal theories as we have will help introduce the reader to a set of texts that are often treated in isolation from one another, while also opening up debates about the categories in which we have placed them.

Finally, we must also note that this volume focuses largely on Ashkenazic legal theories (that is, legal theories developed by Jews either living in or descended from those who lived in Europe, many of whom immigrated to the United States and Israel), to the exclusion of Sephardic Jewish legal theories (that is, legal theories developed by Jews descended from those who were expelled from Spain or Portugal in 1492, many of whom immigrated to North Africa, the Balkans, and countries along the Mediterranean). Only in part 4, "Jewish Law and the State of Israel," do we present Ashkenazic and Sephardic legal theories in conversation with one another. Constraints of space necessitated that the focus of this volume be narrower than is perhaps ideal, but at the same time our focus on Ashkenazic thinkers reinforces the historical and theoretical framework that undergirds this volume—which is the encounter between the realities and ideologies of premodern Jewish law and the modern nation-state. This initial encounter took place largely within areas populated by Ashkenazic Jews.[52] It will be one of the tasks of future research on modern Jewish legal theories, some of which has already taken place in the secondary literature in Hebrew, to more fully integrate conversations between Ashkenazic and Sephardic thinkers.[53]

Conclusion

Hart began his now classic *The Concept of Law* by observing that "few questions concerning human society have been asked with such persistence and answered by serious thinkers in so many diverse, strange, and even paradoxical ways as the question of 'what is law?'"[54] As we have suggested in this introduction, modern Jewish arguments about Jewish law are, in Hart's words, "diverse, strange, and even paradoxical." Yet the framework and choice of selections in this volume part ways with Hart's formulation in insisting that the question "what is law?" is not a timeless one, but rather one that is particularly modern in its basic assumption that it is both possible and desirable to isolate the sphere of law from all other purported domains of human life, such as economics, morality, politics, and, of course, theology.[55] Taken as a whole, this volume suggests that modern Jewish legal theories either share this assumption or in some way react to it.

A final note on terminology helps us appreciate the particular Jewish dimension of this problem. Today the Hebrew word *dat* is most often translated as "religion," but historically the term referred to law. The word is biblical and appears in Esther 3:8. There it means law, both the Jewish people's and the king's: "And Haman said unto king Ahasuerus: 'here is a certain people scattered abroad and dispersed among the peoples in all the provinces of your kingdom; and their laws (*dateihem*) are different from those of every people; neither do they keep the

king's laws (*datei hamelekh*); therefore it does not profit the king to suffer them.'"
As Avraham Melamed (b. 1944) has shown, up until the early modern period,
Jewish thinkers such as Saadia Gaon (c. 892–942), Maimonides, Joseph Albo
(c. 1380–1444), Judah Messer Leon (c. 1420–25–c. 1498), and Nissim of Marseilles
(fourteenth century) used the term "dat" in a variety of ways, but all of these usages referred to law, whether human or divine, and not to particular beliefs, Jewish or otherwise.[56] Simone Luzzatto's (1583–1663) *Discorso circa il stato degl' hebrei
et in particolar dimoranti nell'inclita città di Venetia* marks a change in the meaning of
dat. Luzzatto describes Judaism as a religious faith like Christianity by translating dat as "religio" and "religione." Spinoza would follow Luzzatto in distinguishing between law (*lex*) and religion in his *Theological-Political Treatise*. This brings us
full circle to the challenge that Spinoza presented to modern Jewish thinkers. If
law and religion are mutually incompatible categories, can or does Jewish law
fit into either category? Just as the story of Esther describes a king who cannot
suffer a people that has its own dat, a major factor in the development of modern Jewish law has been—in response to the demands of a sovereign with even
more far-reaching claims—the transformation of dat into something (religion)
that will not compete with its claims.

The modern history of the Hebrew term "dat" captures the tension that the
readings in this volume seek to resolve. Some of the thinkers included in the
volume use the term to refer to Jewish law, while others use it to refer to religion
—and which thinkers fall into which group may surprise the reader. To return
to Hart's formulation, modern Jewish legal theories are indeed "diverse, strange,
and even paradoxical." But unlike Hart, we believe that the varied and not always
fully consistent nature of the answers to the question "what is Jewish law?" constitute what is vital and interesting about modern Jewish legal theories. The fact
that this volume does not offer one definitive answer to the question of what
Jewish law is testifies to both the importance and the difficulty of answering
this question. The task, we believe, is to appreciate these theories in their differences while also recognizing that their divergences stem from a common challenge: how to reconcile Jewish law, if not Judaism, with the rise of the modern
nation-state.

Notes

1. For an overview of academic scholarship on the Talmud and rabbinic literature, see
Charlotte Elisheva Fonrobert and Martin S. Jaffe, *The Cambridge Companion to the Talmud and
Rabbinic Literature* (Cambridge: Cambridge University Press, 2007). For premodern arguments

about Oral Torah, see Moshe Halbertal, *People of the Book: Canon, Meaning, and Authority* (Cambridge, MA: Harvard University Press, 1997). For modern claims about the Oral and Written Torah, see Jay Harris, *How Do We Know This? Midrash and the Fragmentation of Modern Judaism* (Albany: State University of New York Press, 1994). For a helpful discussion of the theological issues at stake in considering the scope of Oral Torah, see Benjamin Sommer, *Revelation and Authority: Sinai in Jewish Scripture and Tradition* (New Haven, CT: Yale University Press, 2015).

2. Moses Maimonides, *Mishneh Torah*, "Laws of the Foundations of the Torah," 9:1.

3. Ibid., "Laws of Rebels," 1:2.

4. Ibid., 2:1.

5. For an overview of this subject, see Gerald Bildstein, "Maimonides on 'Oral Law'," *Jewish Law Annual* 1 (1978): 108–22.

6. Ronald Dworkin, *Taking Rights Seriously* (Cambridge, MA: Harvard University Press, 1977), 75.

7. See the text by him in part 1.

8. See the text by him in part 4.

9. For a lucid overview of the topic of the philosophical issues at stake in discussions of ta'amei ha-mitzvot, see Josef Stern, *Problems and Parables of Law: Maimonides and Naḥmanides on Reasons for the Commandments* (Albany: State University of New York, 1998).

10. This claim might seem to have the potential to undermine the authority of many laws, and later commentators were quick to criticize Maimonides on this point. See Stern, *Problems and Parables of Law.*

11. Ashkenazim and Sephardim are the two major ethnic groups of diasporic Jews, which began to diverge around 1100. Broadly speaking, Ashkenazim are the Jews of northern Europe, especially the Yiddish-speaking communities of Central and Eastern Europe, and Sephardim are the Jews of southern Europe and the Mediterranean countries. The laws, liturgy, and customs of these two ethnic groups differ in various ways.

12. Haym Soloveitchik, "Rupture and Reconstruction: The Transformation of Contemporary Orthodoxy," in *Jews in America: A Contemporary Reader*, edited by Roberta Farber and Chaim Waxman (Waltham, MA: Brandeis University Press, 1999), 322. Soloveitchik focuses largely on transformations of Modern and Ultra-Orthodox communities in the late twentieth century, but the changes he describes began earlier.

13. Jean Bodin, *On Sovereignty*, edited and translated by Julian H. Franklin (New York: Cambridge University Press, 1992).

14. Julian H. Franklin, *Jean Bodin and the Rise of Absolutist Theory* (Cambridge: Cambridge University Press, 1973).

15. For general background, see the essays collected in *The Cambridge History of Medieval Political Thought c. 350–c. 1450* (Cambridge: Cambridge University Press, 1988) and in *The Cambridge History of Political Thought 1450–1700* (Cambridge: Cambridge University Press, 1991), both edited by J. H. Burns.

16. Jean Bodin, *Six Books of the Commonwealth*, abridged and translated by M. J. Tooley (Oxford: Basil Blackwell, 1967), 35.

17. Thomas Hobbes, *Leviathan*, edited by Karl Schuhmann and G. A. J. Rogers (New York: Thoemmes Continuum, 2003).

18. Bodin, *Six Books of the Commonwealth*, 38.

19. Ibid., 35.

20. Bodin and Hobbes argue the former, while Benedict de Spinoza and Jean-Jacques Rousseau (1712–78) argue the latter.

21. The Treaty of Westphalia of 1648 began the process of institutionalizing the secularization of politics through modern systems of law.

22. For an overview, see Richard Tuck, *The Rights of War and Peace: Political Thought and the International Order from Grotius to Kant* (New York: Oxford University Press, 2001).

23. Ian Hunter, *The Secularisation of the Confessional State: The Political Thought of Christian Thomasius* (Cambridge: Cambridge University Press, 2008).

24. New natural law theories would emerge in the mid-twentieth century with Jacques Maritain's *Les droits de l'homme et la loi naturelle* (New York: La Maison Française, 1942) and later with the Oxford legal philosopher John Finnis's *Natural Law and Natural Rights* (Oxford: Clarendon Press of Oxford University Press, 1980). For the most part, natural law thinking has not been prominent in modern (or premodern) Jewish legal theories. For a systematic attempt to put forward an argument for a Jewish view of natural law, see David Novak, *Natural Law in Judaism* (Cambridge: Cambridge University Press, 1998).

25. Ian Hunter, *Rival Enlightenments: Civil and Metaphysical Philosophy in Early Modern Germany* (Cambridge: Cambridge University Press, 2001); Leo Strauss, *Natural Right and History* (Chicago: University of Chicago Press, 1952); Richard Tuck, *Natural Right Theories: Their Origin and Their Development* (Cambridge: Cambridge University Press, 1982).

26. See Gottfried Wilhelm Leibniz, *Leibniz: Political Writing*, edited by Patrick Riley (Cambridge: Cambridge University Press, 1972); Patrick Riley, *Leibniz' Universal Jurisprudence: Justice as the Charity of the Wise* (Cambridge, MA: Harvard University Press, 1996).

27. Riley, *Leibniz' Universal Jurisprudence*, 141–98; Jeremy Bentham, *An Introduction to Principles of Morals and Legislation*, edited by Jonathan Bennett, accessed January 15, 2017, http://www.earlymoderntexts.com/assets/pdfs/bentham1780.pdf.

28. Immanuel Kant, *The Critique of Pure Reason*, edited and translated by Paul Guyer and Alan Wood (Cambridge: Cambridge University Press, 1999), A235/B294–A261/B315. See also Immanuel Kant, *Groundwork of the Metaphysics of Morals*, edited and translated by Mary Gregor and Jens Timmermann (Cambridge: Cambridge University Press, 2012).

29. Immanuel Kant, *Religion within the Boundaries of Mere Reason*, edited by Allen Wood and George di Giovanni (Cambridge: Cambridge University Press, 1999).

30. Roger Berkowitz, "From Justice to Justification: An Alternative Genealogy of Positive Law," *UC Irvine Law Review* 1, no. 3 (2001): 611–30.

31. John Austin, *The Province of Jurisprudence Determined*, edited by Wilfrid E. Rumble (Cambridge: Cambridge University Press, 1995), 184.

32. H. L. A. Hart, *The Concept of Law* (Oxford: Clarendon Press of Oxford University Press, 1961); Hans Kelsen, *Pure Theory of Law*, translated by Max Knight (Berkeley: University of California Press, 1967).

33. Friedrich Carl von Savigny, *Of the Vocation of our Age for Legislation and Jurisprudence*, translated by Abraham Hayward (London: Littlewood, 1831), 46.

34. Many of the thinkers included in part 1 of this volume make this claim.

35. See, for instance, Leon Pinsker, *Auto-Emancipation* (New York: Maccabaean, 1906). This argument is also made from an anti-Zionist perspective. For example, see Shlomo Sand, *The Invention of the Jewish People* (London: Verso, 2009).

36. For an excellent essay on this subject, see Ismar Schorsch, *On the History of the Political Judgment of the Jew* (New York: Leo Baeck Institute, 1976).

37. For a general overview of the relationship between premodern and modern Judaism, see Jacob Katz, *Out of the Ghetto: The Social Background of Jewish Emancipation* (Cambridge, MA: Harvard University Press, 1973).

38. On the issue of the rabbis' political power, see Catherine Hezser, *The Social Structure of the Rabbinic Movement in Roman Palestine* (Tübingen, Germany: Mohr-Siebeck, 1997).

39. Salo Baron, "Ghetto and Emancipation," *Menorah Journal* 14 (June 1928): 519.

40. On Spinoza's life and beliefs, see Steven Nadler, *Spinoza: A Life* (Cambridge: Cambridge University Press, 1999) and *A Book Forged in Hell: Spinoza's Scandalous Treatise and the Birth of the Secular Age* (Princeton, NJ: Princeton University Press, 2011).

41. Benedict de Spinoza, *Theological-Political Treatise*, edited by Jonathan Israel and translated by Michael Silverthorne and Jonathan Israel (Cambridge: Cambridge University Press, 2007), 68.

42. Jacob Katz, *Toward Modernity: The European Jewish Model* (New Brunswick, NJ: Transaction, 1987), 1.

43. For a comprehensive discussion of Maimonides' political philosophy and his view of law, see Gerald J. Blidstein, *Political Concepts in Maimonidean Halakhah* [in Hebrew] (Ramat Gan, Israel: Bar-Ilan University Press, 1983). See also Menachem Lorberbaum, *Politics and the Limits of Law: Secularizing the Political in Medieval Jewish Thought* (Palo Alto, CA: Stanford University Press, 2001).

44. Moses Maimonides, *Guide of the Perplexed*, edited and translated by Shlomo Pines, introduction by Leo Strauss (Chicago: University of Chicago Press, 1963), 3:27.

45. Ibid., 2:40.

46. Moses Maimonides, *Mishneh Torah*, translated by Eliyahu Touger (New York: Moznaim, 1987), "Laws of Divorce," 2:20.

47. Maimonides, *Guide of the Perplexed*, 3:28.

48. Moses Maimonides, *Moreh nevukhim le-Rabenu Moshe ben Maimon* [Guide of the Perplexed], translated by Mikhael Shvarts (Tel Aviv: University of Tel-Aviv, 2002), 3:27 and 2:40.

49. Moses Maimonides, *Dalālat al-ḥāirīn*, edited by Solomon Munk (Jerusalem: Y. Yunovits, 1929), 3:27.

50. For an overview of the transformation of eastern European Jewry, see Israel Bartal, *The Jews of Eastern Europe, 1772–1881*, translated by Chaya Naor (Philadelphia: University of Pennsylvania Press, 2006).

51. Carl Schmitt, *Political Theology: Four Chapters on the Concept of Sovereignty*, translated by George Schwab (Chicago: University of Chicago Press, 1982), 36.

52. For a helpful English-language overview of Sephardic approaches to Jewish law, see Zvi Zohar, *Rabbinic Creativity in the Modern Middle East* (London: Bloomsbury Academic Press, 2013).

53. Zvi Zohar has done some of the groundbreaking work in Hebrew in this area. For a complete list of his publications in Hebrew, see http://law.biu.ac.il/en/node/373.

54. Hart, *The Concept of Law*, 1.

55. Notably Hart decides to immediately limit his history of arguments about the concept of law to the last 150 years.

56. See Avraham Melamed, "De la loi à la religion: Mètamorphoses du concept de *dath* dans la tradition politique juive," in *Entre ciel et terre, le judaïsme: Les sources de la loi*, edited by Shmuel Trigano (Paris: YYB, 2010).

1 | Jewish Law and the Rise of the Modern Nation-State

Each of the thinkers included in part 1 grapple in one way or another with what Jewish law can and might be once Jews are living in a modern state in which they are treated legally as individuals and not as part of a Jewish collective. The famous statement by Stanislas Marie Adélaïde, comte de Clermont-Tonnerre, to the French assembly in 1789 that "one must refuse everything to the Jews as a nation, but one must give them everything as individuals; they must become citizens"[1] reflects what became a new political and religious reality for Jews. If law and nation are inextricably tied, as they are in the modern nation-state, then what can Jewish law be? In different ways, all the thinkers represented in part 1 attempt to answer this question.

Benedict de Spinoza and Moses Mendelssohn lived in times and places in which the modern nation-state was not yet a reality. In attempting to articulate the ideals of what such a state should be, they set the framework used by many subsequent liberal and conservative Jewish thinkers to articulate what Jewish law could be in the context of the reality of the modern nation-state. And in their correspondence, Mendelssohn and Jacob Emden articulate different conceptions of Jewish law that would be echoed by later Orthodox and Ultra-Orthodox thinkers. The next five thinkers represented in part 1 (Abraham Geiger, Samson Raphael Hirsch, Zacharias Frankel, Heinrich Graetz, and Hermann Cohen) wrote after the emancipation of the Jews in what became the German state. Largely through their respective conceptualizations of Jewish law, four of these thinkers (Geiger, Hirsch, Frankel, and Graetz) formulated the philosophical and ideological bases of the three modern Jewish denominational movements: Reform, Orthodox, and Conservative Judaism. The last

---

1. Quoted in Arthur Hertzberg, *The French Enlightenment and the Jews* (New York: Columbia University Press, 1968), 360.

two thinkers included in this part, Robert Cover and Menachem Elon, wrote in the American and Israeli contexts, respectively. In these contexts, Cover and Elon attempt to envision what Jewish law could be within the larger political frameworks of the United States of America and the State of Israel.

1

Benedict de Spinoza, *Theological-Political Treatise*

Benedict de Spinoza (1632–77) was excommunicated from the Jewish community of Amsterdam in 1656. His *Theological-Political Treatise* was published anonymously in 1670. The *Treatise* raises doubts about the truth of revealed religion generally, and Spinoza is particularly critical of any notion of religious law that implies that there is a personal, supernatural God who communicates God's will to people. Spinoza excoriates the notion that God would elect the Jews or any other people, and in this context he denies that Jewish law is divine in origin. Divine law, Spinoza claims, is by definition universal, just as the laws of nature are. Jewish law, he maintains, has meaning only within the political structure of the Hebrew commonwealth, which no longer exists. Jewish law is thereby rendered problematic for Spinoza, in that it does not correspond to the state and nor is it religious.

Benedict de Spinoza, *Theological-Political Treatise*, edited by Jonathan Israel
and translated by Michael Silverthorne and Jonathan Israel (Cambridge:
Cambridge University Press, 2007), 43–55 and 58–61.

CHAPTER 3: ON THE VOCATION OF THE HEBREWS

True joy and happiness lie in the simple enjoyment of what is good and not in the kind of false pride that enjoys happiness because others are excluded from it. . . . [A] person's true joy and felicity lie solely in his wisdom and knowledge of truth, not in being wiser than others or in others' being without knowledge of truth, since this does not increase his own wisdom which is his true felicity. . . .

When therefore Scripture states that God chose the Hebrews for himself above other nations (see Deuteronomy 10:15) so as to encourage them to obey the law, and is near to them and not to others (Deuteronomy 4:4–7), and has laid down good laws solely for them and not for others (Deuteronomy 4:2), and has made himself known to them alone, in preference to others (see Deuteronomy 4:32), and so on, Scripture is merely speaking according to their understanding . . . as Moses also testifies (see Deuteronomy 9:6–7), they did not know true happiness. . . .

. . . Moses desired to teach the Hebrews in such a manner and inculcate into them such principles as would attach them more closely to the worship of God on the basis of their childish understanding. . . . [T]he Hebrews excelled [over] other nations neither in knowledge nor piety but in something quite different, or (to speak in terms of Scripture, according to their understanding) that the Hebrews were chosen above others by God not, despite their being frequently admonished, with a view to the true life and elevated conceptions but rather for something completely different. . . .

For as regards comprehending reality, it is clear . . . that they had entirely commonplace notions of God and nature. . . . Nor was it for their virtue or [attainment of] the true life; for in this respect too they were on the same footing as other nations and very few were chosen. Their election and vocation therefore lay only in the success and the prosperity at that time of their commonwealth. . . . I would add merely that the laws of the Old Testament too were revealed and prescribed only to the Jews; for since God chose them alone to form a particular commonwealth and state, they had necessarily to have unique laws as well. . . .

Since therefore it is true that God is equally kind, merciful, etc., to all men and that the duty of the prophet was not so much to prescribe the particular laws of his country as to teach true virtue and to admonish men concerning it, there is no doubt that all nations have had prophets, and that the prophetic gift was not peculiar to the Jews. . . .

Thus the Jews today have absolutely nothing that they can attribute to themselves but not to other peoples. As for their being dispersed and stateless for so many years, it is not at all surprising that, after separating themselves from all the nations in this way, they brought the resentment of all men upon themselves, not only because of their external rites which are contrary to the rites of other nations, but also by the sign of circumcision which they zealously maintain. But experience has shown that it is the resentment of the gentiles to a large extent that preserves them. . . .

Furthermore, I think that the sign of circumcision has such great importance as almost to persuade me that this thing alone will preserve their nation for ever, and in fact, were it not that the principles of their religion weaken their courage, I would believe unreservedly that at some time, given an opportunity, since all things are changeable, they might reestablish their state, and God will choose them again. . . .

CHAPTER 4: ON THE DIVINE LAW

. . . What is commonly meant by a law (lex) is a command which men may or may not follow, since a law constrains human powers within certain limits which they naturally exceed, and does not command anything beyond their scope. Law therefore seems to have to be defined more precisely as "a rule for living which a man prescribes to himself for others for some purpose." But the real purpose of laws is normally evident only to a few; most people are more or less incapable of grasping it, and hardly live by reason at all. Hence legislators have wisely contrived (in order to constrain all men equally) another purpose very different from the one which necessarily follows from the nature of laws. They promise to those who keep the laws things that the common people most desire, and threaten those who violate them with what they most fear. . . .

Since law, accordingly, is nothing other than a rule for living which men prescribe to themselves or to others for a purpose, it seems it has to be divided into human and divine. By human law I mean a rule for living whose only purpose is to protect life and preserve the country. By divine law I mean the law which looks only to the supreme good, that is, to the true knowledge and love of God. . . .

If we now consider the character of the natural divine law, as we have just explained it, we shall see:

(1) that it is universal or common to all men, for we have deduced it from universal human nature, and

(2) that it does not require belief in any kind of historical narrative. Since the natural divine law is inferred from the consideration of human nature alone, it is certain that we can conceive it in Adam as much as in any other man, as much in a man who lives among his fellow human beings as in a man who leads a solitary life. Belief in a historical narrative, however reliable it maybe, can give us no knowledge of God nor consequently love of God either. For love of God arises from knowledge of him; and knowledge of him has to be drawn from universal notions which are certain in themselves and well known, and so it is by no means the case that belief in a historical narrative is a necessary requirement for us to reach our highest good. But although belief in such histories cannot give us a knowledge and love of God, we do not deny that reading them is very useful for the purposes of civil life. The more we observe and the better we understand the manners and conditions of men, which can best be learned from their actions, the more wisely shall we be able to dwell among them, and the better we shall be able to adapt our actions and our lives to their ways.

(3) We shall also see that the natural divine law does not require ceremonies. Ceremonies are actions which are indifferent in themselves

and are called good only by convention or which represent some good as
necessary to salvation, or actions (if you prefer) whose rationale is beyond
human understanding. For the natural light of reason requires nothing
that this light itself does not reach; it requires only what carries the clearest
evidence of being a good or a means to our happiness. Things that are good
only by command or tradition or because they are symbolic representations
of some good, cannot improve our understanding; they are no more than
shadows and cannot be counted among actions that are the product or fruit,
so to speak, of mind and sound understanding. . . .

(4) Finally, we see that the supreme reward of the divine law is to know the
law itself, that is, to know God and to love him in true liberty with whole and
constant minds; the penalty is lack of these things and enslavement to the
flesh, or an inconstant and wavering mind.

Selections from the Writings of Moses Mendelssohn and an Associated Text

Known as the Socrates of Berlin, Moses Mendelssohn (1729–86) was challenged to defend Judaism philosophically or convert to Christianity. His 1783 *Jerusalem, or On Religious Power and Judaism* offers a sustained argument for Judaism's rationality and the complementarity of the Jewish religion and modern citizenship, which was not yet a reality. In the excerpts of *Jerusalem* included here, Mendelssohn affirms Spinoza's assertion that after the destruction of the Hebrew Commonwealth, Jewish law has no political dimension. But in contrast to Spinoza, Mendelssohn avers that Jewish law is fundamentally religious in nature. Mendelssohn defines Jewish law in terms of the Oral Torah, which he calls the "living script," and claims that the genius of Jewish law is that it requires interpretation and reinterpretation.

In his correspondence with Jacob Emden (1697–1776), a leading Jewish legal authority, Mendelssohn considers not what Jewish law is as such but rather how one might think about changing particular Jewish laws in light of modern circumstances. The impetus for this correspondence came from a 1772 law enacted by Duke Friedrich of Mecklenburg-Schwerin, which mandated delayed burial to make sure that no one was accidently buried alive. This law directly opposed Jewish law, which demands a quick burial. In his letter to Emden, Mendelssohn argues that by sharply distinguishing between law and custom, it is possible to reform modern Jewish law by looking to a particular law's original meaning and intention. Emden's response is largely animated by his alarm that Mendelssohn gives credence to non-Jewish sources.

Moses Mendelssohn, *Jerusalem, or On Religious Power and Judaism*, translated by Allan Arkush (Hanover, NH: University Press of New England, 1983), 102–3 and 127–34.

. . . The ceremonial law itself is a kind of living script, rousing the mind and heart, full of meaning, never ceasing to inspire contemplation and to provide the occasion and opportunity for oral instruction. What a student himself did and saw being done from morning till night pointed to religious doctrines and convictions and spurred him on to follow his teacher, to watch him, to observe all his actions, and to obtain the instruction which he was capable of acquiring by means of his talents, and of which he had rendered himself worthy by his conduct....

These laws were *revealed*, that is, they were made known by God, through *words* and *script*. Yet only the most essential part of them was entrusted to letters; and without the unwritten explanations, delimitations, and more precise determinations, transmitted orally and propagated through oral, living instruction, even these written laws are mostly incomprehensible, or inevitably became so in the course of time. For no words or written signs preserve their meaning unchanged throughout a generation....

...I cannot see how those born into the House of Jacob can in any conscientious manner disencumber themselves of the law. We are permitted to reflect on the law, to inquire into its spirit, and, here and there, where the lawgiver gave no reason, to surmise a reason which, *perhaps*, depended upon time, place, and circumstances, and which, *perhaps*, may be liable to change in accordance with time, place, and circumstances—if it pleases the Supreme Lawgiver to make known to us His will on this matter, to make it known in as clear a voice, in as public a manner, and as far beyond all doubt and ambiguity as He did when He gave the law itself. As long as this has not happened, as long as we can point to no such authentic exemption from the law, no sophistry of ours can free us from the strict obedience we owe to the law; and reverence for God draws a line between speculation and practice which no conscientious man may cross....

"Exchange of Letters with Jacob Emden Regarding Delayed Burial," in Moses Mendelssohn, *Gesammelte Schriften Jubiläumsausgabe*, volume 19, edited by Haim Borodianski (Bar-Dayan) (Stuttgart, Germany: Frommann-Holzboog, 1973), 156–57 and 161–63 (translated by Matthew Miller).

To the Jewish Community of Schwerin
Berlin, 9th of June 1772 (8th of Sivan, 5532)
Tuesday, the Day after the Festival of Shavuot, 5532, Berlin.

Their pleasant letter from the last month has arrived, and I saw within it that the leader and ruler of the land [Duke Friedrich of Mecklenburg-Schwerin] has decreed that they must leave out their dead three days before they are buried. My masters have been pained and distressed regarding this, thinking that the [Duke] wants to cause them to violate religion (dat), God forbid, or to make them stumble over a biblical prohibition or a rabbinic decree. However, I was a dolt, without knowledge[2] of why they thought [it was forbidden], nor the cause of this great tremor over this matter. . . . If I have erred, then let my words be considered as nothing;[3] but according to my humble opinion this matter does not involve any sort of violation of religion (dat), God forbid, as they have thought. Although the sages of blessed memory said that those who delay [the burial of the] dead violate a negative commandment, they nonetheless permitted to delay [burial] if it is for the honor of the dead, for example to bring him a casket, burial shrouds, women to lament, so that relatives can come, and so that announcements can be made in the city ([*Shulḥan Arukh*,[4]] Yoreh De'ah, 357[:1]). If for the sake of such minor things they [are] permitted to delay [burial], then how much the more so should [someone] not be buried if there is any sort of doubt concerning whether he is still alive, for all is permitted when it comes to saving a life (*pikuaḥ nefesh*).

. . . [I]t seems obvious to me that the reason the sages of blessed memory did not explicitly mention this concern [about burying someone alive] is due to the fact that it was unnecessary in their days, since they buried their dead in caves and alcoves, and they would watch over [the bodies] for three days to see if they were still alive or if they would come back to life, as it says in m. Semaḥot [8: 1]: "They would go out to the cemetery and would watch over the bodies for three days. This is not to be considered [a violation of the prohibition of walking in] the ways of the Amorite.[5] Once, they were looking after a body [and it came back to life], lived another twenty-five years and then died. Another [came back to life], sired five children, and then died." If the matter is so, then [the sages] spoke well when they said, "All who hasten burial are praiseworthy,"[6] for there is no concern [that they will bury someone alive]. However, since we bury our dead in a way that it is not possible to watch over them . . . , it is certainly fitting for us to delay burial until there is no longer any doubt that they might be alive. If an incident like the one cited in m. Semaḥot occurs [but we bury the individual alive], God forbid, how will we justify ourselves?

2. [Ps. 73:22.]

3. [See Job 24:25.]

4. [*Shulḥan Arukh* (The set table), a comprehensive Jewish legal by Yosef Karo (1488–1575) and published in 1565. Its principal sections—Oraḥ Ḥayyim, Yoreh De'ah, Even Ha-Ezer, and Ḥoshen Mishpat—correspond to the sections in the earlier code, *Arba'ah Turim*, also known as the *Tur*, by Ya'akov ben Asher (1270–c. 1340).]

5. [The Amorites were a Canaanite people whose practices, especially those related to sorcery, the Israelites were cautioned not to imitate. See Lev. 18:3.]

6. [b. Mo'ed Katan 22a.]

Behold, all medical doctors testify and say that they do not have any decisive sign for death, and that sometimes a person may faint to the extent that his heartbeat is silent and his breathing completely ceases. Those who see him consider him to be dead, [even though] it is not the case. Rather, one must wait until the flesh is decomposed and rotted. It is evident from the words of the sages of blessed memory in the story in m. Semaḥot, in which they would take the dead to the cemeteries and bury them in alcoves and subsequently they would rise to their feet and come alive, that they agree with the medical doctors. [This is also evident] from what is taught in the Mishnah: "A man with an abnormal seminal discharge (zav), a woman with an abnormal vaginal discharge (zavah), a menstruating woman (niddah), or a postpartum woman that die[s] makes others impure through carrying [the body] until their flesh decays."[7] . . .]

Behold, their Excellencies will see the content of the memorandum that I believe is fitting to be sent to the [Duke], and I believe he will be appeased by it, and every man will sleep in peace. However, if [the Duke] will not be appeased, then there is nothing better to do than to follow in the footsteps of our ancestors of blessed memory, to build a cave in the cemetery in order to purify the deceased there according to custom and to watch over them three days, and then to bury them. In my opinion, this is an obligation incumbent on all holy communities, so that they do not stray from the ways of our ancestors of blessed memory to the left or right since their ways are ways of pleasantness.[8] It is worthy for the sages of the generation to stir [the communities] to do so. Although I know that they will not heed me, since the power of custom (minhag) is resolute and strong, and perhaps I will seem to them as if I am leading them astray, nonetheless I have saved my soul and that shall afford safety.[9]

The insignificant Moses from Dessau

From Jacob Emden
. . . July 3, 1772 . . .
Bless be God, Tammuz 2, 5532, Altona.
Greetings to the honored master, the captain of Torah, the enlightened one, Moses, may his Rock protect him and keep him alive.

7. [m. Niddah 10:4.]
8. [Prov. 3:17.]
9. [Mic. 5:4.]

His pleasant letter from the 29th [of last month] came to me after the holy Shabbat, and I saw in it his desire to understand my opinion, and how I defended the custom (minhag) of Israel [to bury the dead immediately]. . . . I supported [my position] with beautiful proofs from the Bible which are straightforward to the intelligent man.[10] . . . I thought it right to expound according to the person [who asked], so I quickly found as much support as is necessary for the matter from the Bible with the help of God, even though the ways of the sages do not need strengthening. . . .

I only now need to respond to the claims of his Excellency [Mendelssohn] and to resolve the doubts that have arisen for him in this matter.

First, [Mendelssohn] has written [to me], "I do not know how we have strayed from the custom of our holy forefathers, who would bury their dead in alcoves and caves and would watch over them for three days, as it says in m. Semaḥot. From the story that is brought there, it is evident and proven that there is only a clear-cut sign for death after three days." I say to this, God forbid! It is profane to question the custom of our forefathers who are scattered throughout the four [corners of the earth] (even if there is variation in custom in matters where it is of no significance), for in this matter the Ashkenazim, Sephardim, Easterners and Westerners are in accordance.[11] We do not know nor have we heard of any part of the world to which our brothers have been scattered where Jews practice a different custom from what we practice in these lands with regards to burying their dead.

So that we do not contradict an explicit law (din) in the Mishnah, [we will say that] it used to be among [the nation of] Israel that when they lived in their land in peace they would bury [dead] bodies in alcoves. Now, however, this practice has disappeared even in the Holy Land, as is known. (In earlier times, when the land was in our hands, it was easy to do as our ancestors did, to bury in alcoves, since they had an expansive burial plot, and since it is a land of mountains and rocks, as well as one congenial to caves). This is not the case nowadays, since in these lowlands one will hardly even find the necessary space in a plain or valley

10. [Prov. 8:9.]

11. [Ashkenazim and Sephardim are the two major ethnic groups of diasporic Jews, which began to diverge around 1100. Broadly speaking, Ashkenazim are the Jews of northern Europe, especially the Yiddish-speaking communities of Central and Eastern Europe, and Sephardim are the Jews of southern Europe and the Mediterranean countries. The laws, liturgy, and customs of these two ethnic groups differ in various ways.]

(see *Tur*,[12] Yoreh De'ah, 362, in the [Vilna] Gaon,[13] 259; however, [the latter's opinion] is difficult to reconcile, but in my work *Mor u-Ketziah* I explained [it], with the help of God). Whatever the case may be, far be it, God forbid, for one to even raise the thought of the possibility that all of the Diaspora from one end of the earth to the other should have erred in this matter. Let Israel be. If they are not prophets, then they are the children of prophets.[14] They have been assured that they will not forget the Torah, neither them nor their descendants for all times.

Even if such a case is unique because there is a concern for saving a life, according to the opinion of his Excellency [Mendelssohn], far be it [from him] to suggest that none of the leaders of the generations, the shepherds of the holy flock, paid attention to it until now, when the matter was raised by the nations who are seeking a pretext to act according to their practices, [and] when we have been commanded to separate from them and their statutes (especially in such a case as this one which is a long-standing practice from their forefathers, in which they would seek council from the dead, even if nowadays they have forgotten the cause or reason for delaying the burial of their dead and for having the impurity with them in their home for a measure of eight or more days).

Not like these is the Portion of Jacob.[15] . . . Through it we live today; in its shade we shall live amongst the nations; for it we die; and [we] dedicate our lives to not stray from it, either to the left or right as we have been commanded. I have already dealt with what is said in m. Semaḥot, "they would watch over the dead," as well as the many stories [contained therein], in my aforementioned lengthy responsum to the community of Schwerin. . . .

Nonetheless, [watching the bodies for three days] is not necessary as an absolute obligation. Rather, [it only is] in a case in which there is a concern that some dead [individual] was buried and the investigation, supervision, and appropriate interval was harried in a pressing circumstance when they hastened to bury [him] because of some occasional cause. However, when the body is treated

12. [*Tur* refers to both the book *Arba'ah Turim* (Four rows) written by Ya'akov ben Asher (1270–c. 1340), and its author. The title alludes to the rows of jewels in the High Priest's breastplate, and the book is organized in four sections: Oraḥ Ḥayyim, Yoreh De'ah, Even Ha-Ezer, and Ḥoshen Mishpat.]

13. [Eliyahu of Vilna (1720–97).]

14. [b. Pesaḥim 66a.]

15. [Jer. 10:16.]

properly, deliberately, and with the appropriate supervision, as is the custom of the Burial Society in these days, in a time of peace, we are completely and entirely unconcerned for the minutest of minute possibility.

... Even in such a grave matter as [saving a life], doubtless, there is still a distinction to be made between [a case] that is [only] slightly common to one which is non-existent, which would only arise by way of a marvel....

Regarding that which his Excellency [Mendelssohn] has written about the consensus of the medical doctors, [I say] far be it from us to pay attention to them [in a matter] strictly related to the laws of the Torah, for then [the Torah's] foundations will weaken and [its] pillars will quake.[16]...

Regarding that his Excellency thought that he had a support and proof for the words of human beings who have no wisdom, from the *mishnah* in the tenth chapter of m. Niddah, which states that it is impossible to distinguish between death and fainting until the flesh has decayed, our Exaltedness was not precise in interpreting the Talmud [regarding the statement:] "[it is] a decree lest he faint." [Mendelssohn] understands that the concern of fainting is referring to the man with abnormal seminal emission (zav) who has died, that we are concerned that he has not [actually] died, and the uncertainty about whether he is still alive is not removed until his flesh has decayed.

This is not the case, this is not correct, my son, rather this is the [proper] interpretation: The rabbis were concerned that perhaps a live, [otherwise] healthy *zav* would faint and be thought to have died suddenly, even though he is still alive ("fainting" is a common occurrence even among those who are healthy, especially those who are suffering from emissions). [Others will think he is dead] and will conduct [the preburial] purifications [on his body] on top of an emplaced stone, but [since] he is alive, [he] will render impure [other objects that are situated underneath the rock] by being on top of [the] rock, and this is a stumbling block leading to sin.[17]

Therefore, [the sages] decreed due to this case that even in case of a *zav* who

16. [See Job 9:6.]

17. [The impurity of an individual suffering from bodily emissions differs from the impurity of a corpse in the case of a large and heavy stone. Whereas a corpse that is placed on such a stone does not render objects underneath the stone impure, individuals suffering from bodily emissions who lie on top of such a stone do render objects underneath the stone impure. Consequently, following b. Niddah 69b, Emden understands the mishnah as establishing a precaution regarding impurity.]

is certainly and absolutely dead, nevertheless the corpse renders other objects impure [qua zav] until the flesh decays. . . .

In regards to what his Excellency [Mendelssohn] concludes, "And if the matter is in doubt until three days, then certainly this is not a violation of delaying [the burial of] the dead, since it states [in the Mishnah] that they would delay in order to bring him a casket, etc. How much the more so in a case of saving life." Beware! Do not turn to mischief.[18] Who would think to say thusly? I do not suspect that his Excellency wants to completely uproot a law (din) from the *mishnah*, which says, "All who delay [burial of the] dead has violated, except. . . ."[19] But, according to his opinion, the extension necessarily follows that one who delays [the burial] has not transgressed. On the contrary, the opposite is obligatory, for one is obligated always to delay [the burial of] the dead. What then shall be done with the *mishnah* which has no meaning according to your premise? Far be it from you, who I love like a son[, to do so]. Certainly an error has been made without analysis and examination. Rather, my son, heed the discipline of a father,[20] do not swerve from my words,[21] and do not turn to the words of idolatrous doctors. . . .

> *The lover of your soul, the words*
> *of a speaker of peace to the true seed,*
> *Jacob Israel [Emden], called Ya'avetz*
> *Written by night and sealed by [the next]*
> *day, so as not delay the commandment.*

18. [Job 36:21.]
19. [See m. Sanhedrin 6:4. This is a gloss of the mishnah.]
20. [See Prov. 1:8.]
21. [Prov. 4:5.]

Abraham Geiger, *Posthumous Writings*

Writing after the emancipation of the Jews in 1812, Abraham Geiger (1810–74) served as a rabbi in several Reform congregations and was one of the early founders of the academic study of Judaism (*Wissenschaft des Judentums*). Geiger's theological and scholarly undertakings converge in his commitment to applying modern historical methods to the study of Judaism. In 1840, Geiger assumed a rabbinic position in Breslau. His response to the opposition of Rabbi Solomon Tiktin and his supporters to this appointment provides the context for the selection included here. Geiger invokes both Naḥmanides (Moses ben Naḥman [1194–1270], also known as Ramban) and Maimonides (Moses ben Maimon [1135 or 1138–1204]) to defend his reformist view that Jewish law, which he defines in accordance with the sincere if ultimately erroneous interpretations of scripture by particular rabbis in particular times and places, has always changed in accord with its historical circumstances. Geiger suggests that in calling him a heretic, Tiktin and his supporters would by extension also be calling Naḥmanides, Maimonides, and the rabbis themselves heretics. As one practical outcome of his arguments, Geiger considers the ceremony of ḥalitzah, as described in Deuteronomy 25:9, in which a woman is released from the obligation of a levirate marriage—that is, the obligation to marry her brother-in-law if her husband has died before they had children. Geiger contends that this ceremony should be entirely dispensed with, since rabbinic law no longer sanctions levirate marriage and the obligation to conduct the ceremony often harms widows.

Abraham Geiger, *Nachgelassene Schriften* (Breslau: W. Jacobsohn, 1885), 103–12 (translated by John Raimo).

I assume that the Bible explications the Talmud undertakes toward the establishment of religious prescriptions are earnestly intended as explications; yet with this . . . [my critics[22] say] I insult the teachers of the Talmud, since these explications are in no way earnestly intended and should be [understood as] mere mnemonic devices (*Erinnerungsbelege*), for which he calls upon the declared

---

22. [Israel Deutsch (1800–3) and David Deutsch (1810–73), brothers who were both German Orthodox rabbis and opposed Geiger's appointment as rabbi at Breslau.]

authorities [including Maimonides].[23] . . . As concerns Maimonides, I bid . . . [my critic] to take the *Sefer ha-Mizvot* [Book of the commandments][24]—which he likely does not know at all—and to read there the second principle, along with the comments of Nahmanides. In his quest to satisfy his exegetical conscience—and in the process also to vindicate the Bible explications of the Talmudists—Maimonides also comes back to this . . . assumption that the exegesis (*derash*) is not earnestly intended, but rather with few exceptions is a support (*Anlehnung*) [for an already existing principle].[25] Yet Nahmanides refutes him most thoroughly, proving that this is definitively erroneous and a false attempt at accommodation and he concludes that all those exegeses undertaken by the Talmudists were intended as actual explications, [otherwise] they would have needed to explicitly state that it is a mere mnemonic. . . .[26]

If I now thus derived (*leitete*) . . . that they [the Talmudists] have in general not made much effort towards the correct exegesis—this is merely what they themselves declare. "I was already eighteen years old," says one of the most prominent Talmudists, R. Kahana, "and had already studied the entire Talmud, however I did not yet know that the verses of the Bible are explained according to the natural sense" (b. Shabbat 63a.) . . . That now the later generations in general always and without awe have strayed from the explications of the Talmudists is well known. I refer only to the position of Maimonides in the [*The Guide of the Perplexed*] (3:41) where he explains and adds the law "eye for an eye" according to its

23. [Geiger and Israel Deutsch agree that many rabbinic explications of the Bible do not reflect the correct or plain meaning of the text. But they differ on whether the rabbis earnestly intended their poor exegesis (Geiger), or whether they were not attempting to explicate biblical texts correctly but rather were using them as supports or mnemonics for rabbinic principles (Deutsch).]

24. [First printed 1497.]

25. [This is a reference to the rabbinic concept of *asmakhta ba-alma* (literally, "a mere support," the term also means a mnemonic device) when a biblical verse is merely a support for a rabbinic law, as opposed to the law being exegetically derived from the Bible.]

26. [Nahmanides' *Hasagot* on Maimonides' *Sefer Ha-Mitzvot*, Principle 2. Nahmanides uses the word "asmakhta" for what Geiger is translating as a mnemonic. The dispute between Maimonides and Nahmanides refers to whether a certain type of biblical exegesis yields laws that have biblical authority or merely rabbinic authority. If the exegesis is meant "earnestly" (in Geiger's words), all the laws derived from this type of exegesis would be biblical (Nahmanides' position). If the exegesis is not meant earnestly but is rather merely a support, then these laws are not counted among the 613 commandments (Maimonides' position).]

literal sense and not according to the Talmudic reinterpretation whereby monetary compensation is discussed. [Maimonides states:] "Do not distract yourself with [the fact] that we now impose fines, because my intention here is to state the basis for biblical prescriptions and not for Talmudic reinterpretation.... [ellipsis in original]."

... [Solomon Eiger in Posen[27] claims] that I have allowed a divergent reading and interpretation of the Talmudic prescriptions as regards phylacteries (tefillin)![28] Strange! While [my above-mentioned critics] assert that the exegesis of the Talmudists is absolutely not intended earnestly—rather it is merely a testimony of memory . . .; Herr Eiger does the reverse and asserts that he who concedes a "divergent interpretation and reading taken from the words of the Talmud" is himself a heretic, and now ... Maimonides and R. Samuel ben Meir (Rashbam)[29] [fall into this category]. The latter clearly says in regard to the words: "it shall be as a sign on your hand and as a memory between your eyes" [Exod. 13:9], which ... the Talmud use[s] ... as a foundation for the command to create phylacteries: "The meaning according to sound and natural explanation is that it (the Exodus from Egypt) should always be for you a memory, as though it were written on your hand . . . [ellipsis in original] likewise between your eyes as an ornament or a golden ring, which one wears as a jewel upon the forehead."[30] Therefore the command of phylacteries does not result for him [Rashbam] from the verses adduced by the Talmud for this purpose, but is rather a statute [*Satzung*] like many others having a general application without explicitly being in the Bible. I said the same, only far less apodictically.... In what company does Herr Tiktin [who also accuses me of heresy] now hold himself? Does he concur with the "competent" chief rabbis of Posen, so that I—and with me Maimonides and [Rashbam] and so many others . . . —am a heretic because I say there exists a natural exegesis of texts that does not coincide with the Talmudic [explication] or [does he] agree with [my above-mentioned critics] . . . so that I—and with me Naḥmanides and many others, and even Herr Eiger in Posen—am a heretic because I say: The Talmudists have earnestly intended their explications of the scripture? . . .

27. [Solomon Eiger (1785–1852), a son of Akiva Eiger (1761–1837), inherited his father's position as chief rabbi of Posen. He sided with Tiktin in the dispute with Geiger.]

28. [Tefillin are small black leather boxes containing scrolls inscribed with verses of the Torah. Attached by leather straps, they are worn on the head and left arm by observant Jews during weekday morning prayers.]

29. [France, c. 1085–c. 1175.]

30. [Commentary on Exod. 13:9 by Rashbam.]

I wish only to return to the similar accusation regarding ḥalitzah. . . . I say that ḥalitzah—as an act that should effect the dispensation from levirate marriage—has lost its proper meaning and persists only as old custom now that Jewish law no longer admits levirate marriage, especially if the brother-in-law is already married. Yet this custom has a very injurious effect in some cases; namely when the brother-in-law is hostilely disposed toward the woman, refuses the ḥalitzah and cannot be forced to it or when the brother-in-law is absent and one does not know his whereabouts, so that naturally the ḥalitzah cannot be carried out, and the woman must see the flower of her youth wither. . . . Such a grievance (*Misstande*) should be redressed, and the remedy rests nearby. It is a principle in the Talmud. . . . . [T]he Talmudists dissolve the bond of matrimony in cases that occasion the unnecessary confinement of women. . . . [T]he teachers of the Talmud as well as the later rabbis searched for grounds for mitigation to make it possible for a woman whose widowhood was not completely certain to remarry; the testimony of one individual, a woman, [or] one who heard from another party was valid for the confirmation of the husband's death, and so forth . . . all not to expose the woman to eternal widowhood (*takanot agunot*).[31] Likewise one even had regulations (*Einrichtungen*) for the benefit of women later in the eleventh century, namely that no man should be permitted to marry more than one wife and that divorce should not be performed without the woman's consent.[32] "According to these qualifications," I remarked . . . , "the grievance touched upon above could be easily redressed: Namely, it [could be redressed] by a determination of a meeting of an assembly of rabbis that the earlier marriage be considered not consummated once the brother-in-law who has to perform the ḥalitzah could not be found, or if the brother's wife laid insurmountable obstacles in the way."[33] This [was] my proposal grounded upon Talmudic and rabbinic prac-

31. [b. Gittin 33a, commenting on m. Gittin 3:1, refers to a ruling (takanot agunot) by Rabbi Gamaliel (Jerusalem, first century CE) that placed limits on how a husband could nullify a writ of divorce, so that the husband would be prevented from "chaining" his wife as an *agunah* through arbitrary nullification of a divorce.]

32. [Geiger refers to the enactments of Gershom ben Yehudah (France, 960–1040), who is famous for a synod he convened around 1000 at which he instituted, among other things, a ban on polygamy and a requirement that both parties, not just the man, must consent for them to be divorced.]

33. [Abraham Geiger, *Die Stellung des weiblichen Geschlechts in dem Judenthume unserer Zeit* (The position of the female sex in the Judaism of our time), in *Wissenschaftliche Zeitschrift für Jüdische Theologie* 3 (1837): 10.]

tice and made for the same genuine well-being of the faith as of the confessors (*Bekenner*)!

... What do these men believe the result will be, if they drive their thoughtlessness and unscrupulousness so far as to represent—through contortions—a great part of their own community, that is, a respectable number of recognized German rabbis as "unbelievers excluded by the Israelite society" and "as impermissible credible witnesses"? ... Is this not hypocritical, not the same method as those who torture and burn alleged heretics, yet indeed do not decapitate so as not to spill any blood? ... [T]hese men only concern themselves with the Talmud so long as it is employed to their own ends, and they say that only those alone who swear by their professed views can be considered Jewish. And now, what can, what should the result of such a presumptuous and obstinate pursuit be? ...

But all you, my brothers who seriously care about the religion of the fathers and take no part nor joy in controversy, all you who wish to instill in your children a sense of religion and are eager to equip them for life that they do not perish in the storms, all you whose eyes are not shut before the present conditions, all you I implore by the sacred goods appointed to us to preserve and to guard over: Do not bring the religion to dead letters ... and turn away from the spirit. ... [F]ollow in the tracks of wiser ancestors and perceive how they—holding fast to the eternal rewards (*Gehalte*) of Judaism—have acknowledged the conviction of the time and the appropriate influences of its ever-shifting customs! Yet the differences that necessarily emerge from a living controversy and those [differences that emerge] from the God of spirits who "does not make the minds (*Ansichten*) of men equal to one another just as he does not make their features the same,"[34] are permitted; these differences countenance one another in friendly, mutual recognition as anciently shown (*wie weisen alten*) by Shammai and Hillel![35] Then will we delight in a true peace, which hypocritical lips do not proclaim, but which is rather the fruit of the earnest endeavor that is blessed by God.

34. [b. Berakhot 51a.]

35. [Shammai (Jerusalem, 50 BCE–30 CE) and Hillel (Jerusalem, c.110 BCE–10 CE) were the founders of two Jewish legal schools, whose members often disagreed.]

4 | Selections from the Writings of Samson Raphael Hirsch

Samson Raphael Hirsch (1808–1888) is generally credited with being the intellectual founder of Neo-Orthodoxy, now more commonly referred to as Modern Orthodoxy, which developed in Germany in response to Jewish reformers. In contrast to Geiger and others, Hirsch contends that Jewish law does not change over time, and neither does its binding nature for Jews. The first selection from Hirsch's writings in this volume comes from *Horeb*, his theological treatise of 1838, in which he maintains that the Oral Torah and the Written Torah were revealed together and that the law was closed with Moses. The second selection is from Hirsch's commentary on the Torah portion *Mishpatim* (Exod. 21:1–24:18), which introduces the first body of civil legislation in the Bible. Hirsch offers an account of the relation between the Oral and Written Torah in which the Written Torah is but a set of notes reflecting the complete Oral Torah, which was fully revealed with the written law. Like legal formalists, Hirsch insists that law is a self-generating, internally coherent, and autonomous system. His denial of rabbinic mediation and indeed of rabbinic interpretation in making Jewish law (his claim that the law is discovered and not created) goes hand in hand with his apolitical conception of the law. Geiger made precisely the opposite argument to claim that contemporary Jews could also make such judgments in nullifying the law in light of new historical circumstances.

Samson Raphael Hirsch, *Horeb: A Philosophy of Jewish Laws and Observances*, translated by Isidore Grunfeld (London: Soncino, 1962), 20–21.

REVELATION

... There are here four things which every generation of Israel is bidden to take to heart: (1) the fact and manner of the Revelation of the Torah at Sinai; (2) the fact and the definition of the continuous revelation in prophecy; (3) the attestation and the signs of a true prophet; (4) the signs of and warning against a false prophet.

The law was not brought to Israel by an intermediary, whether accredited by signs or not; all Israel, numbering two and a half million souls, were assembled at Horeb, and heard directly the voice of the Lord when He began, amid universal turbulence, to reveal the law of life. The whole of Israel became in that moment prophetic and climbed to the highest reaches of prophecy. . . . The beginning of the Revelation of the law at Sinai is the guarantee of the completion of the law through Moses. . . . [T]he Torah declares itself to be closed for all time. . . .

. . . They were not to be law-giving prophets, for the law, both written and oral, was closed with Moses, and transmitted to the people directly, and it stood above the prophets. . . .

The Torah directly revealed at Horeb . . . is the touchstone of the prophet; and since the completion of the Written and Oral Law at Horeb, the determination of its content is not tied to prophetic inspiration from heaven. Do not be led astray. . . .

Samson Raphael Hirsch, *Pentateuch: Translation and Commentary*, translated by Isaac Levy (Gateshead, UK: Judaica, 1973), 288.

COMMENTARY TO EXODUS, CHAPTER 21; *MISHPATIM*[36]

"1. Now these are the rules that you shall set before them. 2. When you acquire a Hebrew slave, he shall serve six years; in the seventh year he shall go free, without payment."

V.2. ["When you acquire a Hebrew slave"] To the unprejudiced mind, nothing can show so strikingly the truth of the traditional oral-law as the first two paragraphs, V.2–6 and 7–11, with which this "Mosaic Lawgiving" starts. The civil and criminal laws of the Nation are to be given, the fundamental basis and the ordinances of justice and humaneness are to be laid down, which are to govern the relationship and behavior of man to his fellowman in the state; the first matter to be dealt with, quite naturally deals with the rights of man, and this starts with the sentences *"When a man sells another man,"* and *"when a man sells his daughter"*!!! What an unthinkable enormity if actually this "written word" of the "book of Law of the Jewish Nation" should really be the one and only, sole source of the Jewish conception of "Rights." What a mass of laws and principles of jurisprudence must have already been said and fixed, considered, laid down and explained, before the Book of Law could reach these, or even speak of these,

---

36. [Compare Hirsch's perspective on the Oral Torah as expressed in this commentary to that of Eliyahu of Vilna, in part 2 of this volume, who also comments on these texts. Also compare Hirsch's view of servitude in Jewish law to that of his grandson, Isaac Breuer, which is included in part 3.]

which, after all, are only quite exceptional cases. And it is with these sentences, the contents of which deny and limit the very holiest personal right of man, the right to personal freedom, that the Law *begins*. But it is quite a different matter if the written word, the "Book" is *not* the real source of the Jewish conception of rights, if this source is the traditional law, which was entrusted to the living word to which this "book" is only to be an aid to memory and reference, when doubts arise; if, as indeed is stated in the "book" itself, the total and complete Law had been given over to the people in its complete form, and had been impressed upon them, and explained to them and lived by them for full forty years, before Moses, just before his death, was to hand them this written book. Then we can well understand that it is just the exceptional cases which principally come to be described, so that just from them, the normal general principles of justice and humanity may be more strikingly realized. Then we can understand how it is that general principles of justice are altogether not so much given in this "book," but preferably single concrete cases, and these are described in the "book" in such an instructive manner that the principles which underlie them, and which had been entrusted to the living minds and living practice of the people, can easily be seen from them. Then we understand how the language that is used in this "book" is so skillfully chosen that often by the use of a striking expression, an unusual or altered construction, the position of a word, a letter[,] etc., a whole train of ideas of justice and human rights is indicated. AFTER ALL, IT WAS NOT OUT OF THIS BOOK THAT THE LAW WAS TO HAVE BEEN ACQUIRED. This book was to be given into the hands of those who were already well informed in the Law, simply as a means of retaining and of reviving ever afresh this knowledge which had been entrusted to their memories; and also to the teachers of Law as a means of teaching to which the students can go for references to the traditional actual laws, so that the written sentences lying before them would make it easy for them to recall to their minds the knowledge they had received orally.

The Written Torah is to be to the Oral Torah in the relation of short notes on a full and extensive lecture on any scientific subject. For the student who has heard the whole lecture, short notes are quite sufficient to bring back afresh to his mind at any time the whole subject of the lecture. For him, a word, an added mark of interrogation, or exclamation, a dot, the underlining of a word[,] etc.[,] etc., is often quite sufficient to recall to his mind a whole series of thoughts, a remark[,] etc. For those who had not heard the lecture from the Master, such notes would be completely useless. If they were to try to reconstruct the scientific contents of the lecture literally from such notes they would of necessity make many errors. Words, marks, etc., which serve those scholars who had heard the lecture as instructive guiding starts to the wisdom that had been taught and learnt, stare at the uninitiated as unmeaning sphinxes. The wisdom, the truths, which the initiated reproduce from them (but do NOT PRODUCE out of them) are sneered at by the uninitiated as being merely a clever or witty play of words and empty dreams without any real foundation.

When the word of God, wants us to realize what are the principles of rights and humaneness which it demands for the respect of the human being, it starts off with the criminal . . . who in all other states, is threatened with the direst punishment to body and freedom, and it shows us what is the treatment that God's idea of rights in His State dictates. Let us read this law:

["When you acquire a Hebrew slave."][37] The oral tradition teaches us that the case dealt with here is that described in [Exodus] 22:2, that a thief who cannot restore the value of the theft of his victim is sold to help him make this restoration. If he has nothing [with which to make restitution] then he shall be sold for his theft. Such a sale can only be made to make up the value of the actual theft itself, but not to bring it up to the double value where this is imposed as a fine. Such a sale is only imposed on male thieves, not on females. The written note on this [rule (halakhah)] is that there it does not say in a general term ["if he has nothing then he shall be sold"] which would sufficient but adds ["for his theft"] and also it does not say ["for the theft"] (which would suffice) but ["for his theft"] and not ["her theft,"] excluding female thieves. The case where a man sells himself out of dire poverty is provided for elsewhere, ["if your kinsman under you continues in straits and must give himself over to you"] (Lev. 25: 39). That is why it says only ["When you acquire a Hebrew slave"—] he is already a slave before you buy him, has been declared one by the court, and it is from the court only, that you can buy him. Nevertheless, as the Mekhilta remarks, to you he must remain a Hebrew, your fellow-national, it is only that the court has no option but to call him "slave." ["Perhaps he should not be called 'slave'" at all, it being a term of opprobrium. But it says: "When you acquire a Hebrew slave." The Torah designates him a slave against his will.]

37. [Except where otherwise noted, Hirsch's source for what follows is Mekhilta DeRabbi Ishmael, a collection of midrashic exegesis on Exodus 12–23 that includes both legal and narrative exegesis (halakhah and *aggadah*). For an English translation, see *Mekhilta De-Rabbi Ishmael*, translated by Jacob Z. Lauterbach (Philadelphia: Jewish Publication Society, 1935). At various points Hirsch cites, in Hebrew, alternative versions of the Mekilta. Lauterbach includes these alternatives in his notes to the Hebrew text.]

Zacharias Frankel, "Judicial Evidence
According to Mosaic Talmudic Law"

A rabbi and a historian of Judaism, Zacharias Frankel (1801–75) was one of the founders of the school of Positive-Historical Judaism, which later became known in the United States as Conservative Judaism. Like other proponents of Positive-Historical Judaism, Frankel contends that Geiger and other Jewish reformers depict Jewish history, especially the history of Jewish law, in wholly passive terms. In contrast, Frankel maintains that the history of Jewish law is an expression of the organic growth of the Jewish people's spirit over time. In the selections included here, Frankel emphasizes the ways in which the historical development of Jewish criminal and civil law reflects the customs and self-consciousness of the Jewish people as they unfolded over time. The Oral Torah is the expression of this unfolding. Frankel was self-consciously influenced by the German historical school of law, and especially by Friedrich Carl von Savigny (1779–1861), who insisted that law is tied to the common life of the people. Like Savigny, Frankel emphasizes the organic link between Jewish law and Jewish peoplehood and is ambivalent about equating law with rules. While recognizing Maimonides' genius, Frankel laments the systemization at the heart of Maimonides' *Mishneh Torah*, which for Frankel limits the scope, meaning, and vibrant life of Jewish law.

Zacharias Frankel, *Der gerichtliche Beweis nach mosaisch-talmudischen Rechte* (Berlin: Verlag von Veit, 1846), 55–62 and 97–111 (translated by John Raimo).

The object of the revealed law generally concerns an injured relation (*Rechtsverhältniss*), a loss, which someone suffers . . .; the object of the positive law is generally the acquisition of a right, which precedes from a mutual will (contract). . . . The latter considers in detail the acquisition of movable and immovable goods, lease holding and rent, mortgages, buying and selling, association, and other private law relations. This law flowed from disparate elements; it partly loses itself in time-honored traditions, some were partly from the laws of nations . . . under which the Jews lived—those of the Greeks, Romans, and Persians. In doing so, the Talmudic law nevertheless kept its independence. . . .

. . . Now, what Talmudic law has most in common with Roman [law] are legal cases; the same matters are often discussed here and there, and they form the basis upon which the ideas of law (*Rechtsideen*) are applied. This commonality lay in the circumstances and the needs of the time . . .; such contact of peoples with one another [is] nearly unavoidable. But these legal determinations differ from one another in almost all cases, clearly demonstrating that they have not taken one legal doctrine from the other. Thus the mortgage law of the Talmud is quite different from that of the Romans, they diverge in [in their understanding of] bonds and subjection, and thus in principal parts of the law. What Talmudic law roughly incorporated from Roman law had to be expressed in a completely different way according to the spiritual direction of the oriental and occidental mind. . . . Talmudic law retained a religious coloring through its connection to Mosaic laws . . . [which was] the ultimate preserver and guardian of the law. This came about from the idea of justice itself, which in the sacred scriptures is frequently represented by the divinity. . . . The Talmudic law by no means concludes with this. . . . [Its] jurisprudence is manifold and does not derive its legitimation only from scripture. Still, it retained a religious character in its entirety, which joined law to revelation (*Geoffenbarte*). . . . The Talmudic civil law also recognizes regulations from ancient times, which it traces from the period of the first conquest of the land by Joshua. . . .

. . . [M]ore fixed guidelines (*Grundlinien*) were recorded as time moved on, and the civil law gradually gained consistency both through some principles and through practical application and diligent treatment. . . .

No practical necessity pressed for the preparation of a code, which would have also further suffered from its fragmentariness. . . .

. . . The undertaking of a scholar of the twelfth century was epoch making in bringing the existing material into a system and establishing a universal code. *Moses ben Maimon* from Cordova, [who became] famous under the name of *Maimonides* [and] whose mind was trained in the Peripatetic School and had taken the Aristotelian method of logical schematizing for his own, authored with astonishing learning and cautious mastery of these materials his great work the *Mishneh Torah*, in which he reproduced the whole of the law, both the Written (Mosaic) and the Oral (Talmudic). He arranged the results in this work without going into further disputations and explanations, [and] ordered the material with an admirable architecture according to divisions, sections, chapters, and paragraphs so that every object in group-like formation of all its surrounding particulars could be treated completely and exhaustively by species, division, and subdivision according to its genus. The fourth part of this work includes the criminal and civil law; and here is the first completed legal code. What Maimonides accomplished—just as if he were the creator of a systematic presentation of Talmudic learning—can only be appreciated by a deeper entry into the work, for which he gathered the building blocks from the most neglected corners of the almost incalculable Talmudic literature and bought it together by his comprehensively ordering mind; time will not withhold its admiration from him. Yet this work also has its deficiencies: it is too much of an artwork, and some imperfections depend upon this both in its construction and in its execution. . . . Maimonides established firm, inescapable standards in criminal law that remain far from reality. . . . Maimonides' desire to give his work the greatest possible thoroughness further induced him to gather everything that each Talmudic author omitted and perhaps only jotted down as an opinion: and so the criminal law had to appear completely disfigured and embody the fluency of its speculation in useless, withered theorems. Moreover, Talmudic research on criminal law could not serve as the basis of a reasonably complete criminal code because it survived only in the confines of the old law and left significant gaps. Maimonides admittedly tried to fill these gaps in some places; but how poorly! And as a result he indeed stepped directly away from the Talmudic criminal law! The work demonstrates a further deficiency in its execution. The author did not append his sources, nor did he explain through a commentary how he chose in his work the received opinion from among the often dissenting earlier opinions. . . .

Heinrich Graetz (1817–91) began his career dedicated to continuing the fight against reform and as a student of Samson Raphael Hirsch. Unlike Hirsch, however, Graetz believed that the only way to take on the reformers was on their own terms. He embraced historical scholarship to show that Geiger's vision of Judaism was narrow and incomplete, especially when it came to his rejection of the modern relevance of Jewish law. The author of the eleven-volume *History of the Jews*, from which the selection here is taken, Graetz continues to be hailed as one of the most important modern historians of the Jews as well as a crucial ancestor of Conservative Judaism. Arguing against Geiger's account of the history of Jewish law as the passive result of changing historical circumstances, Graetz highlights the difference between what he calls Rabbi Akiva's "revolutionary" view of the Oral Torah and Rabbi Ishmael's more "moderate" voice. Graetz contends that these differences reflect the dynamic and plural character of rabbinic conceptions of the oral law. From Graetz's point of view, this was a defense of the enduring value of Jewish law against reformers who wanted to do away with Jewish law, as well as an argument that Jewish law was subject to change, in spite of what the Neo-Orthodox claimed.[38]

Heinrich Graetz, *History of the Jews* (Philadelphia: Jewish Publication Society, 1893), 2:351–56.

Amongst the personages of [the classical rabbinic] period, Akiba ben Joseph[39] was unquestionably the most talented, original and influential. . . . According to one legend, he was a proselyte. . . . Another legend represents him as a servant of Kalba-Sabua, one of the three richest men of Jerusalem, who, by their provisions, wished to prevent for many years the famine occasioned by the siege. The legend adds that the daughter of one of these wealthy men of Jerusalem, named Rachel, had bestowed her love on Akiba, on the condition that he should follow

---

38. [Abraham Joshua Heschel offers an account of the dynamic nature of rabbinical theology on the basis of a similar distinction between Akiva and Ishmael in his *Heavenly Torah: As Refracted Through the Generations*, translated by Gordon Tucker (New York: Continuum, 2006).]

39. [Lived in the latter part of the first and early part of the second century CE.]

the study of the Law. In those days this meant to acquire culture, and thus, in his fortieth year, Akiba entered a school, in order to take his first lessons to obtain the knowledge in which he was deficient. . . .

. . . In this [Akiba's] system, the law was not considered as a dead treasure incapable of growth or development. . . . As the fundamental doctrine of his system, Akiba maintained that the style of the Torah, especially in parts relating to the laws, was quite different from that of other writings. Human language, besides the indispensable words employed, requires certain expressions, figures of speech, repetitions, and enlargements—in fact it takes a certain form which is almost unnecessary for conveying the writer's meaning, but which is used as a matter of taste, in order to round off the sentences and to make them more finished and artistic. In the language of the Torah, on the other hand, no weight is put on the form; nothing is superfluous, no word, no syllable, not even a letter; every peculiarity of expression, every additional word, every sign is to be regarded as of great importance, as a hint of a deeper meaning that lies buried within. Akiba added a number of explanatory and deductive rules. . . . When a deduction had been obtained by the correct use of the rules, such conclusion might again be employed as the foundation for fresh deductions and so on. . . .

Akiba was not to be restrained in this course by any consequences whatsoever. He had opened up a new path with his system, and a new point of view. The Oral Law, of which it had been said that it hung on a hair and had no firm ground in Holy Writ, was thus placed on a firmer basis, and the dissensions concerning the [rules] were to a considerable degree diminished. Akiba's contemporaries were surprised, dazzled, and inspired by his theories, which were new and yet old. . . . With exaggerated enthusiasm, it was said that many enactments of law, which were unknown to Moses, were revealed to Akiba. . . .

In the development of Jewish law, in which Akiba had wrought such changes, Ishmael ben Elisha[40] took an important part. He demanded the explanation of the written law from the common-sense view, and was thus one of the chief opponents of Akiba's system. According to Ishmael, the divine precepts of the Torah are expressed in human language, in which various figures of speech, linguistic repetitions and oratorical modes of expression occur, on which, however, no weight should be laid, as they are a mere matter of form. . . . Ishmael had his own school. . . . He there developed the rules which were to be employed in explaining and applying the Written Law. . . .

40. [Lived in the latter part of the first and early part of the second century CE.]

Selections from the Writings of Hermann Cohen

Initially a student of Graetz's at the Breslau Jewish Theological Seminary, Hermann Cohen (1842–1918) pursued a career in philosophy. Remarkably for a Jew who remained openly Jewish, Cohen became a professor of philosophy at the University of Marburg and was the founder of a highly influential philosophical school known as Marburg Neo-Kantianism. Cohen sought to resuscitate a broad concept of law and make it the center of ethics. The first selection is from Cohen's 1904 treatise on ethics. Here, Cohen argues that law constitutes the state and gives the state its ethical foundation. Of particular note is the centrality of Cohen's account of the contract, which he claims embodies the ethical relationship between the rights of individuals and their obligations to one another. It is those obligations that the state protects. The second selection is from Cohen's last work, *Religion of Reason out of the Sources of Judaism*, published posthumously in 1919, which is a Jewish philosophical corrective to Immanuel Kant's (1724–1804) *Religion within the Bounds of Mere Reason*. Cohen defends Jewish law as the religion of reason, which he defines as the absolute truth of pure monotheism. God is for Cohen the ideal against which reality must always be measured. Strikingly, despite the fact that a cornerstone of his philosophical system is the claim that law is the foundation of the state, Cohen in no way associates Jewish law with the state or with any political task. Instead, Jewish law symbolizes Jewish teaching, which is fundamentally religious and ethical in character. In this connection, Cohen's preferred translation for the Hebrew word Torah is *Lehre* (teaching), as opposed to *Gesetz* (law), which was commonly used to translate the word Torah.

Hermann Cohen, *Ethik des reinen Willens*, in *Werke*, edited by Helmut Holzhey and H. Weidebach, (Hildesheim, Germany: G. Olms, 2012), 7:228, 241–49, and 260–62 (translated by Shira Billet).

Not only is the law (*Recht*) dependent on ethics, but ethics must also trace itself back to the science of law. . . .

We usually think about the concept of the state under the concept of dominion, according to the Roman state's laws of *imperium* and *dominium*. Under these concepts, the boundaries of public and private law easily and often spill over into one another. . . . Nevertheless, the state . . . fundamentally cannot free itself from the task, which is designated through the formula *pacta servare* [agreements must be kept]. . . . In contracts, the state preserves fidelity. And in spite of all abuses of dominating power, this fidelity forms the state's foundation and its ethical (*ethisch*) right (Recht); its right to be recognized as a legal person and to serve as the highest and most exact model of ethical self-consciousness.

The self-consciousness of the legal person is the self-consciousness of the unity of the will, which is capable of accomplishing the totality.[41] And ought this highest unity [of the will] be cognized in the state? . . .

Rousseau already distinguished the general will . . . from the will of all.[42] . . . Does that now mean, however, that it does not depend at all on single wills, so that only a general will comes about? How could this general will come to be universal, a will of the totality, if single wills can be disregarded? . . .

. . . We must now turn to the concept of the legal person, and to the methodological meaning that is due to this concept. . . . The distinction between the cooperative (*Genossenschaft*) and the majority[43] (*Mehrheit*) lies precisely in its [the cooperative's] independence from actual particularity; [the cooperative's methodological] worth as totality and as a legal person lies [in this independence from actual particularity]. . . . *Its* [the cooperative's] *significance lies not in its actual reality (Wirklichkeit) but rather in its worth as an ethical guiding concept of self-consciousness.* . . .

We made the logical meaning of totality . . . independent of the realization of all single wills. But . . . [t]he unity of the state is mutilated . . . if it lacks even one member. Every being that is competent (*fähig*) as ethical, as legal subject of the pure will, must be called to the fulfillment of the self-consciousness in the state. . . . [W]ithout [the participation of each member], the unity of the state . . . contains a gap that . . . prevents the coherence of the ethical world that the state must represent. This unity must not be suspected as [being] a mere abstraction; it is the most real (*realst*), the most vital, the highest human good. [T]he state —[which we have described] as the task of self-consciousness, in the task of the

41. [Self-consciousness (*Selbstbewusstsein*) is a German philosophical term that connotes an unfettered, free, rational awareness of the self. In nineteenth-century German idealism, this term took on social and collective connotations. By "totality," Cohen designates a human collective that is an abstraction beyond any naturally existing collective (for example, a family or tribe) and is accomplished through philosophical concepts.]

42. [Jean-Jacques Rousseau, *Du contrat social ou Principes du droit politique* (1762), vol. 2, chapter 3.]

43. [For Cohen, the majority—as distinct from the totality—is a collective that is discovered empirically.]

unity of the will of all its members—should represent for us *the constitution of the ethical subject*. . . . [T]he subject . . . consummates itself in the will. Here . . . "spirit" (*der Geist*) is designated as the being (*Wesen*) . . . of this pure will.[44] Spirit signifies more than merely the restricted exercise of the intelligence, but certainly never more than the life of culture. Self-consciousness finds its succinct (*prägnant*) expression . . . in the spirit. *And so the state becomes the world of the spirits*; [the state becomes] . . . the legal constitution of the spirits.

That [could] seem to be a peculiar use of the word "spirit." Yet the appearance of peculiarity reflects [a] prejudice. One is accustomed to allow spirit to relate only to the religious constitution and to the religious form of the human being. One considers *the church* alone to be the kingdom of the spirits. One thereby overlooks [the fact] that the formation of consciousness of cognition has never been entrusted to the church by culture. One thus thinks [of] spirit without the scientific content of spirit, when one believes one . . . must understand it in a spiritual [that is, religious] sense. Yet . . . the ethical type and power of spirit first arises from within theoretical culture. So the basic law (*Grundgesetz*) of truth requires it [spirit]. And so it [spirit] continues to positively have an effect in the content of the state concept. *Thus the fiction of the legal person comes to be the hypothesis of the subject in its* [the subject's] *highest expression as spirit.*

We have already drawn attention to the juridical basic concept (*Grundbegriff*) of the contract: how all legal action can be understood as a contract. One can almost view contracts as equivalent to *inter vivos* [the transfer of a gift during one's lifetime, rather than after death, and] legal transactions in general (*Savigny*[45]). One-sided legal transactions always consider the other [individual]. . . .

Thus all right [Recht] . . . is led back to contract. . . . . [If] the contract is seen . . . as the general form of right, the state is then allowed to recognize in it its deepest methodological ground. . . .

. . . The contract is a claim: a claim of right that I bring to the other. . . . Now *the contract renders speech (Ansprache) out of the claim (Anspruch). And thereupon the other transforms* [itself] *into I and You. You is not He. He would be the other. He comes in danger of being treated as It. You and I belong absolutely together.* I cannot

44. [Spirit (*Geist*) is German philosophical term that was especially significant in nineteenth-century philosophy and was made famous in the work of Georg Wilhelm Friedrich Hegel (1770–1831). Cohen uses the term here as an expression of the collective cultural consciousness of a people.]

45. [Friedrich Carl von Savigny, founder of the historical school of jurisprudence, insisted that law is tied to the common life of the people.]

say You without relating you to myself, without uniting you in this relationship with the I.

But the enhanced requirement also lies therein: that I can also not think I without thinking You. So the other has transformed itself in self-consciousness, as it were, into the dual (*in den Dualis*) of the I. If self-consciousness wants to signify the unity of the will, thus must it construct the unification from I and You. *The will unites me and you; you and me. This unity signifies the task of self-consciousness.*

That is the progress of the other to the You. And this progress substantiates the legal fiction. So the legal person proves itself as the moral person. And this reality of the moral person represents the state, as the task of self-consciousness. The contract consummates (*vollziehen*) the unity of I and You. This contract is not an endeavor of caprice (*Willkür*) and experiment; rather, it is the condition, the necessary and sufficient condition, for the consummation of self-consciousness. In the state the I is brought to the purest unfolding, in which the other is transformed into the You....

We come here to a new concept, to that of law (Gesetz).[46] *The action of the state consists of laws* (Gesetzen). The task [of self-consciousness] must be thought of as and determined to be law. The will of the state expresses itself in laws. The self-consciousness of the state must thus fulfill itself and unfold in laws, as its actions.... Why have we until now avoided this word [law], this basic word of all culture?

The closest answer could be found in the reference to a well pondered difficulty that lies in Kant's concept of the Ought in distinction from the Is.... [T]he ambiguity, which lies in the *natural laws* (Naturgesetze) and which lets the law thus appear as a law in my limbs, surfaces.... [This is how] the methodological idealism of ethics is confused and crippled from the beginning.

The law, as it is meant here, does not concern the unity and the paragon of the laws which the basic law, the constitution, constitutes; rather [law concerns] the particular laws through which the tasks of the state's will express and activate themselves. Without law, no will—thus also no self-consciousness of the state. *This state concept of law must become the guiding concept for personal self-consciousness....*

46. [Cohen turns here to the concept of law as Gesetz (statutory law), as opposed to law as Recht (right).]

Hermann Cohen, *Religion of Reason out of the Sources of Judaism*, translated by Simon Kaplan (Atlanta, GA: Scholars, 1995), 366–70.

We are . . . on the classical ground of Jewish thinking when we try to answer the question of the relation between law (Gesetz) and religion (*Religion*) not in the dogmatic sense, but in accordance with our method. The ancient thinkers have proved with audacious clarity how various biblical laws were already changed in the Talmud. Moreover, they drew attention to the distinction between the Torah as the whole and the number of the particular commandments (*Geboten*). The problem for us can only be the general concept of the law. This concept of law means, in particular, its appropriateness for the preservation and the development of religion. The statutes (Satzungen) and ordinances (Rechte) are comprised under the supreme concept of the Torah. The law (Gesetz) consists of laws (Gesetzen). The unity of the laws, however, is the teaching, the religion. . . .

The continuation of the Jewish religion, of Jewish monotheism, is therefore bound to the continuation of the law in accordance with its general concept—not to the particular laws—because the law makes possible that isolation which seems indispensable to the care for, and continuation of, what is, at once, one's own and eternal.

Isolation in the world of culture! Does not what is required from the point of view of the law constitute a condemnation of Judaism? However, one should bear in mind that, in the final analysis, isolation is not demanded from the point of view of the law, but from that of pure monotheism. Monotheism is at stake; in the face of this how could the community of the world of culture be its legitimate tribunal? With monotheism the world of culture is at stake. . . .

The law, even if it were adhered to only on the holidays, and even, for some or for many, only on the Day of Atonement, is a bulwark against leveling pure monotheism, with its teaching of the reconciliation of man with God, as the salvation of man by God. . . .

Isolation is not the unique end of the law, but rather the idealization of all earthly activity by the divine. Worship is not limited to the synagogue; the law fulfills and permeates the whole of life with it. Of course, through this the whole of life is directed to the unique end. However, it is only opportunistic to fear withdrawal and alienation from culture in this positing of an end. Culture is given a firm center through this, and isolation, so far as it is unavoidable, may nevertheless permit and promote dedication and familiarity with all of the branches of culture. . . . In this historical power lies the meaning of the law as a symbol. Of course, it has no value of its own, but this exactly is the value of a symbol, that it is able to awaken the genuine value. What is not a symbol is therefore limited to the form that it may be able to represent through action or image.... If we finally consider the law as a symbol, we exceed the expression with which the Mishnah distinguishes the law from the teaching (Lehre), calling the law the "fence around the teaching."[47] The law is not only a fence, which isolates the teaching in order to guard and protect it, but, considered as a symbol, it becomes a lever which is not only a positive support of the teaching but a means for engendering the teaching....

47. [m. Avot 1:1: "They (the men of the Great Assembly) said three things: Be measured in judgment; raise up many disciples; and make a fence around the Torah." Cohen translates "Torah" as teaching and identifies it with pure monotheism, while he identifies the "fence" with Jewish law. Classical rabbinic commentators interpret "Torah" as referring to biblical law and identify the "fence" with rabbinic law.]

Menachem Elon (1923–2013) was born in Germany and immigrated to Palestine in 1935. He taught law at the Hebrew University of Jerusalem until he was appointed to Israel's Supreme Court in 1977, where he served until his retirement in 1993. His three-volume study, *Jewish Law: History, Sources, Principles*, originally published in Hebrew in 1973, remains the seminal textbook on Jewish law. Elon was an advocate of Mishpat Ivri (Hebrew Law), which he defines "as referring to those matters of Jewish law whose equivalent is dealt with in modem legal systems—matters pertaining to relations between man and his fellow and society."[48] Since it brackets the religious or ritual components of Jewish law, Mishpat Ivri for Elon serves as a basis of law for the State of Israel. According to him, "Jewish law," which he often used synonymously with Mishpat Ivri, could be understood within the positivist framework of the Jewish legal theorist Hans Kelsen (1881–1973). Kelsen argued that "the basic norm" (*Grundnorm*) is a logically presupposed norm that formally provides a legal system with its validity.[49] For Elon, the written Torah is the Grundnorm of Jewish law.

Menachem Elon, "The Legal System of Jewish Law," *New York University Journal of International Law and Politics* 17 (1984–85): 221–43.

. . . While the civil and ritual areas of Jewish law share a common source, methodology, and conceptualization, there is a fundamental difference between these two areas. This distinction was already pointed out in the *Mishnaic* era when the sages differentiated between *issura*, religious matters, and *mamona*, mostly matters of civil law. . . .

. . . [H]alakhah is, on the one hand, uniform and interrelated in that its components have a common religious source, a common method of thought and analysis, and an interdependence between its *ritual* commandments and its *civil*

48. Menachem Elon, "The Legal System of Jewish Law," *New York University Journal of International Law and Politics* 17 (1984–85): 227, note 28.

49. Hans Kelsen, *Pure Theory of Law*, translated by Max Knight (Berkeley: University of California Press, 1967), 212.

precepts. Conversely, *halakhah*, as it has crystallized, has recognized an essential and fundamental distinction between *issura* and *mamona*, the latter generally corresponding to most of what is included in the corpus juris of contemporary legal systems. This basic distinction offered greater flexibility and an extraordinary potential for development to the civil part of *halakhah*, that part which is most affected by and subject to changes in economic and social life. . . .

To analyze the corpus of Jewish law as a legal system with methods of classification and legal principles equivalent to those of modern jurisprudence, we must briefly consider the historical development of Jewish law. The foundation of Jewish law and its basic norm, or as Professor Kelsen put it, its *Grundnorm*, is the written Torah, and the body of oral law which grew continually until it was crystallized in the teachings codified in the *Mishnah* and in both the Jerusalem and the Babylonian Talmuds which followed it. This Talmudic literature is the basic material of Jewish law and constitutes the point of departure of any study or discussion of *halakhah*. . . .

. . . Most significantly, this enormous mass of material came into being against the background, and as a result of, the application of Jewish law to practical day-to-day life. . . . Law, as a reflection of life itself, constantly evolves. Its function is to find solutions for problems which arise out of life in every generation and in every place. The existence of Jewish judicial autonomy and the fact that *halakhah* functioned as a living body of law guaranteed the continuous development of Jewish law. In Jewish law, as in any other legal system, development occurs by way of its creative sources—the legal sources. . . .

A fundamental change took place in the practical application of Jewish law at the end of the eighteenth century. Jewish judicial autonomy in Europe was annulled at the onset of the Emancipation. Practical judicial activity in the Jewish communities became limited to the ritual aspects of the *halakhah*. With the end of Jewish judicial autonomy, the subject matter of the responsa changes drastically. The vast majority of the responsa now dealt with ritual matters—such as laws relating to prayer, benedictions, holy days, and dietary matters—and to a limited extent with matters of family law. Conversely, matters from the legal system of Jewish law constitute a negligible proportion of the post-Emancipation responsa. The few responsa which deal with civil law matters seem divorced from a living body of law. . . .

Law in the modern state is territorial. The same courts judge all people without regard to religion or national origin. A modern state is not prepared to grant judicial autonomy to an ethnic minority living within its boundaries. The only possibility for again applying Jewish law to practical life, therefore, lay in its being incorporated into the legal system of a modern state. That possibility arose with the advent of the Zionist movement which ultimately led to the establishment of the Jewish state. . . .

The subject of Jewish law should not be confused with the problem of the relationship of religion and the state, an extremely sensitive issue which is greatly disputed by various groups in Israeli society. What is proposed is the incorporation of that part of *halakhah* which is included in the various legal systems of modern states, that is, the legal sections of *halakhah*, not its ritual portions. As was demonstrated, even in previous times *halakhic* scholars drew a distinction between the civil and ritual components of *halakhah*. While the line they drew is not identical to that between law and religion, the existence of such a division in the world of *halakhah* is itself sufficient to serve as a guideline for discussion of the place of Jewish law in the State of Israel. . . .

The teaching of Jewish law and its renewed application as a legal system to everyday life must be implemented in a method that is acceptable to other legal systems. Jewish law must be interpreted according to accepted jurisprudential principles and the accepted categories of legal classifications and terminology. This approach is essential for the understanding and teaching of Jewish law as a legal system comparable to other modern legal systems. At the same time, great care must be exercised to avoid forcing Jewish law into the framework of another legal system and thereby to prevent the adoption into Jewish legal thought of alien legal principles, classifications, and terminology which have no place in the structure and basic concepts of Jewish law.

9

Selections from the Writings of Robert Cover

Robert Cover (1943–86) taught at Yale Law School from 1972 until his untimely death in 1986. His 1983 essay "Nomos and Narrative," an excerpt from which appears here, rejects different forms of legal positivism that deny the political and moral framework that, Cover argues, constitutes law and legal meaning. Law is inextricably tied to the stories we tell about ourselves, and Cover maintains that the enforcement of these stories is almost always bound to coercion and violence. In his posthumously published 1987 essay, "Obligation: A Jewish Jurisprudence of the Social Order," a short excerpt from which also appears here, Cover begins to unravel the Jewish story told by Jewish law—which, he claims, is about obligation, not rights. As such, the Jewish narrative offers an important counterbalance to the dominant social contract framework of American legal theory, which emphasizes rights as opposed to obligations. Cover's arguments are especially influential to some of the Jewish feminist considerations of Jewish law, included in part 5.[50]

Robert Cover, "Nomos and Narrative," *Harvard Law Review* 97, no. 1 (1983): 4–5, 7, 9–10, 25, 40, 42, 44, and 53.

We inhabit a nomos—a normative universe. We constantly create and maintain a world of right and wrong, of lawful and unlawful, of valid and void.... The rules and principles of justice, the formal institutions of the law, and the conventions of a social order are, indeed, important to that world; they are, however, but a small part of the normative universe that ought to claim our attention. No set of legal institutions or prescriptions exists apart from the narratives that locate it and give it meaning. For every constitution there is an epic, for each decalogue a scripture. Once understood in the context of the narratives that give it meaning, law becomes not merely a system of rules to be observed, but a world in which we live....

The normative universe is held together by the force of interpretive commitments—some small and private, others immense and public. These commit-

---

50. For a critique of Cover's use of Jewish law as an alternative model for secular law, see Suzanne Last Stone, "In Pursuit of the Countertext: The Turn to the Jewish Legal Model in Contemporary American Legal Theory," *Harvard Law Review* 106, no. 4 (1993): 813–94.

ments—of officials and of others—do determine what law means and what law shall be. . . .

Law may be viewed as a system of tension or a bridge linking a concept of a reality to an imagined alternative—that is, as a connective between two states of affairs, both of which can be represented in their normative significance only through the devices of narrative. . . . A nomos, as a world of law, entails the application of human will to an extant state of affairs as well as toward our visions of alternative futures. A nomos is a present world constituted by a system of tension between reality and vision. . . .

. . . The very imposition of a normative force upon a state of affairs, real or imagined, is the act of creating narrative. . . . To live in a legal world requires that one know not only the precepts, but also their connections to possible and plausible states of affairs. It requires that one integrate not only the "is" and the "ought," but the "is," the "ought," and the "what might be." Narrative so integrates these domains. . . .

The biblical worlds of normative meaning were built around a sacred text that included both precept and narrative. . . . In our own normative world, there is no obvious central text, certainly none that exhaustively supplies both narrative and precept. Nonetheless, the Constitution of the United States declares itself to be "supreme Law." . . .

In an imaginary world in which violence played no part in life, law would indeed grow exclusively from the hermeneutic impulse—the human need to create and interpret texts. Law would develop within small communities of mutually committed individuals who cared about the text. . . . But . . . [i]nterpretation always takes place in the shadow of coercion. . . .

. . . [T]he statist position may be understood to assert . . . a convention of legal discourse: . . . The position that only the state creates law. . . . [This position] . . . confuses the status of interpretation with the status of political domination. . . .

. . . By exercising its superior brute force, however, the agency of state law shuts down the creative hermeneutic of principle that is spread throughout our communities. The question, then, is the extent to which coercion is necessary to the maintenance of minimum conditions for the creation of legal meaning in autonomous interpretive communities. . . .

Judges are people of violence. Because of the violence they command, judges characteristically do not create law, but kill it. . . . Confronting the luxuriant growth of a hundred legal traditions, they assert that *this one* is law and destroy or try to destroy the rest.

But judges are also people of peace. Among warring sects, each of which wraps itself in the mantle of a law of its own, they assert a regulative function that permits a life of law rather than violence. . . .

Robert Cover, "Obligation: A Jewish Jurisprudence of the Social Order,"
Journal of Law and Religion 5, no. 1 (1987): 65–68.

The basic word of Judaism is obligation or *mitzvah*. It, too, is intrinsically bound up in a myth—the myth of Sinai. Just as the myth of social contract is essentially a myth of autonomy, so the myth of Sinai is essentially a myth of heteronomy. Sinai is a collective-in-deed, a corporate-experience. The experience at Sinai is not chosen. The event gives forth the words which are commandments. In all Rabbinic and post Rabbinic embellishment upon the biblical account of Sinai this event is the Code for all Law. All law was given at Sinai and therefore all law is related back to the ultimate heteronomous event in which we were chosen—passive voice.

Now, just as the social contract theories generated Hobbes and others who bore a monstrous and powerful collective engine from the myth of individualism, so the Sinaitic myth has given rise to counter myths and accounts which stress human autonomy. Indeed, the Rabbinic accounts of law-making autonomy are very powerful indeed, though they all conclude by suggesting that everything, even the questions yet to be asked by the brilliant students of the future and the answers to those questions—everything was given at Sinai. And, of course, therefore, all is, was, and has been commanded—and we are obligated to this command. . . .

Indeed, to be one who acts out of obligation is the closest thing there is to a Jewish definition of completion as a person within the community. A child does not become emancipated or "free" when he or she reaches maturity. Nor does she/he become sui juris. No, the child becomes bar or bat mitzvah, literally one who is of the obligations. Traditionally, the parent at that time says a blessing. Blessed is He that has exonerated me from the punishment of this child. The primary legal distinction between Jew and non-Jew is that the non-Jew is only obligated to the seven Noachide commandments. Where women have been denied by traditional Judaism an equal participation in ritual, the reasoning of the traditional legist has been that woman are not obligated in the same way as are men with respect to those ritual matters (public prayer). It is almost a sure sign of a nontraditional background for someone to argue that women in Judaism should have the right to be counted in the prayer quorum, or to be called to the Torah. Traditionalists who do argue for women's participation (and there are some who do), do so not on the basis of rights. They argue rather that the law, properly understood, does or ought to impose on women the obligation of public prayer, of study of Torah, and so forth. For the logic of Jewish Law is such that once the obligation is understood as falling upon women, or whomever, then there is no question of "right" of participation. Indeed, the public role is a responsibility.

II | Eastern European Views of Law
Dissolution of Jewish Communal Power

Beginning in 1764 with the dissolution of the Council of the Four Lands by the Polish government and continuing throughout the eighteenth century as the Austro-Hungarian, Ottoman, and Russian Empires absorbed all of the previously independent countries of Eastern and Central Europe, Jewish communal structures weakened, and Jewish communities increasingly lost aspects of the political autonomy that they had previously possessed. Jewish law, which had regulated many parts of such communities' public life, ceded that role to state law and retreated into the home, synagogue, and yeshiva. While none of the thinkers included in this part of the volume would deny that Jews should observe Jewish law in all areas of their lives, they responded to this new situation by developing privatized theories of Jewish law. Strikingly, while the thinkers included in this part offer different answers to the question "What is Jewish law?," none of them describe Jewish law as a means—even a divine means—for regulating Jewish public life.

Two main strategies or tendencies for redescribing Jewish law emerge in the Eastern European context: Some thinkers understand Jewish law as an object of intellectual engagement almost to the exclusion of practical concerns, while others maintain an interest in the practice of Jewish law but emphasize the religious individual, almost to the exclusion of the collective.

In terms of the first strategy, a Lithuanian tradition, which begins with Eliyahu of Vilna and his student Ḥayyim of Volozhin and continues with Ḥayyim Soloveitchik and Shimon Shkop, privileges the analysis of Jewish law over its implementation. As a result, these thinkers generally prefer the study of the Talmud and its interpreters to the study of legal codes. With Soloveitchik and Shkop, reflection on Jewish law reaches a level of abstraction that would not be possible were the study of Jewish law geared only toward practice. In terms of the second strategy, Yisrael (Lipkin) Salanter stresses ethical formation alongside observance of the commandments as the two elements of Torah. Yisrael Meir Kagan fully synthesizes Jewish law and ethics by injecting ethical considerations into Jewish legal decision making and by applying the full technical apparatus of Jewish law to ethical concerns.

Other positions share both tendencies. Shneur Zalman of Liady, the founder of Ḥabad Hasidism,[1] rejects the intellectualism of the Lithuanian tradition and advocates the practice of the commandments even when it is unaccompanied by understanding. Yet, for Shneur Zalman, the practice of the commandments is understood to have important theological consequences. Naḥman Krochmal, though influenced by contemporary jurisprudence, interprets Jewish law as a practice for stimulating reflection on philosophical truths. Intellectual engagement with Jewish law is central as well as its practice, but only insofar as it promotes reflection. Joseph Soloveitchik, the grandson of Ḥayyim Soloveitchik, continues the tradition of abstract analysis of the Talmud and its interpreters but also claims that Jewish law ought to be the source for Jewish philosophy. Still, he insists that it is "religious" and cannot be reduced to other interests.

---

1. Hasidism is an Orthodox Jewish spiritual revival movement that began in the eighteenth century. The Ḥabad branch of Hasidism, founded in 1775 by Shneur Zalman (1745–1812), is also known as Lubavitch Hasidism (from the name of the Belorussian village where the leaders lived for a hundred years).

Selections from the Writings of
Eliyahu of Vilna and Associated Texts

Eliyahu of Vilna (1720–97), also known as the Vilna Gaon (the genius of Vilna), may be considered one of the founders of modern Judaism.[2] Precisely at the time when Jewish communal authority was disintegrating, Eliyahu's approach to Jewish law emphasized its study as opposed to its implementation. Eliyahu stressed the authority of rabbinic interpreters, which he identified with the Oral Torah, over scripture, the Written Torah, in determining Jewish law. Furthermore, as described by his student Ḥayyim of Volozhin, he also rejected the mediation of Jewish law by the various legal codes that had been developed—in particular, Yosef Karo's *Shul-ḥan Arukh*,[3] as supplemented for Ashkenazi Jewry by Moshe Isserles's *Ha-Mapah*.[4] Indeed, his own commentary on these texts, while affirming them by commenting on them, can also be understood as a critique of them and other commentaries on them by marshaling Talmudic sources and their interpreters who disagree with their rulings. In the last selection presented here, Eliyahu objects to a ruling that codified a custom not supported by the Talmud and its interpreters. In his view, neither codes nor custom can stand in the way of direct intellectual engagement with the sources of the Oral Torah.

Eliyahu of Vilna, *Mishlei im Bi'ur ha-Gr'a* (Vilna, 1931), 24
(translated by Elli Fischer).

"Let your mind hold on to my words" [Proverbs 4:4]—for the Torah is like bread, which nourishes the heart of man, as it says, "Come, eat my bread."[5] And

2. For a full development of this argument, see Eliyahu Stern, *The Genius: Elijah of Vilna and the Making of Modern Judaism* (New Haven, CT: Yale University Press, 2013). The choice of these selections and their significance are indebted to this work as well as conversations with its author.

3. *Shulḥan Arukh* (The set table), a comprehensive Jewish legal code by Yosef Karo (1488–1575) and published in 1565. Its principal sections—Oraḥ Ḥayyim, Yoreh De'ah, Even Ha-Ezer, and Ḥoshen Mishpat—correspond to the sections in the earlier code, *Arba'ah Turim*, also known as the *Tur*, by Ya'akov ben Asher (1270–c. 1340)

4. Moshe Isserles (Poland, 1520–72), *Ha-Mapah* (The tablecloth), a gloss on *Shulḥan Arukh*.

5. [Prov. 9:5; New Jewish Publication Society (NJPS) of America Tanakh translation, modified.]

it must be consumed constantly, thus "recite it day and night."[6] The commandments (*mitzvot*), however, are like confections, which are good at the right time and on occasion, like a confectioner who visits from time to time.

Eliyahu of Vilna, *Aderet Eliyahu al ha-Torah* (Warsaw, 1887), 63
(translated by Elli Fischer).

"[He shall be brought to the door or] the doorpost" [Exodus 21: 6]—the straightforward meaning of scripture (*pashta di-kira*) [is that] a doorpost [alone, without a door,] is also fit [to be the site of the Hebrew slave's ear piercing on the occasion of his choosing to remain with his master after his initial six-year period of servitude].[7] However, Jewish law (halakhah) uproots scripture [and establishes that both a door and a doorpost are necessary]. So it is with most of this passage and several passages in the Torah. They magnify our Oral Torah (torah she-be'al peh), which is the rule (halakhah) given to Moses at Sinai, and [these passages] become inverted, like wax imprinted by a seal, with the exception of the commandments that stem from "MNTzPK," which are upright.[8] It is similarly written: "How stupid are those people who rise before a Torah scroll [but not before a great man, for in the Torah scroll "forty (lashes)"[9] is written (as punishment for transgressions)], and the rabbis came [and subtracted one] (b. Makkot 22b). The same is true of . . . the majority of the Torah. Therefore, one must know the straightforward meaning of the Torah, so that he is familiar with the seal [itself]. The same applies in the case of the ear piercing [of the Hebrew slave].

6. [Josh. 1:8.]

7. [See selection 4 for commentary on this passage by Samson Raphael Hirsch.]

8. [See *Zohar Ḥadash* to Song 1:4, which associates the five Hebrew letters that have two forms (one when they appear in the middle of the word, and one when they appear at the end of the word)—*mem, nun, tzade, peh,* and *kaf*—with the word *meisharim* (upright), as opposed to all other letters. The meaning of "the commandments that derive from MNTzPK" is uncertain. A grandson of Eliyahu of Vilna explained that it refers to the five cases in the Torah in which Moses required divine assistance because he did not know what law to apply. See Eliyahu of Vilna, *Zikhron Eliyahu* (Bnei Brak, Israel, 1991), 2:11–12. See also b. Shabbat 104a and Tosafot *ad loc., s.v. geru'ei,* as well as Eliyahu's commentary on *Sefer Yetzirah* 1:3 (Eliyahu of Vilna, *Sefer Yetzirah im Peirush Rabbeinu Ha-ga'on . . . Eliyahu Me-Vilna* [Jerusalem: Ariel, 1874], 32b.])

9. [See Deut. 25:3.]

Eliyahu of Vilna, *Mishlei im Bi'ur ha-Gr'a* (Vilna, 1931), 58
(translated by Elli Fischer).

["Negligent hands cause poverty, but diligent hands enrich." (Proverbs 10:4)]
This . . . refers to the Torah. For "negligent hands" means one who studies lazily,
that is, he does not study the source of the laws (dinin) but only the abridged
laws, to show that he knows all of the laws. This "causes poverty," for ultimately
he will forget even that since he does not know the sources. However, "diligent
hands"—one who studies the law (ha-din) along with its source and knows every
statute and law (dat ve-din)—"enrich"—for he knows it all.

Hayyim of Volohzin, introduction to Eliyahu of Vilna, *Bi'urei ha-Gr'a al Shulḥan
Arukh Oraḥ Ḥayyim* (Vilna, 1860), i (translated by Elli Fischer).

. . . Our masters, the early authorities (rishonim)[10] of blessed memory, saw,
after the sealing of the Talmud, that due to the weight of exile the academies had
shrunk, and they saw that there are few elites who swim in the sea of Talmud to
find therein the action for every specific detail of the laws (dinim). Our brothers,
the Israelites, have been scattered in every corner of the exile; Jewish communities have proliferated; and those who offer instruction based on the Talmud have
decreased. To that end, they authored works that contain codified rulings (halakhot pesukot). This continued in the following generations, and the generations
that followed those generations, depending on the uncertainties and the uncertainties about uncertainties that arise anew in each generation. Finally, our rabbis, the authors of *Shulḥan Arukh*,[11] arose and set the table (arkhu ha-shulḥan) for us
to eat and taste their words from that blessed source. Indeed, they have become
our guides,[12] showing the people of Israel the way they are to live and how they
are to behave.[13] For one whose apprehension falls short of understanding and
deriving instruction from the Talmud [itself], how goodly and how sweet are
the words of the upright codified rulings; the righteous can walk on them [while

10. [Leading rabbis and legal decision makers from the eleventh to the mid-sixteenth
century.]

11. [Both Yosef Karo, the Sephardic author of the *Shulḥan Arukh*, and Moshe Isserles, the
Ashkenazi who wrote a gloss on it in *Ha-Mapah*.]

12. [Literally, "as our eyes." See Num. 10:30.]

13. [See Exod. 18:20.]

sinners stumble on them],[14] for it shall cause many to stumble and remove from themselves the yoke of toiling and studying the Talmud to derive the law from it. They say that studying to ascertain practice is solely the study of *Shulḥan Arukh*. Even if they study the Talmud, they do so only to sharpen their minds. Some even neglect the Talmud entirely and are content to study *Shulḥan Arukh* only. This is not the straight path for which God graced us with intelligence to plumb the depths of the Talmud. Every novel idea that a diligent student will suggest is already included in their holy words.[15] The just shall walk in the uprightness of their path, so that their instruction will primarily be derived from the Talmud, while the study of *Shulḥan Arukh* will serve as a cue to remind them of the laws, for it is the refined flour that is gathered up from all the commentaries on the Talmud.

Thus, anyone who scrutinizes this work, which was authored by the great and holy rabbi whose Torah and righteousness heralded him from one end of the world to the other, whose good name is greater than the title *Rabban*,[16] the honor of his sanctity and Torah, the eminent Rabbi Eliyahu the Pious, may his soul rest in Eden, [as a commentary] on *Shulḥan Arukh*, will see that the method of our great rabbi, may his soul rest in Eden, is to evoke and remind one of the source in the Talmud, based on its commentaries, while one is studying *Shulḥan Arukh*. This is aside from the sweet and profound novellae contained within his holy words. Even though his words are brief, they are like stars that appear small, yet the entire world stands below them. . . .

Yosef Karo, *Shulḥan Arukh*, Oraḥ Ḥayyim 490: 9 (translated by Elli Fischer).

When Shabbat coincides with the intermediate days of the festival (*ḥol ha-mo'ed*).[17] . . .

14. [Based on Hos. 14:10. The conclusion of the verse ("while sinners stumble on them") is not included in the original text, as the author assumed an educated reader would recall it and understand his attitude toward codes.]

15. [See y. Pe'ah 2:4 and Midrash Leviticus Rabbah 22:1.]

16. [See m. Eduyot 3:4.]

17. ["Profane (days) of the appointed time." The week-long festivals of Passover and Sukkot distinguish between the first and last days of the festival, which are subject to all the observances of holidays, and intermediate days, when some of the holiday observances and restrictions are relaxed.]

Moshe Isserles, *Ha-Mapah, ad loc.* (translated by Elli Fischer).

. . . It is customary to recite the Song of Songs on Shabbat of the intermediate days of the festival [of Passover]. . . . The same applies to [the festival of] Sukkot with Ecclesiastes. It is customary to recite the Book of Ruth on [the festival of] Shavuot. The people customarily do not recite the blessing "regarding the reading of a scroll book" or "regarding the reading of holy writ" [before these special readings for the festivals].

Eliyahu of Vilna, *Bi'ur ha-Gr'a, ad loc.*, note 14 (translated by Elli Fischer).

"It is customary [to recite the Song of Songs on Shabbat of the intermediate festival [of Passover]"—for it speaks about the redemption from Egypt. This is the formulation in *Darkhei Moshe*:[18]

Abudraham writes:[19] "Everyone customarily recites the Song of Songs on the festival of unleavened bread[20] . . . and on [the festival of] Shavuot, the Book of Ruth . . . , and on [the festival of] Sukkot, Ecclesiastes. . . . And it is stated in m. Soferim [14: 3]: 'One who recites one of the five scrolls[21] recites [the blessing] "regarding the reading of a scroll-book," even if [the scroll] is written among the other holy writings [and not on its own].'" Maharil[22] similarly writes that one should recite this blessing, even if it is not written in a scroll. . . . This is the custom; and it is against *Mordekhai*,[23] which states in the first chapter of [b.] Megillah that one recites the blessing "regarding the recitation of holy writ."

So too, *Bayit Ḥadash*,[24] *Levush*,[25] *Minhagim*,[26] and *Mateh Moshe*[27] state that one

18. [(Ways of Moses), a commentary by Moshe Isserles (Rema) on the *Arba'ah Turim*.]

19. [David ben Yosef Abudraham (also Abudarham and Abudirham) (Spain, fourteenth century).]

20. [Another name for Passover.]

21. [That is, the Song of Songs and the books of Ruth, Esther, Lamentations, and Ecclesiastes.]

22. [Ya'akov ben Moshe Levi Moelin (Germany, c. 1365–1427).]

23. [Commentary by Mordechai ben Hillel (Germany, 1220–98) on the Talmud.]

24. [*Bayit Ḥadash* (New house; also known as *Baḥ*), written by Yoel Sirkes (Poland, 1561–1640).]

25. [*Levush Malkhut* (Robes of royalty), by Mordecai ben Avraham Yoffe (Poland, c. 1530–1612).]

26. [*Sefer Minhagim* (Book of customs), first printed in 1566, by Yitzḥak Tyrnau (Austria-Hungary, late fourteenth century).]

27. [(Staff of Moses) first printed in 1591 by Moshe ben Abraham of Przemysl (Poland, c. 1550–1606).]

recites a blessing [over the reading of these texts] even if they are not written on scrolls, a fortiori if they are written in scrolls like a Torah scroll. This is the custom of all the early authorities [rishonim], as stated in *Magen Avraham*.[28] And the statement [in *Magen Avraham* that we recite this blessing on all such readings] "with the exception of Ecclesiastes" can be discounted, since at the end of the third chapter of m. Yadayim, the Mishnah concludes that it was disputed and then decided that Song of Songs and Ecclesiastes are equal when it comes to rendering the hands impure.[29] Maimonides also explained thus in [*Mishneh Torah*] "Laws of Sources of Impurity," 9: [6].[30] . . . So too states the glosses of *Mordekhai* on the first chapter of b. Megillah: "They are all equal vis-à-vis this blessing." This is the primary view.

28. [(Shield of Abraham), first published in 1692, by Avraham Abele Gombiner (Poland, c. 1635–82).]

29. [Somewhat counterintuitively, sacred texts render hands that touch them impure. Thus, two texts that both render the hands impure are of equal sanctity.]

30. [Moses ben Maimon, also known as Rambam (Morocco, Egypt; 1135 or 1138–1204), the author of the *Mishneh Torah*.]

Ḥayyim of Volozhin (1749–1821) was a disciple of Eliyahu of Vilna and the founder of the Etz Ḥayyim Yeshiva in Volozhin, which institutionalized their shared vision of the dedicated study of Jewish law disconnected from any practical application of that study.[31] Rather than producing a code of Jewish law, Ḥayyim of Volozhin composed *Nefesh ha-Ḥayyim* (The soul of life), which provides the theoretical underpinnings for study of the Talmud and its interpreters. On the one hand, drawing from Kabbalistic ideas, Ḥayyim of Volozhin asserts that the commandments derive from the supernatural world and that their performance affects that world. On the other hand, rejecting certain antinomian tendencies in Hasidism, he insists that the authority and value of the commandments are mediated by the revelation of the Torah, the origin of which is one of the highest supernatural realms. Thus, one may no longer alter the commandments in view of their supernatural origin or effects, and study of the Torah is of greater value than the performance of the other commandments. Nevertheless, Ḥayyim of Volozhin also relativizes both the Torah and its commandments by claiming that they express only the human perspective —in which there are distinctions between, for example, prohibited and permitted foods—whereas from the divine perspective everything is God and is thus holy. Still, he argues that since human beings cannot transcend their human perspective, they must obey the rules entailed by such distinctions. In these ways, Ḥayyim of Volozhin constructs a theology for the followers of an antitheological movement (the Mitnagdim, or those who oppose Hasidism), which from a legal theoretical perspective combines features of natural or supernatural law and positivism.

Rav Chayyim of Volozhin, *The Soul of Life: The Complete Neffesh Ha-Chayym*, translated by Eliezer Lipa (Leonard) Moskowitz (Teaneck, NJ: New Davar, 2014), 66–78, 150–56, 307 and 485–93 (translation adapted by the editors).

. . . [T]he essential point of the matter is that He, blessed be His Name, after He created all the worlds, created man, last of all creations . . . , the final integrating

---

31. [On the place of this institution in the development the Lithuanian tradition of learning, see Shaul Stampfer, *Lithuanian Yeshivas of the Nineteenth Century: Creating a Tradition of Learning*, trans. Lindsey Taylor-Guthartz (Oxford: Littman Library of Jewish Studies, 2012). On Ḥayyim of Volozhin, see Norman Lamm, *Torah Lishmah: Torah for Torah's Sake in the Works of Ḥayyim Volozhin and His Contemporaries* (Hoboken: Ktav, 1989).

power for all the camps. . . . And so all of the commandments are connected to and dependent upon the source of their supernal root in the structures and processes of the components of the Chariot [*merkabah*][32] and the measure of the [divine] body (*shi'ur komah*)[33] of all the worlds taken together. . . . And when man performs his Master's . . . will, and fulfills one of God's commandments with a specific limb and the power within it, the rectification (*ha-tikkun*) that is caused relates to that world or lofty power. . . . And so too the converse, heaven forbid: when he blemishes one of his powers or limbs via his sin . . . , the blemish also reaches . . . to that specific world and lofty power that corresponds to it in the structure of the measure of the [divine] body. . . .

And this was also the entire matter of the service of the Patriarchs . . . who fulfilled the Torah before it was given. . . . It is not that they were commanded and [thus] acted as they did from a legal perspective (*mitzad ha-din*), for if it were so they would not have taken positions, heaven forbid, based on their own intellect and attainment, even if they had grasped that based on the essential feature of the root of their soul it would have been necessary to trespass and to change even a small part of one of all of God's commandments. Jacob the Patriarch, peace be upon him, would not have married two sisters, nor would have Amram married his aunt, heaven forbid.[34] [They acted] only from the perspective of what they could grasp, in the purity of their rationality, of the awesome rectifications (*tikunim*) that would be accomplished for each commandment, in the worlds and powers above and below, and the large blemishes, the destruction and ruin, heaven forbid, that they would cause if they did not perform them. . . . But from when Moses came and brought [the Torah] down to Earth, "it is no longer in the heavens."[35] And lest a great person whose attainments are vast become wise and says: "I am one who sees the secret and reasons of the commandments in the powers and upper worlds that are appropriate for me according to the root of my soul," or for anyone else according to his root, to violate, heaven forbid, any commandment or to neglect any of the smallest of details of performance . . . ,

32. [Following certain strands in Kabbalah, the created universe, including supernal and mundane realms, is described as God's chariot.]

33. [*Shi'ur Komah*, translated here as "the measure of the [divine body]," is the name of an early work of Kabbalah, as well as its content—which describes the measurements of God's body. According to Ḥayyim of Volozhin, these measurements are a description of creation keyed to the parts of the human body, which are integrated with them.]

34. [Such marriages are forbidden by the Torah.]

35. [Deut. 30:12.]

for this reason the Torah concluded with (Deut. 34:10): "no other prophet like Moses arose." . . . For the reasons for the commandments and their final effects have not yet been revealed to any person in the world, not even to Moses our master, peace upon him, other than First Adam before the sin. . . . For the holy Torah is emanated from above human comprehension, beyond all conceptual grasp. How would it be possible for this matter to be placed within a human's grasp, to change its rules (halakhot) and the organization of its times according to the expanse of his knowledge? . . . And once the holy Talmud was sealed, for us there's nothing to do but scrupulously guard and perform everything recorded in the holy Torah, Written and Oral, according to all their laws and mandates . . . without deviating from them even to the smallest degree. And when the person of Israel fulfills them properly, even without intention, and even if he has no comprehension of the reasons for the commandments and secrets of their intentions, even so, the commandments are fulfilled, and thereby the worlds are rectified. . . .

. . . [A]ll of the fundamental principles of the holy Torah, every one of the warnings and commandments, positive and negative, all operate within this point of view (beḥinah): from our perspective (mitzad hasagateinu) there absolutely exist differences and variations between places. In clean places we are permitted and also obligated to discuss and to reflect on the Torah's words. And in filthy places we are prohibited even to reflect on the Torah's words. And so it is with all the matters and the system of behavioral obligations that we are directly commanded in the holy Torah, and lacking this, our perspective, there would not be any room for the Torah and commandments at all. And even though, in truth, from His, blessed be He, perspective, which has the capability of grasping His essential nature, He permeates everything with complete uniformity. . . . However, we are not able—and also not permitted—to engage in any way [in] contemplating and understanding of this awesome matter. . . .

Let us now . . . explain a bit about the difference in quality and greatness that the light of the holy Torah has relative to the commandments. . . . We find that the sages of blessed memory stated (b. Sotah 21a): "Rabbi Menaḥem expounded on, 'For a commandment is a lamp and Torah is light' (Prov. 6:23). The verse linked the commandment to a lamp and the Torah to light to teach you that just as a lamp only protects temporarily, so too a commandment only protects temporarily. And just as light illuminates forever, so too Torah shields forever. . . ." . . . [E]ven that holiness and the enlivening forces and lights of the commandments that make a person holy and enliven the person who performs them are taken from and have influence based only on the holiness and light of the holy Torah, for a commandment has no inherent vitality or holiness or light of its own at all. It is only due to the holiness of the letters of the Torah that are written in relation to the context of that commandment. And we can also apply the matter in the verse: "For a commandment is a lamp and Torah is light," to the context of the lamp that has no light of its own—it only has the light that illuminates within it.... And the reason for this is ... that the commandments, in the source of their root, are connected and dependent upon the design of the components of the Chariot: the worlds and the supernal powers. And the supernal source of the root of the holy Torah is very lofty, above the totality of all the worlds and the powers. And it unfolds downward within them all, and they receive from it the essence of their vitality and the overflowing abundance of their holiness. For that reason, it is the provider of, and what impresses, vitality, holiness, and light upon all of the commandments.

Selections from the Writings of Shneur Zalman of Liady

Shneur Zalman of Liady (c. 1745–1812) is a major figure in Hasidism. At least in part, Hasidism arose in response to the elitist intellectualism that characterized Lithuanian Judaism, epitomized by Eliyahu of Vilna. In contrast to the view of Ḥayyim of Volozhin, Shneur Zalman privileges other commandments over Torah study; it is their performance that truly expresses love and fear of God. Yet Shneur Zalman, who founded Ḥabad Hasidism, also pushes back against certain anti-intellectual and antinomian tendencies within Hasidism. He propounds a theology, drawn from Kabbalah, in which the practice of the commandments draws a transcendent God into the world. These consequences occur, Shneur Zalman claims, whether or not one understands the reasons for the commandments. Indeed, it is better to perform the commandments simply because they are God's will than because one comprehends their metaphysical effects.

Shneur Zalman of Liady, *Tanya* (Brooklyn NY: Kehot, 1984), 49a
(translated by Zalman Rothschild).

Our Rabbis of blessed memory said, "Study is not the essential thing, but rather action is"[36] and "today to do them,"[37] as it is written, and thus one interrupts Torah study to fulfill an actionable commandment when it cannot be fulfilled by others, because this is the entirety of man and the purpose of his creation and descent into this world, which is for God to have a home in the lower [region]s (*dirah be-taḥtonim*) specifically, to transform the darkness to light and that God's glory should fill all of the physical earth, specifically. . . .

Shneur Zalman of Liady, *Tanya* (Brooklyn NY: Kehot, 1984), 8a
(translated by Zalman Rothschild).

. . . [L]ove is the source of all 248 positive commandments and from [it] they are derived and without it they have no true existence, for the one who fulfills

36. [m. Avot 1:17.]
37. [Deut. 7:11.]

them truthfully he is the one who loves God's Name and desires to cleave to Him truthfully. And it is impossible to cleave unto Him truthfully other than through fulfilling the 248 [positive] commandments, which are the 248 limbs of the King, as it were. . . .[38] And fear is the course of the 365 negative commandments, for he [who fears God] will fear rebelling against the King, King of Kings, the Holy One, blessed be He. . . .

Shneur Zalman of Liady, *Likkutei Torah* (Brooklyn, NY: Kehot, 2002), Deuteronomy 1a (translated by Zalman Rothschild).

And the purpose is to draw down the infinite light (*or ein sof*),[39] blessed be it, which is of Godliness that transcends (*sovev*),[40] and this is done through Torah and commandments. . . . For it is today, in this world, that one can draw down from the level of the essence of God and of God Himself, unlike tomorrow in the world to come. . . .

Shneur Zalman of Liady, *Torah Or* (Brooklyn, NY: Kehot, 1991) 23a (translated by Zalman Rothschild).

[This was] the concept of the generation of the desert, which was from the level of [the matriarch] Leah,[41] the world of thought, and [which] complained "Why must we descend into the level of the world of speech which is the level of kingship (*malkhut*),[42] the lower land, to fulfill the commandments in speech and action? Is it not also possible to fulfill them through the Torah and command-

---

38. [The 248 positive commandments correspond to the 248 parts of the human body. See *Tikkunei Zohar, Tikun* 30.]

39. [Kabbalists, including Shneur Zalman, were deeply skeptical about the ability of the mind to comprehend God in essence (as opposed to emanations or manifestations —that is, the *sefirot*), and thus referred to God beyond the *sefirot* as *ein sof* (literally, "without limit") or *or ein sof* (limitless light).]

40. [*Sovev* literally means "surrounds" and refers to the godliness that transcends the world, especially as compared to *memaleh* (filled), which refers to the godliness that is within the world.]

41. [The matriarchs Rachel and Leah serve as Kabbalistic symbols that connote speech and cognition respectively. See, for example, Zohar 2:126b.]

42. [In Kabbalah, speech is usually associated with the final one of God's emanations, the sefirah of malkhut. See, for example, *Tikkunei Zohar* 17a.]

ments in spirituality (*ha-torah u-mitzvot be-ruḥniut*), that is, by way of thought?"[43] However, in truth, they were gravely mistaken, for it is through speech and action specifically [that the] revelation of the infinite light (or ein sof), blessed be it, is drawn down with ever increasing intensity....

Shneur Zalman of Liady, *Torah Or* (Brooklyn, NY: Kehot, 1991) 9a (translated by Zalman Rothschild).

As it is written "Whom else have I in heaven? And having You, I want no one [on earth],"[44] for one does not want [godliness from lower levels] ..., for these are only [of the level of] ray and reflection alone; rather, [one wants] to cleave to the body of the King which is God's essence, God Himself. ... [A]ll of this [the level of ray and reflection] are the explanation and reasons for the commandments (ta'amei ha-mitzvot) which are the level of the wisdom of the Torah (*ḥokhmat ha-torah*) which are drawn from God's wisdom. However, the body of the commandments of action (*gufei mitzvot ha-massiyot*) such as phylacteries (tefillin)[45] and ... charity, as it is written, "For the work of righteousness"[46] and the like, are the will of God which is above reason (ta'am) and knowledge (da'at) that are drawn from wisdom (*ḥokhmah*).

43. [The generation of the desert was perturbed as to why it should "downgrade" to the level of speech and action, when it could just as well fulfill all commandments by way of thought.]

44. [Ps. 73:25.]

45. [Tefillin are small black leather boxes containing scrolls inscribed with verses of the Torah. Attached by leather straps, they are worn on the head and left arm by observant Jews during weekday morning prayers.]

46. [Isa. 32:17.]

Naḥman Krochmal,
Guide of the Perplexed of the Age

Naḥman Krochmal (1785–1840) was a major influence on the Jewish Enlightenment (*Haskalah*) in Eastern Europe. The selections below are from Krochmal's
Guide of the Perplexed of the Age, published posthumously in 1851. Krochmal interprets Judaism in the intellectual terms of modern German philosophy, while
preserving a role for the commandments and accounting for features of Jewish
law. In the first selection presented here, he offers a general account of religion
as faith in the spiritual as the source of all things, which may be expressed at various levels of conceptual clarity. The Jewish faith is unique because, regardless of
the form of its expression, its content remains the same. Krochmal then shows
how certain commandments serve to stimulate reflection on the spiritual. In the
second selection, Krochmal offers an evolutionary historical account of Jewish law,
which is influenced by the thought of Friedrich Carl von Savigny (1779–1861), the
founder of the historical school of jurisprudence. Krochmal maintains that the Oral
Torah consists of the necessarily unwritten principles for adapting Jewish law from
one generation to the next, while reinterpreting rabbinic claims that seem to conflict with this account.[47]

Naḥman Krochmal, *Moreh Nevukhei ha-Zeman* (Jerusalem: Karmel, 2010),
29–33, 189–191, and 216 (translated by Lawrence Kaplan, supplemented from
Jay M. Harris, *Nachman Krochmal: Guiding the Perplexed of the Modern Age*
[New York: New York University Press, 1991], 248).

CHAPTER 6: THE SPIRITUAL SYMBOL AND THE SIGN

... Know that every religious faith is faith in the spiritual (*ruḥani*). ... And
in light of this, the essence of those many beliefs and rituals, to which we refer
by the general term, idolatry (*avodah zarah*), is [the worship of] those spiritual
forces that can only be grasped by thought, but which are attached to or united
with ... physical objects that can be grasped only by the senses. And we, the

47. [For more on Krochmal, see Jay M. Harris, *Nachman Krochmal: Guiding the Perplexed of
the Modern Age* (New York: New York University Press, 1991).]

community of those who were the first to uphold the divine unity in the purity of its truth, believe and know that all physical things pass away and perish, and are as naught, because they do not possess true reality. And even the spiritual that we apprehend as attached to all physical objects, and which manifests itself more in the human species, and comes to light in unique human beings, even its persistence and the truth of its existence is only via God, may He be exalted, for He alone is the Perfect Rock, "a dwelling place for us from generation to generation" (Ps. 90:1),[48] that is, the cause that encompasses in its uniqueness all the various types of causes and the true existence of all that is. For the true existence and true persistence of all that is are only in Him. For if anything outside of God possessed, in itself, true existence and persistence—then it would be God. And this is the depth of the secret of the verse, "I am the First and I am the Last, and beside Me there is no God" (Isa. 44:6).[49] . . .

Know, furthermore, that this great cornerstone that the theologians maintained on the basis of tradition is the very same principle that the leading philosophers found difficult to grasp. . . . Even more astonishing than this is that every individual who possesses a religion (dat), if he is God-fearing and observes the commandments for the sake of Heaven, is aware of this very cornerstone, but not through intellectual clarity, but on the basis of the knowledge of God that is planted in his heart and bound up with his soul. As the verse states, "All your children are taught by God" (Isa. 54:13).[50] . . . For the apprehension of the believer that all is naught and emptiness except that which relies upon God —this is knowledge of God. And his apprehension that he, in his essence and spirituality, is beloved by Him and can approach Him, and through this he will endure—this is worship of God. . . . However, even though these apprehensions are planted in a person's heart, they, nevertheless, still need to be cultivated and watched over, that is, the powers of the soul need to be aroused to be directed to them by means of study of the Torah and performance of commandments, awe, and guarding the sanctuary and holy things, already from the time of childhood. . . .

From all that has been said, we can derive the definition of Torahitic faith (emunah ha-torayyit): It is knowledge of the absolute truth—God, Blessed be He; and knowledge of that which exists and persists through God—Spirit—as this

48. [NJPS, modified.]
49. [NJPS, modified.]
50. [NJPS, modified.]

knowledge is implanted in the minds and hearts of every person, whether old or young, when the powers of his soul are aroused toward them. . . .

. . . [W]e wish to present here . . . primary symbolic terms as proof for what has been said, namely, that the Torahitic representations possess the wondrous quality of being the same [in terms of content] in their essence for both the simple worshiper and the enlightened individual who delves profoundly, and they differ only in their form and in the manner [in which] they are apprehended. . . .

Aside from the symbolic terms and sacred objects that we have mentioned, the Torah also contains practical commandments that symbolize the spiritual and arouse one to [apprehend] it, like ceasing to work on Shabbat, circumcision, phylacteries (tefillin), and the sounding of the shofar,[51] and all those commandments that are a remembrance for the Exodus from Egypt. And these commandments are referred to as commandments that are signs and remembrances. And Naḥmanides[52] . . . offered a general reason that encompasses many commandments [of this type]. And here is some of what he writes there: "For he who buys a mezuzah[53] for one *zuz* [a small coin] and fixes it in the entrance to his house and directs his intention to its meaning has already acknowledged the innovation of the world, God's knowledge, and His providence, as well as [the truth of] prophecy. And, moreover, he has acknowledged that God's lovingkindness extended to those who do His will is very great, for He took us out of slavery into freedom and great honor. And therefore the sages said (m. Avot 2:1), 'Be as careful with a light commandment as a grave one,' for they are all greatly beloved and precious. For at every moment an individual, through performing them, acknowledges his Lord, etc." The gist of his comment is that all the commandments allude to the spiritual, and arouse and enlighten the heart to apprehend it or an event that symbolizes a primary witness that the spiritual and the spiritual order are to be found in the world. And this is why these actions are themselves holy, that is, symbols of the spiritual that emerge from the inwardness of the soul via the tongue and the organs into external existence. . . .

---

51. [A musical instrument made of a ram's horn. Frequently mentioned in the Bible, it has been used in postbiblical times to announce holidays and features prominently in the New Year liturgy.]

52. [Naḥmanides, *Commentary on the Pentateuch*, Exod. 13:6; see also selection 3 in part 1.]

53. [A mezuzah is a scroll inscribed with specific verses of the Torah, most often inside a decorative case, that is attached to the doorpost of a Jewish home.]

CHAPTER 13: THE ORIGIN OF THE TRADITION OF COMMENTARY AND RULES (HALAKHAH) IN THE MATTER OF THE COMMANDMENTS OF THE ORAL TORAH[54]

... It is logically necessary that regarding every general law (nomos) that is given to an entire community, both to the community as a whole and to the individuals composing it, that is, that the law contains legal and juridical governance (*ḥok u-mishpat*) for the people as a whole, as well as for all its groups, families, and even individuals in their occupations and circumstances—it is impossible that all the law's particulars can be spelled out and explained, for these particulars, in truth, are endless. It is, therefore, necessary that the law be formulated in terms of general principles, in such a way that all the particular [issues] that will arise in the future, over the course of time, will be covered by those general principles. Moreover, if that law (nomos) at the time it was given was set in writing, the only way possible for its general legal judgments (*mishpatim kollelim*) to be formulated is in a very concrete manner, that is, in accordance with the needs, occupations, mode of life, and physical location of that generation concerning which that law's general principles were set in writing. Therefore, it is necessary that those into whose hands the governance [of the community] on the basis of this law was entrusted must possess some methods for how to explain [and apply] these established general principles with regard to a time, place, and mode of life that differs greatly from the time, place, and mode of life that existed in the generation when the law (nomos) was given and in the immediately following generations.

And to elaborate further, we will say that while it is both possible and fitting for that law (nomos) itself in its general principles, which were formulated to accord [to the situation] of the first generation in which the law was given and the immediately following generations, to be set down in writing and for many copies of it to be made, so that it be widely available to all those who are called upon to govern in accordance with it, such is not the case with regard to the methods for how the particulars are to be extrapolated from the general principles. Here it is neither necessary nor even possible that these methods for how

54. [For analyses of this chapter, see Harris, *Nachman Krochmal*, 206–273; and Shmuel Bialoblocki, "Eim le-Masoret ha-Peirush ve-ha-Halakhah" [The origin of commentary and Jewish law], in *Eim le-Masoret* [The origin of the tradition], edited by Shmuel Bialoblocki, (Ramat Gan, Israel: Bar-Ilan Press, 1971), 74–126.]

the particulars are to be extrapolated from the general principles that accompanied the law when it was promulgated be set down in writing. This is true even with regard to [the methods for how the particulars are to be extrapolated from the general principles as applied to] the first generation, and how much more so does this hold true for the methods of comparing the circumstances of earlier periods [close in time to when the law was given] with later periods, and [taking into account] all the changes that occurred over the course of time. . . .

And the discerning individual (*maskil*) will understand that if the original ancient society was not that "numerous and mighty" (see Exod. 1:9) to begin with, and if originally when the law was set down the modes of life were simple and [legal] transactions were not complex and involved, and if the ancient language was limited in terms of the number of words it possessed, but rich and powerful in terms of the content of those words—then the difficulty in attaining this goal [of discovering the proper intention and delimitation of each and every matter] will be very great, as will [conversely] be the need to do so and the effort required.

And if the above holds true for a human political law (*nomos medini*), where its precise observance is not that critical, and there is no prohibition against its changing over the course of time, and it does not, in most cases, encompass all the circumstances of the lives of the individuals [governed by it], and, by its very nature, does not persist for such a long time, as the [circumstances] of different historical periods in the course of events change from head to toe—then certainly with respect to a divine law (*nomos elohi*) that in its essence and nature was set down for eternity, that encompasses both the community as a whole, its every part, as well as all the individuals belonging to it, [governing] all their movements, when they lie down and when they rise up, and the relationship between the community's God and the community as a whole, its every part, as well as all the individuals belonging to it, how much more so will it require from the very beginning of its being promulgated that it be handed over to the community's rulers, and will necessarily be accompanied by all that we have mentioned, so that it may be understood and instituted among the people, and that judicial determinations may be made regarding all the branches that derive from it and all the particular deeds that keep on multiplying, and all the changing historical circumstances—all this almost without limit.[55]

55. [This entire evolutionary historical picture that Krochmal draws is based on—and in places is a close paraphrase of—Friedrich Carl von Savigny, *Of the Vocation of Our Age*

It is, then, one of the cornerstones of our faith that aside from the Torah that we possess in writing, there came alongside it, possessing equal value, matters that were received orally and that are also [considered to be] Torah. And its primary principles were communicated to Moses orally at Sinai, and were transmitted by him to Joshua, and after him to the elders, and to the prophets and the sages of each generation that followed them, in a continuous, unbroken chain, until the time of the sages of the Mishnah and Talmud, who lived in the time of the Second [Jerusalem] Temple and up to four hundred years after its destruction. And these primary principles that were received orally, they and the derivatives that flow from them, as well as everything that the leading sages of each generation innovated and consented to with regard to them over this lengthy period of time of more than eighteen hundred years, all of this, for our sages, is included in the general term, "Oral Torah" (torah she-be'al peh).[56] And the meaning of this name and its intention derive from two considerations: first, that its primary principles were communicated to Moses orally at Sinai; and, second, that during those generations mentioned the sages were not permitted to write down even one single statement from all those things [the different legal categories] we have related—even though, one by one, these statements were fixed and ordered in fixed and ordered formulations, and this occurred in the last third of that lengthy period—just as it was never permitted to recite the written Torah orally, but only from a book. Thus we find the sages reiterating this prohibition in their famous statement "Words that are written, you are not permitted to recite them orally; words that are oral, you are not permitted to recite them from a written text" (b. Gittin 60b), that is, [with regard to the second half of the statement, it is not permitted] that they [the oral teachings] be written down in a well-known and edited book and be publicly taught from it [that book, as opposed to writing down notes for one's private use, which is permitted]. And understand all this. . . .

. . . [T]he speaker [in y. Talmud Pe'ah 2:4, who said, "everything that a diligent student shall innovate was said to Moses our Master on Sinai"] felt that it is the nature of the Spirit, [being] total unity and complete intelligence, to encompass

---

for Legislation and Jurisprudence, translated by Abraham Hayward (London: Littlewood and Co., 1831). See Harris, *Nachman Krochmal*, 226–32.]

56. [As Harris notes, "the formulation here [in this paragraph] is quite traditional" (*Nachman Krochmal*, 265, note 38) and is not entirely consistent with the evolutionary historical picture that Krochmal draws.]

all the offshoots that are united within it, from it they came and to it they shall return, just as the simple idea of the circle . . . already includes all the concepts and properties that were explained by the geometricians. . . . Everything was included in the simple definition of the circle, such that one who defined it already mandated all the wondrous definitions and properties that are known to us today, and which shall be discovered in the future. All the time that they have not been elucidated they are contained within the idea of the circle in potential[lity] only, and when one discovers them through investigation they become, for him, part of the idea of circle in actu[ality]. From here there is a source of the saying above, both in relation to the finite recipient [that is, Israel], although only in potential[lity], and in relation to the giver, may He be blessed, in actu[ality] as well, for Him there is no distinction between potentiality and actuality.

14

Yisrael (Lipkin) Salanter, *Light of Israel*

Yisrael (Lipkin) Salanter (1810–83) founded the Musar movement, which focused on individual ethical formation. He promoted this movement through his journal, *Tevunah: Kevutzat Ḥiddushei Torah Mi-Ḥakhmei u-Gedolei Yisra'el* (Wisdom: collection of Torah novellae from the sages and great ones of Israel), in which the selections below were originally published. Salanter claims that the task of the human being is to master his negative character traits and replace them with positive ones. Though in principle Salanter draws a distinction between this process of ethical development, which requires emotional engagement, and the study of Jewish law, which is purely rational, in practice things are much more complex. Consonant with the insights of Legal Realism and Critical Legal Studies, Salanter acknowledges that subjectivity cannot be eliminated from the determination of Jewish law. He maintains that while rabbinic judges must strive to make the strictly rational judgments characteristic of Torah law, this is ultimately unattainable for human beings. Indeed, he claims that far-reaching disputes between Jewish legal authorities stem from basic differences of temperament. Yet he insists that these emotional intrusions into rational law do not compromise it; rather, they provide opportunities for humans to contribute to the Torah. Moreover, Salanter maintains that, when developed with the proper intention, specifically legal positions that are rejected as practical law are what can be contributed to the Torah.[57]

Yisrael (Lipkin) Salanter. *Or Yisra'el* [Light of Israel], edited by Isaac Blazer (Vilna, 1900), 80–81 and 86–92 (translated by Geoffrey Claussen).

A person should not say, "That which God has done cannot be changed; the Blessed One has impressed an evil force within me, and how can I hope to uproot it?" This is not so! The forces within a person can be subdued—and they can even be replaced. . . . And this is in accordance with the statement of our rabbis of blessed memory (m. Avot 4[:1]): "Who is mighty? One who subdues one's [evil] inclination, as it is written, 'One who is slow to anger is better than the

---

57. [For more on Salanter, see Immanuel Etkes, *Rabbi Israel Salanter and the Mussar Movement: Seeking the Torah of Truth*, translated by Jonathan Chipman (Philadelphia: Jewish Publication Society, 1993).]

mighty, and one who rules one's spirit is better than one who conquers a city' (Prov. 16:32)."[58] "Might" means standing up to one's opponent with strength, and subduing him with fortitude; "conquers a city" means that the people of the city obey their conqueror with love and affection, not finding it burdensome to fulfill his commands but rather enacting his plans with happiness, joy, and delight. So, too, one who subdues one's evil inclination is merely the "mighty" one, who has strengthened himself to restrain one's appetite. This is the level of "slow to anger": the individual is prone to anger yet restrains it, preventing it from erupting. From here, one may slowly, slowly reach the level of the "one who rules one's spirit," such that the spirit of one's appetite will be under the power of one's upright reason—loving righteousness and not desiring its opposite. And this is the whole [purpose] of the human being: to uproot every negative quality and character trait from one's heart. . . .

It is known that there are two kinds of speech and thought: that which is [purely] rational (*sikhli*) and that which is emotionally engaged (*hitpaʻali*).[59] That which is rational is consistent for all people, but this is not true with emotional engagement, where the experience of one person is not comparable to that of another. . . . Thus, when two people differ on a rational matter . . . we say that one of them is mistaken. . . . This is not so with emotional engagement, in which there is no essential contradiction, but rather both [emotional responses] are true (and only [different] because of their causes—different temperaments or a different stimulus).

Thus, reason is enduring—not subject to change or corruption. When a person (using the appropriate ways of wisdom) finds demonstrations or evidence that change [his or her view of] a rational matter, the former is seen as a mistake —imagined, and not in the realm of reason. This is not so with emotional engagement, which is ephemeral and dependent on the situation.

This is perhaps indicated in the statement of our rabbis of blessed memory (b. Shabbat 10a): "Rava[60] saw that Rabbi Hamnuna was prolonging his prayer. He said: 'You are setting aside eternal life (Torah) and busying yourself with the ephemeral!'"—because the Torah is rational, stripped of all of the desire

---

58. [NJPS, modified.]

59. [Or "emotionally excited," as translated in some contexts below.]

60. [Rabbi Abba ben Joseph ben Ḥama, a fourth-century CE Talmudic sage.]

and emotional engagement of the soul . . . , whereas prayer is grounded in the ephemeral emotional engagement of the soul. . . .

Nonetheless, being human, even if a person has the ability and power to strip away his reason from the emotional engagement of the soul-forces,[61] putting them to sleep (so that they are not aroused and cannot interfere with and distort the power of reason—

*Note: . . .

It is perhaps for this reason that our rabbis of blessed memory warned (b. Sanhedrin 7a): "a judge should always imagine himself as if a sword rests between his thighs, and hell (*gehinnom*) is open beneath him." They did not offer this warning for cases of animals unfit for slaughter . . . but rather for monetary cases (din), where the inclination [to bias] is very common. Nonetheless, if a person dedicates his heart and soul to purifying his thoughts in accordance with his knowledge, this is truly the pursuit of justice that God seeks. This is the "truth" of the case [according to which a judge should judge], the definition of truth in legal judgment. . . .

—nonetheless, as a human being, the soul-forces are [still] found within, and one cannot separate them from one's reason. And so it is not within the capacity of a human being to reach "true reason" that is totally disembodied[62] and separate from the soul-forces. And the Torah was given to human beings, to use it to make judgments in accordance with human reason (purified as much as possible—see b. Bekhorot 17b: "the Merciful One said 'Do it, and however you do it will be acceptable to me'"). Matters should be decided through accumulating evidence and weighing it. The side on which the evidence has greater value, whether due to the quantity of evidence or its weightiness, produces the decision, and thus the matter will stand. . . .

When a person discovers a matter of Torah that is accepted as law, it is not "his." It is, rather, the revelation of a matter that was hidden up to that point. Therefore, if it is *not* accepted as law, it is God's Torah nonetheless, and one who meditates on its words receives reward—but it is [also] "his," for through his

61. [*Koḥot ha-nefesh* is translated as "soul-forces," following Hillel Goldberg, *Israel Salanter: Text, Structure, Idea: The Ethics and Theology of an Early Psychologist of the Unconscious* (New York: Ktav, 1982).]

62. [*Mufrash* is translated as "disembodied," following Goldberg, *Israel Salanter*, 119.]

labor he produced it as a new matter for the Torah that did not exist before. All this is on the condition that it is with purity of thought, without personal bias, which is the foundation of that which is "for its own sake." . . .

Thus [the dispute of] the school of Shammai and the school of Hillel[63] can be explained, and we need not wonder how it came about that the students within each school, on the whole, agreed with the other members of their own group, and the significance of this. The reason for their disputes was the difference in the temperament of their soul-forces, which human beings cannot strip away from reason . . . , and one who investigates God's Torah does so only according to what one's eyes see, following one's ability, guarding the measure [of one's soul-forces] so that it does not go beyond its boundary, and purifying one's reason in accordance with the limits of human strength. . . .

And this is the instruction and requirement for a human being: to strive with all of one's might so that one's soul-forces are calm and quiet when one is engaged in reasoned reflection. And when these forces are quiet, they can almost be at a point of equanimity, especially for the "completed human being"—one who guards oneself against those constantly changing, powerful sources of [emotional] arousal that can be implanted in one's soul. . . .

. . . [I]t is known that the Torah of Blessed God can be divided into two general types: 1. The commandments, statutes, and ordinances of Blessed God. 2. The rest of the Torah, the foundation of which is raising up, from the hidden depths, uprightness in character traits and the purification of the soul-forces, until they long only for what is good in the eyes of God and human beings. . . .

63. [Shammai (Jerusalem, 50 BCE–30 CE) and Hillel (Jerusalem, c. 110 BCE–10 CE) were founders of Jewish legal schools, which often disagreed.]

15

Ḥayyim Soloveitchik, *Novellae and Clarifications on Maimonides*

Ḥayyim Soloveitchik (1853–1918), who taught at the Etz Ḥayyim Yeshiva in Volozhin before assuming the position of rabbi of the town of Brest in Belarus, pioneered a novel approach to the study of Talmud and other rabbinic texts, especially Maimonides' *Mishneh Torah*. Called alternatively "conceptualism," "the analytic movement," or simply "the Brisker method" (after the name for Brest in Yiddish), it is characterized by the construction of general, abstract categories to understand particular legal rules or positions. Legal disputes are thus analyzed as reflecting disagreements about these categories as opposed to deriving from differences of historical context, policy aim, or textual interpretation. Therefore, the approach has affinities with the contemporary scholar Ernest Weinrib's legal formalism, since it too aims to expose the "immanent moral rationality" of law.[64] Still, unlike Weinrib's formalism, Soloveitchik's approach retains a residual positivism because the general categories are left independent from any moral, political, or historical explanation. Presumably, they are understood, as in the thought of Ḥayyim of Volozhin, as stemming from God's will. This approach to Jewish law is entirely theoretical and does not concern itself with practical rulings. Indeed, a feature of yeshivot influenced by it is the study of topics that have no practical application, such as the rules of the Temple sacrifice. While Ḥayyim Soloveitchik never expressed his theory of Jewish law, it is displayed in some of his classic analyses, such as the selection below, which first examines a difficulty concerning Maimonides' ruling in the *Mishneh Torah* about the punishment for violation of the prohibition of possessing leavened bread on Passover. Next, it discusses two different ways of understanding the commandment to eliminate leavened bread before Passover and two different ways to conceptualize the relationship between the prohibition of possessing leavened bread and the commandment to eliminate it.[65]

64. Ernest Weinrib, "Legal Formalism: On the Immanent Rationality of Law," *Yale Law Journal* 97, no. 6 (1988): 949–1016.

65. On this method of study, see Norman Solomon, *The Analytic Movement: Hayyim Soloveitchik and His Circle* (Atlanta, GA: Scholars, 1993); Chaim Saiman, "Legal Theology: The Turn to Conceptualism in Nineteenth-Century Jewish Law," *Journal of Law and Religion*

Ḥayyim Soloveitchik, *Ḥidushei Rabbeinu Ḥayim: Ḥidushim u-Biurim al ha-Rambam* (Jerusalem, 2002) 42–43 (translated by Ephraim Meth).

. . . "One is liable to a flogging for transgression of these two negative commandments [that the leavened bread "shall not be seen" and that the leavened bread "shall not be found" on Passover][66] only if he buys leavened bread or ferments dough during Passover, in order to violate the law actively. If, however, one who possesses leavened bread before Passover does not get rid of it at the onset of Passover and allows it to remain on his premises, he is not liable to the flogging prescribed by Scripture despite his transgression of two negative commandments, because his transgression involves no action on his part."[67]

It has already been asked: Why are there any lashes at all for transgressing the prohibition of it "shall not be seen (*lo yira'e*)" and it "shall not be found (*lo yimatz'e*)"?[68] And behold in b. Pesaḥim 95[a] it is explained explicitly that the prohibition of possession is a prohibition that is transformed into the prescription (*la'v ha-nitak le-aseh*) of elimination (*tashbetu*) [of the leavened bread].[69] This is difficult for Maimonides, who rules that one who purchases leavened bread on Passover must receive lashes since his purchase was active.[70] This requires inquiry.

[The answer] may be seen in this: For Rabbi Akiva Eiger[71] questioned Tur,[72]

---

21 (2006): 39–100; Yosef Blau, ed., *Lomdus: The Conceptual Approach to Jewish Learning* (Jersey City, NJ: Ktav, 2006).

66. [See Exod. 12:19 and 13:7.]

67. [From Moses Maimonides, *Code of Maimonides*, vol. 3: *Book of Seasons*, translated by Solomon Gandz and Hyman Klein (New Haven, CT: Yale University Press, 1961), 1:3.]

68. [Despite the fact that Maimonides refers to these as two separate negative commandments, Soloveitchik refers to them as one prohibition. Following him, in the translation they will sometimes be referred to collectively as "the prohibition of possession," the relationship of which to "the commandment of elimination" is the subject of the analysis.]

69. [Violations of such prohibitions do not ordinarily carry a corporal punishment, since compliance with the corresponding prescription rectifies the violation. For example, a violation of the prohibition on stealing does not carry a corporal punishment, since there is a corresponding prescription to return the stolen property. See b. Makkot 16a.]

70. [Maimonides seems to distinguish between passive ownership and active acquisition of leavened bread and then to make this distinction decisive for whether one receives lashes. In contrast, the Talmud in b. Pesaḥim seems to suggest that this distinction is irrelevant because in neither case does one receive lashes, since the prohibition of possession is a prohibition transformed into the prescription of elimination.]

71. [Poland, 1761–1837.]

72. [Ya'akov ben Asher (1270–c. 1340), author of the *Tur (Arba'ah Turim)*.]

who wrote,[73] "According to Rabbi Yehudah, who maintains that the commandment of leavened bread is that it be burned, [the leavened bread's] ashes are permitted just like the law (*ki-din*) of any substance that must be burned, the ashes of which are permitted, whereas according to the Rabbis, who maintain that the elimination [of leavened bread] is in any manner, its ashes[74] are prohibited just like the law of any substance that must be buried."[75] Rabbi Akiva Eiger challenged [Tur's position] based on Tosafot,[76] who write that [the reason that] the ashes of substances that must be burned are permitted, while the ashes of substances that must be buried are forbidden, is because in the case of substances that must be burned, the commandment consists in their [very] burning, and so [once they have been burned] necessarily their commandment has been performed, whereas this is not the case with substances that must be buried, for which there is no commandment in their burial [itself], and it is only in order [to prevent] accident[al benefit from them], which would preclude their commandment from being performed[, that they are buried]. Thus in the case of leavened bread, even if its elimination may be in any manner, still there is a commandment to eliminate it,[77] and thus [both Rabbi Yehudah and the Rabbis][78] should hold that its ashes should be permitted.[79]

[However, i]t seems that the commandment of elimination [of leavened bread] when it can be eliminated in any manner[80] is not similar to the commandment of [elimination when it can only be performed by] burning.[81] For the principle of the commandment (*ikkar ha-mitzvah*) of elimination [of leavened bread] by other means [than burning] is that the owner should [simply] not possess leavened

73. [*Tur*, Oraḥ Ḥayyim, section 445. However, this is not a verbatim quotation.]

74. [Or any other remainder.]

75. [See m. Pesaḥim 2:1 for this dispute.]

76. [Tosafot are medieval commentaries on the Talmud, composed from the twelfth to the mid-fifteenth centuries by numerous rabbis known as the Tosafists. The commentaries were additions (*tosafot*, in Hebrew) to the commentary of Rashi (Shlomo Yitzḥaki, France, 1040–1105).]

77. [The elimination is not just instrumental, to prevent accidental benefit from it.]

78. [They thus disagree with the Tur's construal of the disagreement and its ramifications for the permissibility of the remainder.]

79. [Unable to locate the source in Akiva Eiger's writings where he presents the challenge to Tur that Soloveitchik attributes to him.]

80. [The position of the Rabbis.]

81. [The position of Rabbi Yehudah. Soloveitchik aims to vindicate the Tur's distinction between the two positions and their ramifications, which Eiger had criticized.]

bread, whereas if the commandment [of elimination of leavened bread] is [specifically] by burning, then it is a commandment that devolves on the object of leavened bread, that is, it devolves on [the bread] the requirement to be burned. Now, as to the matter of the permission [to benefit from an object] after its commandment has been performed, [it] requires specifically that its commandment be performed in the object, [only] in that case the object is permitted, and not when the owners have fulfilled a commandment that is incumbent upon them would the object thereby become permitted. And therefore the Tur rightly distinguishes between whether [the leavened bread's] elimination is by any manner[82] and by burning.[83] For if its elimination is by any manner, then the owners have merely fulfilled the commandment that they not possess leavened bread, and therefore the ashes have not become permitted, whereas if its elimination is by burning, then the commandment is done in the object and the commandment has been performed and so the ashes are permitted.

Based on this, [the difficulties with] Maimonides' opinion that we lash for [violations of] the prohibition of it "shall not be seen" and it "shall not be found" are well resolved. For the reason [this prohibition] is not considered to be a prohibition transformed into a prescription[84] must be because [Maimonides] holds that the principle of (ikkaro) [the commandment] of elimination is a prohibition derived from a prescription (issur aseh), that is, one should not possess leavened bread,[85] and it is like all things prohibited through [both] a prescription and a prohibition, which is not transformed into a prescription (nitak le-aseh). Therefore [Maimonides' reasoning] is only applicable if we say that the leavened bread may be eliminated in any manner. . . . [F]or according to the [Rabbis], who hold that its elimination is in any manner, the principle of the verse of elimination is that [individuals] should not possess leavened bread.[86] This is not the case if we say that its commandment is by burning,[87] [for] it would then be a commandment that is performed in the body of the object, and then it is obvious that [the prohibition of it "shall not been seen" and it "shall not be found"] is [a

82. [The position of the Rabbis, according to which the remainder is prohibited.]

83. [The position of Rabbi Yehudah, according to which the remainder is permitted.]

84. [This would make the transgression of it not punishable by lashes.]

85. [A prohibition derived from a commandment is a prohibition not explicitly stated in scripture but implied by a prescription that is explicitly expressed.]

86. [Thus, the commandment of elimination implies the prohibition of possessing bread. It is a prohibition derived from a prescription, for which one may receive lashes.]

87. [The position of Rabbi Yehudah.]

prohibition] transformed into a prescription just like the burning of meat left over from a sacrifice and the like.[88] And even were we to say that [Rabbi Yehudah] too includes in the commandment of elimination the prohibition that they should not possess leavened bread, still it is obvious that the obligation to burn [specifically] the leavened bread is a commandment just like everything else that must be burned, and since this too is included in the verse, [the prohibition of it "shall not be seen" and it "shall not be found"] must therefore be considered a prohibition transformed into a prescription.

So according to this, Maimonides' opinion is easy to understand. The Talmudic passage in b. Pesaḥim 95a that we cited follows the opinion of Rabbi Yehudah, as is evident from the discussion there, and for Rabbi Yehudah, who holds that leavened bread must be burned, it is obvious that [the prohibition of it "shall not be seen" and it "shall not be found"] is transformed into a prescription [of elimination]. In contrast, Maimonides, who rules in "Laws of Leavened and Unleavened Bread," chapter 3, that the elimination [of leavened bread] is by any manner, so [the commandment] of elimination is no more than a prohibition derived from a prescription, [namely] that one should not possess leavened bread, and he ruled correctly that it is not [a prohibition] transformed into a prescription, and one receives lashes for it, as we explained.

88. [Another example of a prohibition transformed into a prescription is the prohibition of leaving meat from a sacrifice unconsumed past its stipulated time period, which is transformed into a prescription to burn such leftover meat.]

Shimon Shkop (1860–1939) studied with Ḥayyim Soloveitchik at the Etz Ḥayyim Yeshiva in Volozhin and later went on to head several other yeshivot, including one in Telisia, Lithuania. Shkop's method of study is significantly influenced by the Brisker method, insofar as it engages in theoretical analysis as opposed to practical rulings and aims to develop abstract categories to use in understanding particular legal rules and positions. However, Shkop's efforts to rationalize and systematize Jewish law extend beyond those of Soloveitchik. For example, in the selection below, Shkop does not begin with a particular difficulty in a rabbinic text but directly asks what the reason is for the various types of liability mentioned in the Mishnah. Indeed, he aims to ascertain the general rationale for liability, rather than to categorize a rule properly. Moreover, once he has ascertained this rationale and surveyed its legal consequences, he views its consonance with non-Jewish law as a point in its favor, which indicates that he believed in a form of universal legal rationality that underlies both Jewish and non-Jewish law.

Shimon Shkop, *Ḥidushei Rebbe Shimon Yehudah ha-Kohen al Mesekhtot Bava Kamma, Bava Metzia, u-Bava Batra* (New York, 1947), 1–2 (translated by Ephraim Meth).

. . . In the Mishnah [Bava Kamma 1:1]: "[There are] four categories of damages:] the ox, the pit, the grazer, and the fire, etc. Their common denominator is that they habitually damage, and [the responsibility] to supervise them is upon you, etc." Behold! In general, [damages] are divided into three categories: [1] Damage that was done by a human body, [2] what his property damaged, and [3] damage that results from an accident that his actions caused (*garmu*), such as [the cases of] a fire or a pit. And to all of them [applies] the principle (*klal*) that "[the responsibility] to supervise them is upon you."

Here it must be explained that even though we have found a way in which a person can be liable in all of the categories [of damage] even when the [damager] is not his property, and even in the cases of the pit and the fire where his actions did not cause (garmu) them, as when he transfers his ox or pit to a guardian who takes the owner's place, and similarly we have found in the case of a thief that he is liable for all the types of damages [by an object he stole], as is explained in the beginning of [b. Bava Kamma Ch 6], and as Tosafot write there[89] that whoever is responsible for supervising (*mutal alav le-shamro*) [something] is its owner in terms of damages;[90] nonetheless, it still requires determination whether the reason for [an individual's] liability (*ha-sibah ha-miḥayyevet*) [to pay damages] in all these cases is [A] the negligence in not supervising the damager, that is to say, that on [account of] this exclusively the Torah made him liable. And the only reason why the [responsibility of] supervision is incumbent on [a particular individual] more than any other individual is because it is his property or because he made and prepared the damager.[91] According to this [position], the reason for the liability for damages would only derivatively be because of the digging of the pit [for instance], for because of his opening or digging the pit the Torah obligated him in supervision and incidentally made him liable afterward for his negligence for not completing the supervision.[92] (Or [B] the obligation to pay damages is because it is his property, as is explained afterward.)[93]

Indeed, it seems, according to the paucity of my understanding, clearly impossible to interpret [the matter] this way.[94] For according to this, it would be the law (ha-din) that if one neglected [to supervise] his ox, [for example,] he did not close [the gate] before it, and it escaped [and caused damage], and by the time of the damage the status [of being the property] of the owner had been removed from the ox, for example if the owner alienated it, then the owner would still be liable since he was negligent at the outset, once everything depends only on the initial negligence, and there is no practical difference at all whether he is the

89. [See b. Bava Kamma 56a, *s.v. peshita.*]

90. [All these cases seem to disconnect the liability for damage from ownership of the damager or direct causation by an individual's own actions, and instead attach the liability to the responsibility to supervise.]

91. [The primary factor for determining liability for damages is whether the individual was negligent in executing his responsibility to supervise the damager. Ownership is only a secondary factor.]

92. [This case seems suited to this position: Digging or opening the pit directly results in a person's responsibility to supervise it, and breach of this responsibility through negligence makes him or her liable for any damage caused by the pit. Ownership does not factor into this particular case at all.]

93. [This is the position that Shkop ultimately champions.]

94. [That the reason for obligation to pay damages is primarily because of negligence and only secondarily because of ownership.]

owner of it at the time of the damage or not. And this is not so, for, according to everyone, one who alienates his damager is only liable in the case of [damage on account of a] pit, but in the case of [damage as a result of] his ox he is exempted. And it is certainly a stretch to say that this [rule] is a result of what the Merciful One innovated[95] that "[an ox that] gored and afterward was declared ownerless is exempted,"[96] since not everyone agrees that this is an innovation. . . .

But, at any rate, the law (ha-din) is clear that it is necessary that [to be liable] they must be the owners of the ox at the time of the damage. From this it is necessarily the case that the reason for the liability here is the fact that [the owner's] property damaged, for just as the Torah made him liable for [the damage done by] his body so too it made one liable for what his property damages. And indeed [even] concerning the pit, he is liable because his damager damaged, and the pit is his because he dug it or opened it, that is, he prepared the damager [to damage], and as a result he is called the owner of it. Just as concerning the right of an individual (zekhut ha-adam) the laws of the Torah (dinei torah) and the laws of the nations (dinei ha-amim) agree that anyone who invents something new in the world is the owner of it for all matter of benefit (davar zekhut), so too the Torah calls someone who prepares an accident [its "owner"]—the pit's owner, the fire's owner—and it made liable for damages the owner of the damager. . . .

It seems, according to the paucity of my understanding, therefore, that the principle of the reason for liability in monetary damages (de-ikkar ha-sibah ha-mihayyevet be-nizkei mamon) follows from his liability for the actions of his ox and pit, and the negligence in supervision is only a precondition for liability. . . .

. . . [W]e say in monetary damages that the Torah made [an individual] liable for his ox's or his pit's damage so long as he is the damager's owner from the outset until the time of damage. The matter of the liability for the damage does not depend specifically on monetary acquisition; rather, whoever controls (shalit) the damager is considered its "owner." And the cause of the control (sibat ha-shlitah) could be a result of various means: either it is truly his acquisition, or he brought it into his domain with a commitment to supervise it, or he stole it, since he becomes its controller de facto by bringing it into his domain.

95. [An anomalous law based on a scriptural verse.]
96. [See b. Bava Kamma 13b.]

17

Selections from the Writings of
Yisrael Meir Kagan and Associated Texts

Yisrael Meir Kagan (1838–1933), often referred to as Ḥafetz Ḥayyim (Desirer of life), which is also the title of one of his famous works, was a scholar, communal leader, and head of the yeshiva in Radin, Lithuania. His approach to Jewish law is marked by two complementary movements that can be referred to as the ethicization of law and the legalization of ethics.[97] In *Mishnah Berurah*, a commentary on the portions of the *Shulḥan Arukh* that concern everyday Jewish life, Kagan often avoids taking sides in disputes between earlier authorities. Instead, he shows how one might act stringently so as not to violate the rule according to either side. *Ḥafetz Ḥayyim* is devoted to clarifying the rules against malicious speech and talebearing. As Kagan admits, these rules had not previously been the subject of attention by legal authorities; nonetheless, he insists that there are not merely counsels of piety, but strict laws. These laws are derived from explicit biblical commandments as well as narratives. Violation of them even entails violations of many other seemingly unrelated commandments. In addition to *Ḥafetz Ḥayyim*, Kagan wrote other works to offer practical guidance in Jewish law, including *Maḥaneh Yisra'el*, which advises Jews on how to observe Jewish law while conscripted into non-Jewish armies. Throughout most of the work Kagan merely summarizes standard Jewish laws on the assumption that it will be feasible to observe them. However, in the selection included below, he acknowledges that Jewish conscripts will likely be required to violate Jewish law yet maintains that they are not liable for such violations because they were done under coercion. Still, he maintains that Jewish conscripts must take every opportunity to leave the army so that they will no longer be subject to such coercion.

97. This analysis has been developed by Benjamin Brown in, among other writings, "'Soft Stringency' in the Mishnah Brurah: Jurisprudential, Social, and Ideological Aspects of a Halachic Formulation," *Contemporary Jewry* 27, no. 1 (2007): 1–41, and "From Principles to Rules and from Musar to Halakhah: The Hafetz Hayim's Rulings on Libel and Gossip," *Dine Yisrael* 25 (2008): 171–256. See also Michael J. Broyde and Ira Bedzow, *The Codification of Jewish Law and an Introduction to the Jurisprudence of the Mishna Berura* (Boston: Academic Studies, 2014). The selections presented here and their significance have been informed by these works and conversations with their authors.

Yosef Karo, *Shulḥan Arukh*, Oraḥ Ḥayyim 437:1 (translated by Ira Bedzow).

If one rents a house to his friend, for the needs of the fourteenth [of Nissan —that is, the eve of Passover], from that day and onward, and [the lessee] acquires it in one of the ways in which renting land takes effect, if [the landlord] does not hand over the keys to him until the fourteenth begins, it is the responsibility of the landlord to check [for leavened bread]; if he has already handed over the key by the fourteenth, it is the responsibility of the lessee to check [for leavened bread].

Yisrael Meir Kagan, *Mishnah Berurah* (Jerusalem, 1894–1907), 437:1 (2) (translated by Ira Bedzow).

"And [the lessee] acquires it"—that is, by money or by deed or by usucaption (*ḥazakah*) or by symbolic acquisition (*kinyan sudar*),[98] but if he has not yet acquired it through one of these [acts] of acquisition, even though the key is in the possession of the lessee, he does not need to check [for leavened bread]. For this would be as if [the landlord] entrusted the key to another; the trustee would not be obligated to check [the house], rather the obligation of checking is on the landlord. You should know that [Yosef Karo] rules categorically like the opinion of Ran[99] and *Maggid Mishneh*,[100] who do not obligate the lessee to check [for leavened bread] except in the case where there are two positive [signifiers that he has ownership of the house], such as [that] he acquired [the property] through one of the effective means to do so before the fourteenth and he was given the key. [However, a]ccording to the opinion of Tosafot and their supporters, handing over the key alone before the fourteenth [is sufficient for] the obligation of checking to fall on the lessee, because the landlord is unable to enter [the premises] since he has no key, thus the obligation falls on the lessee. There are later authorities[101] who write that it is correct to be stringent according to both opin-

98. [Ḥazakah, or usucaption, involves acquiring property by dint of possession over time. A kinyan sudar is a symbolic act in which an object of little value, like a scarf, is exchanged to represent the acquisition of an object of value.]

99. [Nissim ben Reuven of Girona (Spain, 1320–76).]

100. [*Maggid Mishneh* (Second announcement), a commentary on Maimonides' *Mishneh Torah* by Vidal of Tolosa (Spain, latter half of the fourteenth century), first published in 1509.]

101. [The later authorities (*aḥaronim*) are leading rabbis and decision makers who were active since the mid-sixteenth century.]

ions; and, if so, the obligation of checking in this case [falls] on both the lessee and the landlord, and [according to] Pri Ḥadash,[102] [the tenant] may appoint [the landlord] his representative [so that in checking] the obligation of all is fulfilled.

Yisrael Meir Kagan, Ḥafetz Ḥayyim [Desirer of life] (Vilna, 1873), 1–3, 7, 9, 15–20, 24–26, 42–44, 65–66, 69, 124, and 126 (translated by Ira Bedzow).

Blessed is the Lord, God of Israel, who separated us from all of the other nations and gave us His Torah and brought us into the Holy Land. . . .

And when we look at the ways in which we live and investigate them, [and understand] which sins essentially cause [the continuation of] our long exile, we find that there are many. However, the sin of malicious speech (lashon hara) is the gravest. . . .

[I asked myself h]ow has this prohibition become as nothing in the eyes of many people. I observed that it [results] from many causes, [that is] for the masses on the one hand and for the scholars on the other. The masses do not know at all that the prohibition of malicious speech applies even to [speaking] the truth. Regarding the Torah scholars, even those who know clearly and recognize that it applies to [speaking] the truth, there are those among them whom the evil inclination (yetzer hara) leads astray. For some, the evil inclination will immediately rationalize to them [that it is permitted]. . . .

All of these issues are rooted in the fact that with respect to malicious speech and talebearing there is not one [centralized] place that explains their quality and matter in its generalities and its particulars. Rather, the sources [that explain them] are spread out throughout the Talmud and the early authorities [rishonim]. . . .

Therefore, I have strengthened myself, with the help of God, Blessed be He, who graces man with knowledge, and I have collected all of the laws (dinei) of malicious speech and talebearing into a book, and I have taken them from all of the disparate places [where they are found] in the Talmud and [rabbinic] decisors (poskim), . . .

---

102. [Pri Ḥadash (New fruit), a commentary on Yosef Karo's Shulḥan Arukh by Hezekiah da Silva (active in Livorno, Amsterdam, and Jerusalem; 1659–98).]

Out of God's, Blessed be He, love for His people Israel and His desire for their benefit. . . . He distances us from all bad character traits, and particularly malicious speech and talebearing, since it causes conflict and arguments among people, and many times it leads to bloodshed. . . .

Because of the great evil that is found in this reprehensible character trait, the Torah warns us in particular about this in the prohibition (Lev. 19:16) "Do not go about as a talebearer."[103] . . . Moreover, there is another obvious reason why the Torah warns about this [transgression] in particular. When one is truly precise in analyzing in particular malicious speech and talebearing, one finds that they encompass almost all of the prohibitions and commandments regarding how a person should act toward his fellows, and also many [commandments] that prescribe the relationship between man and God. . . .

First, one needs to know the principles (klalim) of malicious speech and talebearing; ("malicious speech" is when one speaks disparagingly about a friend, and "talebearing" is when one tells a person what bad thing another friend said about him or bad thing he did to him). . . . Each one of these principles has in it an essential aspect (sharashim) [literally, "roots"] and consequences thereof (anafim) [literally, "branches"]. . . .

First, I will explain several prohibitions that one may transgress by speaking maliciously or by talebearing, and afterward several prescriptions, and after that several curses that a person brings on himself because of them, and then still after that several [other] major prohibitions [the transgression of which] are caused by [malicious speech and talebearing].

Prohibitions

(1) One who gossips (meragel) about his friend transgresses a [Torah] prohibition, as it says (Lev. 19:16): "Do not go about as a talebearer (rakhil) among your countrymen." . . .

(3) The speaker also transgresses that which is written (Deut. 24:8): "In cases of skin affliction (ha-tzara'at) be most careful to do. . . ." The Sifra[104] explains (Behukotai, 1:3) that when the Torah writes "be most careful to do," the intention is

---

103. [NJPS; using the literal rendering noted in this edition.]

104. [Sifra (also known as Torat Kohanim) is a midrashic legal commentary to Leviticus. It dates to the first or second century CE, but its authorship is uncertain.]

that one should not forget to be careful with respect to malicious speech, so that he not be stricken with skin affliction because of this kind of talk.[105] . . .

(6) Both speaker and accepter of the information also transgress the prohibition of (Lev. 22:32): "You shall not profane My Holy Name," since there is no physical desire or satisfaction in [speaking maliciously or talebearing] that one's evil inclination can use to overpower one. Therefore, the sin is considered simply to be a rebellion [against God] and a breaking of the yoke of the Kingdom of Heaven, as well as a desecration of the Name of Heaven. . . .

Prescriptions

(1) Through [speaking maliciously and talebearing] one transgresses the positive commandment (Deut. 24:9): "Remember what the Lord your God did to Miriam on the journey. . . ."[106] [Through this commandment] the Torah warns us about this [speaking maliciously and talebearing], that we should constantly make mention of the great punishment that God, Blessed be He, gave to the righteous woman Miriam the prophetess, who . . . spoke about her brother [Moses]. . . .

(2) One also transgresses through this type of talk the positive commandment (Lev. 19:18): "Love your fellow as yourself." . . .

Curses

. . . (3) If, heaven forbid, a person treats the [prohibition of malicious speech and talebearing] as if it were nothing, in that he refuses to be careful about it, he subjects himself to yet a third curse, which is (Deut. 27:26): "Cursed be he who will not uphold the terms of this Teaching and observe them." The explanation of [this type of person] is one that refuses to uphold the whole Torah. [The one who speaks maliciously and bears tales, however, i]s called an apostate regarding one matter (*mumar le-davar eḥad*) because of [his refusing to refrain from

---

105. [The connection between skin affliction and malicious speech is made by juxtaposition of the former with the sin of Miriam: "In cases of a skin affliction, be most careful to do exactly as the levitical priests instruct you. Take care to do as I have commanded them. Remember what the LORD your God did to Miriam on the journey after you left Egypt" (Deut. 24: 8–9). That Miriam's sin is malicious speech, which is then punished by skin affliction, is suggested by Num. 12:1–10: "Miriam and Aaron spoke against Moses because of the Cushite woman he had married," and "when Aaron turned toward Miriam, he saw that she was stricken with scales."]

106. [On this incident, see Num. 12:1–16.]

speaking maliciously and bearing tales]. [Nevertheless, s]ince he contemptuously continues to transgress this grave sin, he holds this element of God's Torah as naught, and makes him just like one who is an apostate regarding the whole Torah (*mumar le-kol ha-torah kulah*). Therefore, his sin is too great to bear. . . .

THE RULES OF THE PROHIBITION
OF MALICIOUS SPEECH

. . . Chapter 3: (7) And know yet still, another great and essential principle in these matters is that if a person sees another say something or do something, whether it is related to a matter between man and God or between man and his fellow, and there is a way to judge his words or deeds positively or favorably, if the person is God-fearing, we are obligated to judge him favorably, even if the matter seems, based on what one knows, to implicate the person. . . . Also, in a situation where it seems more probable that the action was good, it is certainly forbidden according to the law to consider the action as bad, since when he judges him unfavorably he will go on to disparage him. [Therefore, i]n addition to transgressing "Judge your kinsman fairly,"[107] he also transgresses the prohibition of malicious speech.

BE'ER MAYIM ḤAYYIM
[THE WELL OF THE WATER OF LIFE][108]

11. *He also transgresses, etc.* Even if one's intention is solely out of a zeal for truth. The proof for this is [the incident with] Miriam. By not judging Moses, peace be upon him, favorably and [not] saying that as a matter of course he acted according to the law when he separated from his wife, scripture considers what she said essentially as malicious speech and she was punished because of it with skin affliction. . . .

Yisrael Meir Kagan, *Maḥaneh Yisra'el* [Camp of Israel] (Vilna, 1881), 46a
(translated by Ira Bedzow).

Chapter 37, in which it will be explained that if given permission to go home, one should not dawdle [but rather go home immediately].

107. [Lev. 19:15.]
108. ["Be'er Mayim Hayyim" is Kagan's more detailed commentary on the main body of the text of the *Ḥafetz Ḥayyim*.]

If the government in its grace gives someone permission to travel home in the middle of a term of service [in the army], it is necessary that he not dawdle in doing so even if he needs to spend money on travel, and particularly during the time of the festival since in going home he can fulfill the positive commandment of "You shall rejoice in your festival . . . ,"[109] and [he can fulfill] other laws of the Torah (dinei torah) while he is at home, which would not be the case if he were in military service where he is forced many times to transgress the Torah. But when the government does not allow him to travel home, may God have mercy, he is not punished [for not fulfilling those commandments] since he is compelled (anus). However, if on the part [of the government] there is no concern about his [going home] and only he himself dawdles [for whatever reason], [then] he will be punished for every particular [commandment] that he transgresses, whether it be not fulfilling a positive commandment . . . or whether he transgresses a negative commandment. . . . [The reason is that] now [his dawdling] is considered by Heaven to be an intentional transgression. . . .

109. [Deut. 16:14.]

Selections from the Writings
of Joseph B. Soloveitchik

Joseph B. Soloveitchik (1903–93), the grandson of Ḥayyim Soloveitchik, was the central rabbinic figure of American Modern Orthodoxy, a movement that aims to synthesize traditional Jewish observance with engagement with modern culture. Soloveitchik's thought is itself an attempt to synthesize his grandfather's approach to Jewish law (the Brisker method) with Neo-Kantian philosophy of the early twentieth century. For example, in the first selection presented here, Soloveitchik offers an account of Jewish law as the expression of religious subjectivity and then proceeds to argue that, as such, it must be the basis for the construction of authentic Jewish theology. In the process, he also opposes attempts by medieval thinkers (Maimonides in particular) and modern liberals to instrumentalize Jewish law for ethical or aesthetic purposes; for Soloveitchik, such attempts deny its uniquely religious character. The second selection is a rare instance of Soloveitchik's acting as a decisor of Jewish law; like his grandfather, he generally preferred theoretical analysis to practical responsa. Addressed to Samuel Belkin, the president of Yeshiva University, this letter from 1951 analyzes the permissibility of instituting a lottery among its rabbinic alumni to determine who would be required to volunteer to serve as a chaplain in the United States military during the Korean War. It evidences a distinctive mixture of philosophical reflection, Brisker methodology, and political considerations. In the preliminary remarks, Soloveitchik draws on Neo-Kantian conceptions about the relation between values and inquiry. Additionally, his discussion of coercion progresses from traditional rabbinic categories to meditations on the nature of free will. Still, especially in the first part of the letter, he continues the Talmudic tradition of his grandfather by systematically analyzing the work of earlier rabbinic authorities to construct an overarching conceptual framework to understand the legal effect of situations of coercion on violations of Jewish law. Later in the letter, especially in its second part, Soloveitchik evidences an acute awareness of the political considerations that must factor into his decision. In that connection, it is interesting to compare his discussion of coercion to violate the commandments during military service to that of Yisrael Meir Kagan in the previous selection.

Joseph B. Soloveitchik, *Halakhic Mind: An Essay on Jewish Tradition and Modern Thought* (New York: Seth, 1986), 67–68, 84–99, and 100–102.

There is a definite trend towards self-transcendence on the part of the spirit. It strives to escape its private inwardness and infiltrate the concrete world encompassed by space and pervaded by corporeal forms. . . . This concrete physical order, enveloped by time and space, is coordinated with its correlate in the internal world. The internal subjective correlate is, in turn, the objectified expression of some more primitive subjectivity. Religious subjectivity, for example, finds its correlate in a certain norm. . . . The norm is much nearer to the outer fringes of externality than its counterpart, the quasi-non-normative subjectivity. The norm, in such a semi-objectified state, attempts to break through the barrier separating the physical from the spiritual in order to appear in the arena of life. The consummation of the religious act always takes place in a non-personal world. . . .

Objectification reaches its highest expression in the Halakhah. Halakhah is the act of seizing the subjective flow and converting it into enduring and tangible magnitudes. It is the crystallization of the fleeting individual experience into fixed principles and universal norms. In short, Halakhah is the objectifying instrument of our religious consciousness, the form-principle of the transcendental act, the matrix in which the amorphous religious hylo [that is, matter] is cast.

Rabbinic legalism, so derided by theologians, is nothing but an exact method of objectification, the modes of our response to what supremely impresses us. . . .

Retrospective analysis opens new vistas to the philosopher of religion. The modern philosophy of religion . . . has a cognitive claim and a methodology of its own. It is not interested in the genetic approach to the religious act, nor does it raise the old problem of causality. . . . The focal problem is of a descriptive nature: What is the religious act? What is its structure, context and meaning? . . .

The basic error of religious liberalism is to be discerned less in its ideology than in its methodical approach. Liberalism has travelled in the wrong direction—from subjectivity to objectivity—and in so doing h[a]s misconstrued both. Religious liberalism is based upon a very "simple" methodological principle. Subjective religiosity, the moderns say, is subordinated to the omnipotent authority of time and change. It is impossible therefore to consider any set of religious norms and dogmas as immutable. . . .

The fallacy of this movement lies in its utter lack of methodology. Where is the assurance that these philosophers, while exploring modern religious subjectivism, have not erred and strayed? . . . The liberals of today, instead of religious subjectivity, plunge mistakenly into some other subjective "order"—the moral or aesthetic. There being no boundary lines in the subjective sphere, trespasses upon the territory of ethics and aesthetics occur unwittingly. When viewed from any other aspect but the objective, subjectivity does not present separate realism. It is only the act of a retrospective analysis that classifies religiosity. Religious subjectivity is synonymous with the subjective "order" surveyed from the premises of objectivity. . . .

Although the method of reconstruction can be adopted and utilized by any theistic religion, it is of immense importance in the field of Jewish philosophy. One of the most perplexing problems that has confused the finest of minds is that of the rationalization of the commandments ([ta'amei ha-mitzvot]). The difficulties encountered by Maimonides in his attempt . . . to develop an all-embracing interpretation of religious norms are well known. Twenty-five chapters of the *Guide* [*of the Perplexed*] are devoted exclusively to the solution of this problem. . . . Judging Maimonides' undertaking retrospectively, one must admit that the master whose thought shaped Jewish ideology for centuries to come did not succeed in making his interpretation of the commandments prevalent in our world perspective. . . . Maimonides' failure to impress his rationalistic method upon the vivid religious consciousness is to be attributed mainly to the fact that the central theme of the Maimonidean exposition is the causalistic problem. The "how" question, the explanatory quest, and the genetic attitude determined Maimonides' doctrine of the commandments. Instead of describing, Maimonides explained; instead of reconstructing, he constructed.

As we have previously indicated, whenever the causal question is raised, the philosopher must transcend the boundary line of religion in order to find his answer which lies beyond the religious domain. . . .

Hence a system of commandment rationalization ([ta'amei ha-mitzvot]) is a philosophical possibility if it is determined by descriptive hermeneutics. . . . [B]y continuous observation and analysis of the objectified forms of the religious act, the general tendencies and trends latent in the religious consciousness may be grasped. . . .

. . . [T]here is only a single source from which a Jewish philosophical *Weltanschauung* could emerge; the objective order—the Halakhah. In passing onward from the Halakhah and other objective constructs to a limitless subjective flux, we might possibly penetrate the basic structure of our religious consciousness.

We might also evolve cognitive tendencies and aspects of our world interpretation and gradually grasp the mysteries of the religious halakhic act. Problems of freedom, causality, God-man relationship, creation, and nihility would be illuminated by halakhic principles. A new light could be shed on our apprehension of reality. . . . Modern Jewish philosophy must be nurtured on the historical religious consciousness that has been projected onto a fixed objective screen.

Out of the sources of Halakhah, a new world view awaits formulation.

Joseph B. Soloveitchik, "On Drafting Rabbis and Rabbinical Students for the U.S. Armed Forces Chaplaincy," in *Community, Covenant, and Commitment: Selected Letters and Communications*, edited by Nathaniel Helfgot (Jersey City, NJ: Ktav, 2005), 24–26 and 52–60.

Dear Dr. Belkin:

At your request, I have explored the halakhic aspects of the problem of volunteering as a chaplain in the armed forces. . . . Before I begin the halakhic discussion of the subject matter, I wish to make three relevant observations.

First, . . . [t]he halakhic inquiry, like any other cognitive theoretical performance, does not start out from the point of absolute zero as to sentimental attitudes and value judgments. There always exists in the mind of the researcher an ethico-axiological background against which the contours of the subject matter in question stand out more clearly. . . . From the very outset I was prejudiced in favor of the project of the Rabbinical Council of America[110] and I could not imagine any halakhic authority rendering a decision against it. My inquiry consisted only in translating a vague intuitive feeling into fixed terms of halakhic discursive thinking.

Secondly, I have examined the problem in a double perspective. (A) I employed the method of pure halakhic formalism. . . . (B) I availed myself of the method of applied Halakhah, which transposes abstractions into central realities, theory into facts. No halakhic investigation would be true to itself save as a practical *organon*. . . .

Thirdly, I have worked with the method of retrospective problem organization and formulation. . . .

110. [The project of the Rabbinical Council of America, the major professional organization for Modern Orthodox rabbis, was to institute a lottery to determine who among its members should volunteer to serve as a chaplain.]

[I.]

... In abstract, the problem can be formulated as follows: Is it permissible to become deliberately involved in such situations which may later compel the individual to violate a religious injunction?

Secondly, if this question should be answered in the negative, we may still ask whether the prohibition against creating unfavorable circumstances applies only to situations in which the violation is certain to happen or even to cases in which the violation is only a probability.

Thirdly, if our analysis should show that under certain circumstances voluntary involvement is permissible, a new question would arise. Does the halakhic approval of involvement apply only to situations in which the breach of the law would be necessitated by the principle of *pikuah nefesh*—saving of a life from extinction—or does it also extend to cases in which the law would be violated in order to ward off a lesser evil, as for instance physical injury or pain?

Fourthly, if the limitation suggested by the preceding question is correct . . . , is this limitation universal or are there exceptions to the rule—i.e., in regard to certain religious laws, is involvement permissible in instances when disobedience would not necessarily result in death? . . .

First, involvement is permissible, according to Rabbi Zerahyah ha-Levi[111] and other classics, even in cases where one may anticipate with certainty the inevitability of future violation of the law for the sake of *pikuah nefesh* if the initial action is undertaken while the norm is in a state of suspension. As regards the Sabbath it means the permissibility of involvement during the week.[112] In regards to other commandments whose effectiveness is continuous, the solution would depend upon which interpretation of Rabbi Zerahyah ha-Levi's ruling we prefer. Thus, according to the stricter interpretation involvement would not be permissible if violation of the law would be inevitable. But if the coercive situation is only a possibility, there is no ground for forbidding involvement.

Second, it is still doubtful whether the maxim of permissibility of involvement is also effective in cases of action under constraint which do not imply *pikuah nefesh*. . . .

II.

Let us now view the problem on the practical level and put into effect the

111. [Zerahyah ben Yitzhak ha-Levi (Spain, c. 1125–after 1186).]

112. This opinion was accepted by Rabbi Joseph Karo in his code, [*Shulhan Arukh*] Orah Hayyim 248:4.

method of applied Halakhah. . . . [M]ay a rabbi volunteer as a chaplain in the armed forces, taking into consideration that the discharge of his duties might involve him in situations in which the violation of the law will be necessary? . . . [W]e must infer that the problem is limited to two situations—the possibility of violating the Sabbath law and of violating the law forbidding *kohanim* [priests][113] to come in contact with dead bodies. I do not see any other form of religious observance which should be jeopardized by the wearing of the uniform. . . .

The problem before us is one which deals with the possibility of a chaplain receiving orders either to travel on the Sabbath or to identify dead soldiers and to mark graves; in either case disobedience would imply court martial. Now the problem we face: is this identical with the case mentioned in Rabbi Zerahyah ha-Levi's decision permitting one to depart for a place where [profanation of] Shabbat is inevitable because of the need to the protect his safety?

The case of enlistment differs from the classical one quoted by Rabbi Zerahyah ha-Levi in two respects. First, while in the latter instance the violation of the Sabbath is a certainty, in the case of volunteering as a chaplain it is only a possibility and, at that, a remote one. . . . Second, in the case quoted by Rabbi Zerahyah ha-Levi the alternative to [profanation of] Shabbat is death, so that the violation will occur under circumstances which will warrant the suspension of the law because of the principle of *pikuah nefesh*. . . . In our case, disobedience would not result in capital punishment but in imprisonment or dishonorable discharge. While the lack of inevitability of transgressing in the case of the chaplain is a strong reason for permitting voluntary enlistment, the fact, however, that the violation will be done under the influence of fear of merely great physical and mental discomfort cancels perhaps the permissibility of involvement.

The problem under consideration now is a twofold one. First, does the penalty of imprisonment come under the law of *pikuah nefesh*? Second, can it be considered as virtual constraint? . . .

The practice among the Rabbis of the Talmud and other halakhic scholars throughout the ages has been to consider the threat of imprisonment as a clear case of *sakanat nefashot* [danger to life] and accordingly, it would be proper to apply this criterion to our problem as well. . . .

---

113. [The temple cult in ancient Israel included levites (members of the tribe of Levi) and kohanim (descendants of Moses's brother Aaron). Even after the destruction of the Jerusalem Temple, kohanim were still bound by certain prohibitions attached to their status, including the prohibition against coming into contact with dead bodies.]

Furthermore, if the Orthodox chaplains should refuse to obey orders in the army it might affect the political status of the Jew in this country and prove disastrous. This alone is a legitimate reason for subsuming the coercive situation under the class of *pikuaḥ nefesh*.

Even if we should assume that the evil of imprisonment is not to be identified as a case of *pikuaḥ nefesh*, it certainly falls under the category of constraint —*ones*—taking into consideration the Maimonidean opinion that infliction of great physical or mental hardship is a constraining influence which affects the voluntary character of the action. Operating with this premise, an offense committed by a chaplain who is under legal constraint and under the absolute command of his superior is to be considered to be a compulsory one. In such a case we will have to apply the inferences which we have reached in the first part of our inquiry about the applicability of the law of involvement in a case of coercion (*ones*).

If the chaplain by refusing to obey should not only incur a severe penalty but also subject himself to physical compulsion whereby he will be forced to do the deed regardless, we then would deal with the first group of *ones* in which case the immoral act is absent and involvement might be permissible. . . . However, such a case is very far-fetched. . . .

Accordingly, our case is now classified under the second type of *ones* which constitutes a defense but does not exculpate the deed, and, consequently, any deliberate action leading to violation is prohibited. We might, however, say that due to the specific mentality of the soldier—inculcated with a spirit of absolute blind obedience, the individual completely loses his freedom of will and his faculty of rational thinking so that his action is more the result of an instinctive response to an order rather than of a deliberate choice. In such a case the constraining situation would belong to the third group of *ones* (extreme instances of inner compulsion) which resembles the first type of *ones* and involvement would be permissible. . . .

Moreover, since the violation in the case of a chaplain is only a probability and not a certainty, one is allowed to create, by enlisting in the army, a coercive situation. He would bear no responsibility for the consequences of his action. . . .

We may, therefore, say that enlisting as a chaplain in the armed forces is permissible according to the Halakhah.

Lastly, . . . [d]oes the Halakhah merely permit enlistment as a chaplain or does it also approve of and recommend such action? Since the answer to this question lies in the realm applied Halakhah, . . . it is worthwhile to pause a moment and survey the consequences which might result from an indifferent attitude on the part of our Orthodox rabbis towards the immediate need of the young Jewish soldiers for religious guidance. . . .

The consequences of such an attitude might prove to be disastrous—namely, all courtesies extended by the government to Orthodox religious institutions might be revoked. The deferment of Orthodox theological students would be the first to suffer.

In summing up the aforementioned facts, we cannot help but state that by ignoring political realities we might cause great harm to the prestige of the Jewish tradition and thus defeat the very objective to which we all are dedicated. All this leads to one conclusion: it is our duty to meet the challenge of the hour and see to provide the armed forces with as many chaplains as our quota requires.

. . . [O]ur decision is not primarily an expression of a pragmatic-utilitarian approach but reflects a halakhic-historic tradition which has always wanted to see the Jew committed to all social and national institutions of the land of his birth or choice which affords to him all the privileges and prerogatives of citizenship. Particularly, the Halakhah emphasizes the duty of the Jew to share in the defense of his homeland in the way in which he is best fitted. Since we as rabbis cannot participate in the physical defense effort, the only way in which we are able to serve our country is to offer counsel and spiritual comfort to those who are called upon to perform this great physical task. . . .

This form of service is not alien to the Jewish tradition. On the contrary, the idea that it is not enough to supply the warrior with the material tools of war, but it is essential that he be, also, equipped with moral fortitude and a great faith, is of Jewish origin. This idea asserts itself in the commandment concerning *mashuaḥ milḥamah*—the priest anointed for war.[114] . . . [T]he essence of the [commandment], regardless of its abstract halakhic aspects, expresses the idea that the warrior who performs the greatest of all tasks—the defense of his country —should be given spiritual aid, encouragement and companionship at a time when he needs them most. . . .

Let me conclude this letter with a passage from *The Guide for the Perplexed*:

As I have told you, it is one of the objects of the law [regarding defecation in a military camp] to train Israel to cleanliness. . . . . [A]nother object of the law is to confirm . . . [ellipsis in the original] the belief of the warriors that God

---

114. [See Deut. 20:2–4.]

dwells in their midst. The reason of the law is therefore stated thus: "For the Lord thy God walketh in the midst of thy camp." The mention of this reason gave occasion to add another lesson: "That he see no unclean thing in thee and turn away from thee."[115] These words warn and caution us against the usual inclination of soldiers to fornication. . . . God therefore commanded us to do certain things which remind us that He is in our midst; we will thereby be saved from those evil practices . . . (II:41).

The moral lesson implied in these words is obvious and I hope that the rabbis will be guided by it.

Sincerely yours,
Joseph Soloveitchik

115. [Deut. 23:14.]

III | Ultra-Orthodoxy and the Rejection of the Modern Nation-State

In contrast to the authors in part 2, not all theorists of Jewish law accepted the privatization of Judaism and the construction of Judaism as a religious confession. A group of rabbinic decisors and ideologues—many, though not all, of whom lived in what was then the Austro-Hungarian Empire—rejected pressures to culturally integrate from the non-Jewish government and efforts to religiously reform by other Jews. Instead, they articulated a new form of Judaism—Ultra-Orthodoxy—that asserted the holistic integrity of Jewish law and the distinctiveness of the Jewish people.

Moshe Sofer is the founding figure of this conservative tradition, especially as his thought is extended and amplified by Akiva Yosef Schlesinger. Despite their differences from their predecessors and from each other, Avraham Yeshayahu Karelitz (initially in Mandatory Palestine and later in the State of Israel) and Yoel Teitelbaum (in the United States) can be seen as representatives of Ultra-Orthodoxy, in that each asserts a monolithic conception of Jewish law that is meant to govern the collective life of the Jewish people. Isaac Breuer, though set off from the mainline of this tradition by genealogy, geography, and education, gives Ultra-Orthodoxy a philosophical articulation. For him, Torah as law constitutes the Jewish nation. Yet these authors did not embrace the attempt to establish a state for this nation and its laws. Indeed, some of them were among Zionism's most vocal critics.

The conservatism of these Ultra-Orthodox thinkers should not be mistaken for faithful preservation, however. Ultra-Orthodox legal theorists use novel arguments and controversial sources to assert their view of Jewish law. Indeed, the other figures represented in this part of the volume, though also associated with Orthodoxy, can serve as indexes of Ultra-Orthodoxy's novelty. For instance, Zevi Hirsch Chajes's reaction to Sofer's rejection of innovation demonstrates how new that rejection really was. Moshe Shemuel

Glasner's dynamic view of the Oral Torah indicates the alternative trajectories that were possible from Sofer's thought and anticipates the Zionist writers of the next part. And Moshe Feinstein's debate with Yoel Teitelbaum highlights disagreements over the legitimate sources of Jewish law and the homogeneity of the Jewish people.

The figures in this part of the volume thus represent a third way, relative to those legal thinkers included in the previous and subsequent parts. They reject the privatization of Jewish law as well as its nationalization. Instead, in different ways, they articulate a political but nonstatist Jewish law.

Moshe Sofer (1762–1839) was the leader of what would become known as Orthodox Judaism in its formative struggles against efforts to reform Jewish practice.
Born in Frankfurt am Main, in Germany, he served as the rabbi in several cities in
Hungary before assuming the position of rabbi of Pressburg, where he established
an important yeshiva as well as a rabbinical dynasty. Called by the name of his
collection of responsa, *Hatam Sofer* (Seal of the scribe), his approach to Jewish
law is characterized by a strict conservatism that is expressed in a statement that
would become the motto of his followers: "The new is forbidden by the Torah!"
Sofer asserts what he claims is the authority of an unchanged tradition, which he
simultaneously constructs. Indeed, Sofer's motto itself is based on an innovative
reinterpretation of a classical rabbinic dictum.[1] Sofer's innovative conservatism is
evident in his leveling of previously acknowledged legal distinctions, such as between customs and enactments and between rabbinic and biblical laws, to solidify
Jewish law as a monolithic structure that must be accepted in its entirety. Indeed,
Sofer argues that rabbinically instituted laws possess biblical authority and that
contemporary rabbinical courts cannot modify them. Though Sofer viewed such
stringency as warranted by the threat of reform, other traditional rabbis were troubled by it, as evidenced by the notes of Zevi Hirsch Chajes, a student of Nahman
Krochmal, in his correspondence with Sofer. On a sociocultural level, Sofer insisted
on the maintenance of boundaries between Jews and non-Jews, an idea that would
be emphasized by those who followed him.[2]

Moshe Sofer, *She'elot u-Teshvot Hatam Sofer* (Brooklyn, NY: Grossman, 1958),
1:45a–46b (translated by Elli Fischer).

Abundant peace to the honored master . . . Rabbi Avraham . . . : . . . .
Today my eyes lit up from the sweetness of your statements about the con-
sistory of the province of Westphalia, who attempted to uproot the established

1. b. Ketubot 38b.
2. On Moshe Sofer, see Jacob Katz, "Towards a Biography of the Hatam Sofer," in *Divine
Law in Human Hands*, edited by Jacob Katz (Jerusalem: Magnus, 1998), 403–43.

rules (*halakhot kavu'ot*), the instructions of our fathers and rabbis, to treat species of *kitniyot*[3] as forbidden on the festival of Passover. Yet they stood up on their own to permit this for themselves.

... [P]erhaps they know why they ruled permissively, and we therefore must give them the benefit of the doubt. . . .

This is for them, but for us, who, thank blessed God, do not need this safeguard, it is clear that these species must not be permitted. It goes without saying that it is not possible [to permit them] without the release [from vows] . . . , for that is obvious; who is so prominent, who is so important, who is so perfectly tailored to uproot this enactment and this fixed practice that was established by so many of our French rabbis? For even according to the accepted stance—that a practice that did not spread throughout all of Israel can be annulled by a minor rabbinical court[4]—in the present case this would not apply for several reasons. First, in my humble opinion, the sages who instituted it never enacted it in the first place with the intent that it spread throughout all Israel, only to Ashkenazim.[5] . . . This rationale was written by Tosafot[6] in [b. Gittin] 36b. . . . And it is clear that today we have no great court that can oppose those eminences [who established the prohibition].

Furthermore, according to Maimonides' [*Mishneh Torah*] "Laws of Rebels," [2:3,][7] anything that safeguards the Torah may not even be abolished by a great rabbinical court.

Furthermore, . . . a long-standing practice nevertheless may not be permitted without reason. On the contrary, we must add fences and safeguards, since the

---

3. [Initially, kitniyot referred specifically to legumes (see m. Kil'ayim 2:2), but the word later came to refer to all noncereal species of grain from which Ashkenazi Jews customarily refrained on Passover.]

4. [See below in this section for a discussion of the authority of a "minor" rabbinical court.]

5. [Ashkenazi and Sephardi are the two major ethnic groups of diasporic Jews, which began to diverge around 1100. Broadly speaking, Ashkenazim are the Jews of northern Europe, especially the Yiddish-speaking communities of Central and Eastern Europe, and Sephardim are the Jews of southern Europe and the Mediterranean countries. The laws, liturgy, and customs of these two ethnic groups differ in various ways.]

6. [Tosafot are medieval commentaries on the Talmud, composed from the twelfth to the mid-fifteenth centuries by numerous rabbis known as the Tosafists. The commentaries were additions (*tosafot*, in Hebrew) to the commentary of Rashi (Shlomo Yitzhaki, France, 1040–1105).]

7. [Moses ben Maimon, also known as Rambam (Morocco, Egypt; 1135–1204).]

generation is not worthy. Due to our manifold transgressions, this generation is completely licentious, and therefore it is necessary to continue boldly toward stringency and not be lenient....

... Indeed, *Shulḥan Arukh*,[8] Yoreh De‘ah section 228:28, rules that there is no way to permit a consensus reached on a fence and safeguard. . . . Indeed, God expressed His desire for [such safeguards] when He said: "Enact precautions for precautions."[9] ...

Rabbinical Court of Hamburg, *Elu Divrei ha-Brit* [These are the words of the covenant] (Altona, 1819), iii–vi and 6–11 (translated by Elli Fischer).

ANNOUNCEMENT

... Behold, in our sins, it has been several years since Jewish men began to scorn the word of God, the words of our sages of blessed memory, the authors of the Mishnah and Talmud....

But now, due to our great sins, the malignancy has spread in the Jewish community, for some people have begun to congregate together and make evil statutes to change Jewish custom against the holy words of the sages of blessed memory....

This is what they have begun to do: They have attacked the order and customs of our prayers ... and [they] pray in the German language, against the custom of all Israel.

We have now been asked to render an opinion on this matter, that is, whether those changes to our prayer rites can be permitted. After thoroughly studying the issue, we have issued this ruling (*pesak halakhah*):

(A) It is forbidden to alter any formulation from the prayer rite that has been handed down to us from our late predecessors of blessed memory.

(B) It is forbidden to recite public prayers in the synagogue in any language but the Holy Tongue, as is the custom of all Israel.

8. [*Shulḥan Arukh* (The set table), a comprehensive Jewish legal code by Yosef Karo (1488–1575) and published in 1565. Its principal sections—Oraḥ Ḥayyim, Yoreh De‘ah, Even Ha-Ezer, and Ḥoshen Mishpat—correspond to the sections in the earlier code, *Arba‘ah Turim*, also known as the *Tur*, by Ya‘akov ben Asher (1270–c. 1340).]

9. [In b. Yebamot 21a, Rabbi Kahana interprets the doubled language in Lev. 18:30, "You shall keep My charge (*u-shimartem et mishmarti*)," to mean "enact precautions for my precautions."]

(C) It is forbidden to make music in the synagogue with any instrument on Shabbat and festivals, even by means of a non-Jew who was readied before Shabbat.

We have sincerely hoped that those people would incline their ears to our words and heed the voice of their teachers, who alone are suited to render an opinion on all that pertains to what is permitted and forbidden (*issur ve-heter*). . . .

But our hopes were for naught, for these people disobeyed with their scheming and made themselves low with their sins. They very quickly built a house of prayer that they called a "Temple." They published a prayer book for Shabbat and the festivals. . . . They added and subtracted from the prayer rite as they saw fit. . . . They printed most of the prayers in German, not the Holy Tongue, and worst of all is the sick wickedness that they omitted every instance in which faith in the ingathering of exiles is mentioned. . . .

One who denies this faith denies the principles of the religion (*kofer be-ikkarei ha-dat*). . . .

This is for you, Jewish brothers: the legal ruling (*pesak din*) of the most eminent rabbis of our time. . . . They all, with one voice, respond and say that these men have perpetrated an abomination with their society, called "*Neuer Tempelverein.*" And any man who is called a Jew is forbidden to pray from their prayer books. Away! Touch not![10] . . . Keep your sons away from their house of prayer, even for occasional visits. Keep yourself far away from her; do not come near the doorway of her house.[11] . . .

From the just rabbinical court (*beit din tzedek*), which safeguards the Torah and worship.

Hamburg, Iyar 5579 [1819]

. . . .

A LETTER

From the great, eminent, and renowned for praise Rabbi Moshe Sofer . . .
To the just Rabbinical Court of Hamburg, etc. . . .
Innovations have come but lately,[12] and one of their laws is that their house of prayer is closed up tight all week, but on Shabbat it is open. Would that they

10. [See Lam. 4:15.]
11. [See Prov. 5:8.]
12. [See Deut. 32:17, where this phrase refers to foreign gods.]

close the doors then, too, for they have altered the formulation of our prayers, which we have received from the Men of the Great Assembly,[13] from the sages of the Talmuds, and from our holy forefathers. They have . . . also removed the texts on the offshoot of David, our Messiah, and on the rebuilding and renovation of the holy city of Jerusalem. They appoint a non-Jew to play an instrument for them on the holy day of Shabbat, which is forbidden to us. And most of their prayers are specifically in German.

. . . You have asked me to join the lions, the eminent rabbis of our time, who repair the breaches of the generation, and to express my opinion on whether or not the truth lies with them. What shall I respond? . . .

. . . The Mishnah of our Holy Rabbi[14] and both Talmuds, which were composed after the destruction, are filled with the laws of daily prayers. . . .

It is known that in the days of the Second [Jerusalem] Temple, Israel lived on its land, and they held the ruler's staff with greatness and glory for centuries. And they had great sages, whose entire occupation was Torah. . . . They had large, fine houses of study, like all the academies (universities) that rulers of the land now establish in the great cities under their rule. They had a Sanhedrin[15] to erect safeguards, make decrees, and ensure proper maintenance. After them were thousands and myriads of disciples and disciples of disciples, until our Holy Rabbi, who composed the Mishnah. . . .

Now, these words came from the mouths of sages and men of understanding, whose hearts were filled with ideas and concepts, the breadth and depth of all disciplines, which were increasingly refined over the course of many years, by thousands of sages, and which were fixed in Israel nearly two thousand years ago, without anyone opening his mouth or flinching. Shall a group of little foxes[16] now rise up to breach their walls and ruin their safeguards, changing their formulations and benedictions, and altering the times and hours that have been established for us?

As a matter of law (din), no rabbinical court can annul the words of another

13. [The Great Assembly (*Keneset Gedolah*) was a religious body during the beginning of the Second Jerusalem Temple period. It was thought to have been composed of 120 members and to have established certain rules.]

14. [Rabbi Yehudah the Prince (ha-Nasi) (Eretz Israel, 135–c. 217), also referred to as simply Rabbi and Rabbenu (ha-Kadosh).]

15. [The Sanhedrin was the great rabbinical court of seventy-one members, which sat in the Temple in Jerusalem.]

16. [See Song 2:15.]

rabbinical court unless it is greater in numbers and wisdom. Even if the reason no longer applies, the enactment (*takanah*) has not been annulled. This is especially true of prayer, which has spread through all Israel. Even though the texts have been localized, it is still considered to have spread through all Israel, since one rite was established for Ashkenazim only, whereupon it spread among them without dissent, and another rite for Sephardim, which spread among them without dissent. This is as *Magen Avraham*[17] section 41 states in the name of the Jerusalem Talmud. This reasoning is mentioned in *Tosafot* . . . [b. Gittin] 36b, *s.v. ella*. See also *Magen Avraham* section 468, *Pri Ḥadash*[18] *ad loc.*, and section 726.[19]

Thus, no [rabbinical court] may make changes unless it is greater in number and wisdom than the earlier sages. Were it greater in numbers but not wisdom, or wisdom but not numbers, it may not annul the words of the rabbinical court. Even if the reason that the earlier sages made their decree no longer applies, one may not annul it unless one is greater. And how can we be greater than them in number? Is not every [great] rabbinical court of seventy-one members?[20] This refers to the number of sages of that generation who agreed on and accepted this matter. Maimonides writes in the [*Mishneh Torah*,] "Laws of Rebels," 2:2:

> If a rabbinical court promulgated a decree, established an enactment, or instituted a practice, and the matter spread to all Israel, and another rabbinical court then arose and wished to annul the words of their predecessors and uproot that decree and practice, it cannot do so unless it is greater than its predecessor in wisdom and number. If it was greater in wisdom but not number, or number but not wisdom, it cannot annul. Even if the reason for the decree no longer obtains, later sages cannot annul it unless they are greater. And how can they be greater in number? Is not every rabbinical court of seventy-one members? This refers to the number of sages of that generation who agreed on the matter that the great rabbinical court established and did not disagree with it.

17. [(Shield of Abraham), a commentary by Abraham Abele Gombiner (Poland, 1637–83) to *Shulḥan Arukh*, Oraḥ Ḥayyim.]

18. [*Pri Ḥadash* (New fruit), a commentary on Yosef Karo's *Shulḥan Arukh* by Hezekiah da Silva, (1659–98).]

19. [The version that appears in printed editions of Ḥatam Sofer's responsa has section 496.]

20. [Rabbinical courts are of three sizes, consisting of three, twenty-three, or seventy-one members. Maimonides discusses the great rabbinical court, the Sanhedrin, which always consisted of seventy-one members. This raises the question of how one great rabbinical court can be larger than an earlier one.]

Raavad[21] *ad loc.* adds: "Where the reason [for the decree] has not been voided, even Elijah the Prophet may not annul." However, where the reason no longer obtains, Raavad disagrees [with Maimonides] and maintains that another quorum [of court members], even smaller in number than the earlier court, may permit.

There are two issues here [in Raavad's gloss]. First, if the reason [for the decree] still obtains, then even Elijah the Prophet cannot annul [the decree]. This is what the sages of blessed memory stated in b. Yebamot 102b. . . . Thus even if the reason no longer obtains, and even if we accept Raavad's ruling that a smaller rabbinical court can annul, that is only if they stand up to be counted, for a second quorum is needed to permit [the decree].

So let [the reformers] stand up and be counted! Let them join with the sages of the present generation, may God let them live! These people do not have the right to choose (*mishpat ha-biḥirah*) to separate themselves from the community. And if they say, perhaps, "Your guarantor needs a guarantor; the very fact that it is necessary to convene a new quorum to permit something—who said that? The sages of the Talmud. And we want nothing of theirs. . . ." Yet if they say this, then they bear the yoke of Maimonides' statement ("Laws of Rebels," the beginning of chapter 3): "One who does not admit to the Oral Torah . . . [ellipsis in original] is in the class of heretics (*apikorsim*). . . . [ellipsis in original]" There is nothing else to say.

And if one contends that the reason for praying for the flowering of the Messiah, the son of David, no longer obtains, since we dwell in tranquility and quiet among their majesties, the kings of the nations, God have mercy on them? This is not the case. . . . [E]ven during the days of the Second [Jerusalem] Temple they prayed for the reign of the House of Judah, when we will all be privileged to gaze on God's sweet presence. . . .

. . . However, it is possible that [the reformers] do not anticipate or do not at all believe the words of our prophets regarding the building of the Third [Jerusalem] Temple, the coming of the Messiah, and everything that our sages of blessed memory said on this matter. If that is the case, then we have returned to the aforementioned words of Maimonides at the beginning of chapter 3 of "Laws of Rebels."

Regarding whether it is permitted to play musical instruments in the synagogue: We see that our forefathers who instituted the prayers did not institute

---

21. [Abraham ben David of Posquières (Provence, c. 1125–98).]

musical instruments during prayer even though such song originated with us, in the service in the Holy Temple. Yet our forefathers still abandoned it. We derive from this that they were not pleased with it, since from the day of the [Jerusalem] Temple's destruction there is no rejoicing before [God]. I have written elsewhere that, in my opinion, the verse states, "How can we sing a song of the Lord on alien soil?,"[22] and not "before foreigners," to negate even [singing] before God on foreign soil.... Moreover, [they do so] on the holy Shabbat, which is [a violation] of a [rabbinic decree] to abstain from labor (*shevut*) not for the sake of fulfilling a commandment.[23] For we do not have the power to invent new commandments that our fathers did not know.[24] And prayer is a commandment, and accepted by God, without instruments, so how can we permit a rabbinic prohibition? Far be it from us. This shall not be done in Israel....

Regarding the fact that they pray publicly in a language other than the Holy Tongue, this cannot be permitted in any way. Even though there is an explicit mishnah, "These things may be recited in any language ... [ellipsis in original],"[25] that prayer is included among those matters that one may fulfill his obligation in any language, nevertheless, that refers only to an individual, and only on occasion. But to do so always, and certainly to appoint a prayer leader to pray in a language of the nations, this is undoubtedly completely prohibited. Otherwise, the Men of the Great Assembly would not have instituted prayer in the clear, beautiful Holy Tongue, for in their day, half the people spoke the Ashdodite language.[26] ...

... Perforce, the Men of the Great Assembly, the institutors of the prayer, who included prophets, as Maimonides wrote, knew from God that prayer may not be in just any convenient language. The loss of the service in the holy Temple cannot be replaced in just any way....

... Our sages of blessed memory said that the world was created using the Holy Tongue.... Thus, it is God's language, in which He gave us His Torah....

Therefore, your announcement in your holy synagogue that it is forbidden to pray using their foreign-tongue prayer books, but only in the Holy Tongue and in accordance with the ancient texts, from prayer books printed as before; and

22. [Ps. 137:4.]

23. [Shabbat prohibitions of rabbinic provenance can, in some circumstances, be waived to facilitate the performance of a commandment.]

24. [See Deut. 32:17.]

25. [m. Sotah 7:1.]

26. [Neh. 13:24.]

not to play an instrument (organ) in the holy synagogue, especially on the holy Shabbat—you have acted in accordance with the Torah, and may your hands be strengthened. May God be with you. There is no doubt that all the eminent sages of the time will agree to this ban. They agree, and I agree, to impose a ban on any Jew who changes even one of all these things. . . .

Tuesday, the second day of Rosh Ḥodesh
Tevet, Ḥanukah 5579 [1818]. . . .
The insignificant Moshe Sofer of Frankfurt
am Main

Moshe Sofer, *She'elot u-Teshuvot Ḥatam Sofer* (Brooklyn, NY: Grossman, 1958), 3:20b–21a (translated by Elli Fischer).

The rabbis, teachers of the Torah, have been asked by those on high in the governorship, to clarify and explain which illicit sexual relations (*ha-arayot*) are forbidden to the Jewish people according to the law of our holy Torah, and which of them the sages of the time have the power to permit temporarily or not.

To respond with truth, I will first say that indeed there are some illicit sexual relations that are explicit[ly forbidden] in the Torah, and there are some that the sages forbade as a safeguard and protective fence, but there is no difference between them, because everything is from the Torah (*ki ha-kol min ha-torah*). This is explained by Maimonides [in the *Mishneh Torah*] at the beginning of the "Laws of Rebels," 1:2:

> Whether matters that they learned via oral transmission, that is, the Oral Torah; or matters that they learned from their own intelligence, using one of the hermeneutic rules by which the Torah is explicated, and it is agreeable to them that the matter is indeed thus; or matters that were made as safeguards to the Torah based on the needs of the time—these are decrees, enactments, and practices; there is a positive commandment to heed them regarding any of these three things. One who violates any one of them [also] transgresses a negative commandment. For [the Torah] states: "[You shall act] in accordance with the instructions given you"—these are the decrees, enactments, and practices that they instruct the public in order to reinforce the law (*ha-dat*) and improve the world (*ve-le-takken ha-olam*); "and the ruling handed down to you"—these are the matters that they shall derive logically using one of the hermeneutic rules for explicating the Torah; "[you must not deviate from] the verdict that they announce to you [either to the right or to

the left]"—this is the tradition that they received, one person from another person.[27]

There is no difference whatsoever between biblical and rabbinic prohibitions; one who violates them rebels against God and His Torah. The only difference is with regard to the punishment of the violator. . . . Also, with regard to biblical sexual prohibitions, betrothal is ineffective and no divorce document is required [to dissolve such betrothal]. This is not the case with regard to rabbinic [prohibitions]. . . .

The insignificant Moshe Sofer of Frankfurt am Main

Zevi Hirsch Chajes, *Kol Kitvei Maharatz Chajes* (Jerusalem: Divre Ḥakhamim, 1958), 1:269–72 (translated by Elli Fischer).

This is the response sent . . . by the eminent sage of Pressburg . . . Friday, 12 Adar II, 5597 [1837]

Peace and all the best to my close friend, . . . Rabbi Zevi Hirsch Chajes, . . . the head of the rabbinical court and yeshiva of the holy community of Zolkiev. . . .

Your precious letter reached me just as Shabbat arrived. . . . I will respond immediately, to dispel from your pure heart regarding what I wrote in my previous letter[28] that "the new (*ḥadash*)[29] is forbidden by the Torah." I did not write that "uncircumcised" fruit (*orlah*),[30] cross-bred crops (*kil'ayim*),[31] or "offensive" sacrifice (*pigul*) is not accepted.[32] Rather, only "the new," for I have understood from the elders that it is proper to be among the upholders of the Torah. They were cautious about making openings and seeking leniencies on behalf of the rogues amongst our people, [openings and leniencies] which they desire. Yet if

27. [Deut. 17:11]

28. [*Responsa Ḥatam Sofer, Yoreh De'ah* 338. This responsum is a reply vehemently opposing Chajes's suggestion that a physician who is a priest (kohen) should be permitted to come in proximity to a Jewish corpse to confirm death.]

29. [In its original context, the term refers to the new season's grain, which is not permitted until the *omer* offering is brought on Passover. Sofer borrows the term and applies it to anything "new."]

30. [Fruits from the first three years after a tree is planted, whose use the Torah forbids.]

31. [Grafted or hybrid crops, whose use the Torah forbids.]

32. [Sacrifices offered with the intention to consume them after their mandated time, which are not accepted as an offering; see Lev. 19:7.]

[such rogues] find a crack the size of a beading needle, they will breach, breach after breach.[33] Your exalted honor should see part 4 of *Responsa of Maimonides*, in the laws of mourning, regarding the simple matter of marrying a woman before three festivals have elapsed since one's [original] wife's death. He writes: "Take these words to heart, lest fences are breached as a result, and every man will do what is upright in his heart. For, they will attribute the matter to great people, and thus foxes will make breaches by means of it."[34] I wrote that delaying burial involves the violation of a positive and a negative commandment because, at the very least, Naḥmanides[35] wrote thus. There is no practical difference nowadays [about whether delaying burial involves the violation of only a negative commandment or of both a positive and a negative commandment], and it is best to elevate the prohibition.

(*[Note by Chajes:] In my opinion, his decision, namely, that it is permissible to elevate the prohibition[—that is,] to say of [something prohibited by] a negative commandment alone that it is [prohibited by both] a positive and negative commandment, is incorrect. We see that even though the sages of blessed memory permit threatening language, see Maimonides, *Commentary on the Mishnah* (m. Sanhedrin chapter 7), regarding the punishments for forbidden sexual relations, where he wrote in the middle of his commentary: "The sages have cautioned against sinful thoughts and distanced people from things that lead to them, and they spoke at length to threaten and to strike fear . . . [ellipsis in original] but no lashes are incurred for any of these things or anything like them." Similarly, when [the sages] say, "It is as though he killed someone," "It is as though he worshipped idols," or their statements about many things that they incur the death penalty, these are only threats intended to strike fear. However, to say of a rabbinic prohibition that it is a biblical prohibition, of this Maimonides states in "Laws of Rebels," chapter 2, that this is what the prohibition of "You shall not add [anything to what I command you (*bal tosif*)]"[36] is said about. . . . This is also included in the caution: "Keep far from a false charge,"[37] even though he does so for a reason and purpose. The sages of blessed memory were always careful to clarify which matters derive from the words of scripture (*mi-divrei torah*) and [which matters derive from] the

---

33. [Job 16:14.]

34. [Responsum 20 of those printed after Maimonides' Book of Judges in the *Mishneh Torah*.]

35. [Moses ben Naḥman of Girona, also known as Ramban (Spain, 1194–1270).]

36. [See Deut. 4:2.]

37. [Lev. 23:7.]

words of the scribes (*mi-divrei soferim*), even where there are no practical consequences in law.)

Yet you, sir, rely on the rejected opinion of *Havot Yair*[38] [section 139], which states that the entire root [of this prohibition of delaying burial] is only rabbinic. But we do not reveal this, because, due to our sins, in our times there has been a proliferation of such people who go so far as to say that we are not concerned about the words of the rabbis[, saying] that God did not command [them]. . . . It is about such cases that it was stated: "Sages, be careful with your words."[39] Nowadays, those who come later will certainly drink, and many have already drunk.[40] . . .

This is [the meaning of] "the new is forbidden by the Torah" in all times and all places, and even more so nowadays. . . .

The insignificant Moshe Sofer of Frankfurt
am Main

Moshe Sofer, "Last Will and Testament (1839)," in *The Jew in the Modern World*, edited by Paul Mendes Flohr and Judah Reinharz, translated by Dov Weiss (New York: Oxford University Press, 2010), 196–99.

I. WITH THE HELP OF GOD, MAY HE BE BLESSED, THURSDAY, 15 KISLEV 5597 [1837]

. . . You—my sons and daughters, son-in-laws, and grandchildren, and their children—listen to me and flourish.

Be not inclined to do a wrong thing, to dispute with the wicked "men who are evildoers" (Psalms 141:4), "the new ones, who came but lately" (Deuteronomy 32:17).

Do not live in their vicinity and do not associate with them at all, and never occupy yourselves with the writings of R.M.D. [Rabbi Moses of Dessau]—then your foot will never stumble. . . .]

Be careful not to change your Jewish name (*Shem*), language (*Lashon*), and

---

38. [Responsa by Yair Ḥayyim Bacharach (Germany, 1639–1702), first published in 1699.]

39. [m. Avot 1:11.]

40. [The mishnah uses "drinking from waters" as a metaphor for students taking in a master's poorly chosen words.]

dress (*Malbush*), heaven forbid, and the sign is [the verse] "and Jacob arrived intact (*ShaLeM*)" (Genesis 33:18).[41] ...

And you shall not say that the times have changed, for we have an Ancient Father, may His Name be Blessed, Who has not changed and will not change. ...

II. [TO THE JEWISH COMMUNITY OF PRESSBURG]

With the help of God, May He be Blessed, may your fear of the Lord prolong your life and years. ...

... [P]lease, the seat of the rabbinate should not be vacant for more than two years; and only a renowned man of learning should fill the position. ... And [also] one who has not delved into heretical works.

And he shall not preach in the language of the nations. ...

... God forbid that anyone will introduce changes, either with regard to the structure [of the synagogue], or the prayer book. ...

My daughters and daughters-in-law, beware lest, God forbid and heaven forbid, you reveal a handbreadth of your flesh by shortening the customary clothing. ...

41. [The three root letters of the Hebrew word *shalem*—Sh, L, and M—are read by the rabbis as an acronym: *Shem* (name), *Lashon* (language), and *Malbush* (dress).]

20

Selections from the Writings of Akiva Yosef
Schlesinger and an Associated Text

Akiva Yosef Schlesinger (1837–1922) was an ideologue and publicist of Ultra-Orthodoxy. At the yeshiva at Pressburg, Schlesinger was a student of Avraham Shemuel Binyamin Sofer, the son of Moshe Sofer. Schlesinger was instrumental in mobilizing a self-identified community under the banner of the elder Sofer's conservative approach to Jewish law. His most famous work, *Lev ha-Ivri* (The Hebrew heart), is in part a commentary on Sofer's testament (included in the previous selection), now presented as authoritative for the entire Jewish community. But, though he cast himself as Sofer's disciple, Schlesinger was more than that. Even more clearly than Sofer, he saw that reforms to Jewish law did not just threaten Jewish law; rather, they threatened the Jewish people qua people by construing Judaism as a religious confession and allowing Jews to acculturate to the surrounding society. In response, Schlesinger amplified aspects of Sofer's conservatism by putting his statements of principle into practice. Contrary to efforts to refine Judaism into a form that was compatible with Christianity, Schlesinger claims that every rule in the *Shulhan Arukh* and even every custom is as important as the Ten Commandments. Moreover, he injects a self-consciously nationalist element into his arguments—albeit, at this point, in a deterritorialized form. He maintains that Jews and non-Jews constitute separate categories of humanity with different tasks and duties. Jews ought to preserve their distinctiveness while living among non-Jews; indeed, this distinctiveness is the root of Jewishness. To make these claims, Schlesinger often draws on narrative portions of rabbinic literature, the legal authority of which is debated. Many of his ideas are expressed in the famous 1865 rabbinical decision of Michalowce, which has been described as the manifesto of Ultra-Orthodoxy and which took aim at those Orthodox who were willing to allow certain synagogue and educational reforms in the interests of acculturation. Yet even those rabbis who sympathized with the decision's aims were uneasy about its legal status. This is perhaps indicated by the use of "religious" instead of "legal" language in its conclusion.[42]

42. For more on Akiva Yosef Schlesinger, see Michael K. Silber, "Schlesinger, Akiva Yosef," in *The YIVO Encyclopedia of Jews in Eastern Europe*, accessed January 1, 2017, www

Akiva Yosef Schlesinger, *Lev ha-Ivri* [The Hebrew Heart] (Jerusalem: Hillel Schlesinger, 1990), 1:9–14, 104, and 186; and 2:173 (translated by Binyamin Hunyadi and Roman Levit).

GENERAL INTRODUCTION

. . . One and unique is the Creator of all creatures (*eḥad ha-meyuḥad yotzer ha-yetzurim*),[43] who decreed in his wisdom to separate all creatures of His world into four discrete categories. His supreme knowledge prepared for each and every person, the work of the hands of the Holy One, blessed be He, his station and his way, through which he will attain the purpose that was appointed for him by the Merciful Father, his Creator and Master, for his eternal soul in temporal life by means of fulfillment of His commandments. The Creator thus commanded to the first category of humans to adhere to the seven [Noahide] commandments. . . .[44] The principle appointed to [this first category of humans] was the commandment to inhabit the world[, which means] to investigate and to understand all manner of the workings [of the world], to settle the world, and to extract from the forces of nature in the most effective way [the means] for the settlement of the world, and to glorify in all possible ways the creation of the King of the world. . . .

Afterward the Holy One, blessed be He, distinguished the second category [of humans], and He chose a people for a kingdom of priests[45] from among all the nations and languages, and He took from them the commandment to settle the world. Their sole charge shall be God's Torah, and their purpose in this world [shall be] to keep the six hundred and thirteen commandments, the Written and Oral Torah, and in keeping these commandments they will attain the aim [of

---

.yivoencyclopedia.org/article.aspx/Schlesinger_Akiva_Yosef. On Schlesinger and the larger context of the rise of Ultra-Orthodoxy, see Michael K. Silber, "The Emergence of Ultra-Orthodoxy: The Invention of Tradition," in *The Uses of Tradition: Jewish Continuity in the Modern Era*, edited by Jack Werthheimer (New York: Jewish Theological Seminary, 1998), 23–84.

43. [The first letters of the first four words in Hebrew form the word EHYE, based on Exod. 3:14, one of God's designations in the rabbinic tradition.]

44. [According to the Talmud, there are seven "Noahide commandments" that apply to all "descendants of Noah"—that is, all human beings. Six are negative (not to deny God, blaspheme God, commit murder, engage in illicit sexual relations, steal, or eat from a living animal), and one is positive (to establish courts to uphold the rule of law).]

45. [See Exod. 19:6.]

the] eternal purpose in the world. Again God chose the third category, the tribe of priests (kohanim) and levites.[46] . . . The fourth category [of humans] is the [high] priest. . . . In this way did the Cause of Causes balance, institute, and establish His world, and set each and every person to his station and law (mishpato), the portion of each soul as it was hewn from its quarry, to attain the goal that the Merciful Father desired for it. God commanded that all shall forever fulfill and keep their guard and place, and [so] their charges will preserve their spirits; they shall not change it, nor exchange the charge of the King among themselves. They shall not err and transgress on their limit and statute (ḥukam).

[God] thus commanded that the Torah given at Sinai is the legacy of the community of Jacob, and no one from among the nations of the world is permitted to contemplate the Torah of Israel, especially not the Oral Torah, for such is decreed in the Torah, "a gentile who busies himself with the Torah is liable to the death penalty" (b. San. 59a). For the purpose of this Torah is not the one appointed for [the gentile] from the King of Kings, the Holy One, blessed be He. So too, the Torah decreed the opposite to Israel; [namely,] they should desire only the Torah, and study and discuss it rather than of the wisdom of the nations (b. Yoma 19b); they should follow [the directions of its wisdom], and not [the direction of] the wisdom of the nations (Torat Kohanim, Aḥarei Mot 18, 141).[47] If one violates this [decree], he is liable to the death penalty, for anyone who transgresses the words of the sages is liable to the death penalty (b. Eruvin 21b), and is labeled an evildoer (b. Yebamot 20a).

. . . The Merciful One thus decreed as well that [the Israelite nation] also be distinct in their speech, dress, knowledge, etc. . . . [ellipsis in original] from all the nations of the world, like all that is written in His Torah. . . .

Even though the Holy One, blessed be He, gave permission to a Noahide[48] to change his portion, to choose to convert, and to enter into the community of Israel; nevertheless, the commandment is not to go about searching to accept converts, as it states in the Talmud, b. Yebamot 47b. Similarly, converts will not be accepted [at all] in the messianic age (ibid., 24b) when [the prophesy] that "the land shall be filled with devotion to the LORD [as water covers the sea]" (Isa.

46. [The temple cult in ancient Israel included levites (members of the tribe of Levi) and kohanim (descendants of Moses's brother Aaron). The kohanim had the exclusive right and responsibility for making offerings to God; the levites had subordinate responsibilities in the sanctuary.]

47. [A midrashic legal commentary to Leviticus, also known as Sifra.]

48. [Any human being besides a Jew.]

11[:9]) will be fulfilled. Rather, each and every nation will keep their place, guard, and charge that God appointed them. When they fulfill these commandments, which were commanded to them, they will attain the desired purpose—life in the world to come, as it was said: "the righteous among the nations of the world have a share in the world to come" (Maimonides, [*Mishneh Torah*], "Laws of Repentance," 3:5). Likewise, God commanded that the first of the Noahide commandments is not to practice idolatry, that is, [one violates it] only if he does not worship the Creator [at all]. However, if [a gentile] believes [in the Creator] yet worships the Creator through [the] association (*shittuf*) [of another divinity with Him], [he has not violated the prohibition, for] they were not commanded regarding this [prohibition].[49] This is explained in the *Shulhan Arukh* (Orah Hayyim section 156), in the [gloss of the] Rema[50] of blessed memory (*ad loc.*). . . . Yet an Israelite, if he believes in association, he is an idolater and is deserving of death, for thus has God decreed. . . . [So the sages enacted] a number of safeguards and boundaries so that [Israel] should not succumb to the accoutrements of idolatry (*avizaryehu de-avoda zarah*).[51]

Therefore reader, do not judge it harshly if in my book I learn from [the classical rabbinic] laws concerning idolaters about [how one must treat] the worship of our [non-Jewish] nations. For even if [present-day gentiles] are not idolaters, God forbid, in any case their worship is forbidden for us as if it actually was idolatry. . . . The faithful rabbinical courts of Israel are outraged by [the custom of the nations], not because they are repulsive to them, nor [do they see] their wisdom or worship [of the nations of the world as repulsive], God forbid; rather, they are [simply] forbidden to Israel just like that which is forbidden in God's Torah to each and every nation. Hence [Israelites] would be outraged if they saw gentiles occupying themselves with [the study of] Torah; certainly, not because the Torah is repulsive to them, but because the nations of the world were commanded not to study it. [The gentiles] are similarly outraged by Israel when they see [Israelites] occupying themselves with the wisdom of the nations, and a fortiori changing their Jewish language[52] and adopting the customs of the nations (*numusei umot*). . . .

49. [Shittuf refers to the worship of other deities along with God the Creator. Schlesinger almost certainly has the Christian Trinity in mind.]

50. [Moses Isserles (Poland, 1520–72).]

51. [These actions are prohibited because they can lead to idolatry.]

52. [Yiddish, the traditional language of Ashkenazi Jews.]

Wherein is explained the authority of a testament, and that the testament of a rabbi of [all] of Israel to his descendants is also a clear rule (*halakhah meruvaḥat*) for all of Israel, even for those who are not his descendants.

The observant will see and the studious will understand (*yir'eh ha-ro'eh ve-yavin ha-lomed*),[53] how mighty is the testament of a dying man. . . .

. . . Our rabbis of blessed memory . . . said, "The words of a dying man are like a written document formally delivered" (b. Gittin 13a), and "it is a commandment to fulfill the words of the dead" (b. Gittin 14b). This commandment is incumbent on anyone who is commanded [by a dying testator], all the more so the descendants of the deceased. However, from all this, we have only learned the obligation to [fulfill the testament] by one who was commanded [by the testator], but surely one who was not commanded, obviously he is not obligated to fulfill the testament?

All of this is the law (ha-din) in the case of a common man, but in the case of [a testament made by] the outstanding rabbi of the generation, if he commanded a practice to his descendants, a testament such as this has the force of an express rule (*halakhah berurah*), and it is incumbent on all of Israel to fulfill these words. And so have we found explicitly [taught] in b. Ḥullin (27a), for we rule according to Rabbi Yehudah that [ritual slaughter is invalid] "until the jugular veins are cut." Even though the first opinion [in the mishnah] disputes [his view], and in the case of a contradiction between the opinion of a single sage and the majority of the sages, the rule is according to the majority;[54] nevertheless, since Rabbi Yehoshua ben Levi commanded thus to his children: "Be meticulous regarding the jugular vein like [the view of] Rabbi Yehudah" (b. Berakhot 8b), we necessarily establish the rule (*le-halakhah*) like him. . . .

A rule (halakhah) is similarly established according to a testament in the *Shulḥan Arukh* (Yoreh De'ah section 245:22) in the [glosses] of Rema of blessed memory. . . . From all the foregoing, it is sufficient for us to conclude that the testament of a great rabbi in Israel to his descendants is an express rule (halakhah berurah) for all of Israel. Even when it is disputed [by other sages], even when a majority [of other sages] disagree with it, the [rule] is established according to

53. [The first letters of the first four words form the tetragrammaton YHWH, one of God's designations in the rabbinic tradition.]

54. [The anonymous first opinion in the mishnah is here assumed to be the opinion of the majority.]

the testament of a great rabbi in Israel; a fortiori when none dispute it; a fortiori in the case of the testament of our illustrious teacher and rabbi [Moshe Sofer] of blessed memory, from which everything—the words of the Torah and the words of our sages of blessed memory—are reinforced with fixed nails. Certainly, this is a clear rule for all of Israel.

I have therefore set forth with my pen to interpret his holy writings . . . to derive enlightening lessons [from them] both for us and the future generations. . . .

. . . [C]oncerning the community of Israel, these are things that our forefathers of blessed memory passed on to us, which are the roots of Jewishness (*yehudit*) from times immemorial: [Jewish] names, [Jewish] language, and [Jewish] dress. In their merit [our forefathers] were redeemed [from Egypt]. They are equal to all the commandments of the Torah, as is brought in *Tanna de-Vei Eliyahu.* . . .[55] If these were, God forbid, taken from Israel, then all the commandments would be like an [empty] garment without a body. For these things are the body of Israel, that is, the Jew, and through them we became a nation, "I am a Hebrew, . . . I worship the Lord, the God of Heaven" (Jon. 1:[9]). Even if you do not believe the words of our rabbis of blessed memory, who is so blind, so blind to instincts, who cannot see or understand that if you take away, God forbid, these things, you take away everything. For if there are no roots here, a wind will come, God forbid, and uproot and topple it. So have we seen with our own eyes: In each and every country where [Jews] have uprooted these roots, the Torah of God has been forgotten among them and ultimately they have gone out in general from religion. . . . And so the Torah says, "As I see them from the mountain tops, gaze on them from the heights," which is to say, when they are "a people that dwells apart, not reckoned among the nations," then they are in their strength and might (Num. 21[:9]). [Indeed,] *Targum Jonathan*[56] [glosses the verse]: "and in the customs of the nations (*nimusei amemaya*) they do not follow." We should, therefore, stake our lives on this foundation of foundations of our [social] standing. . . .

. . . .

It has also been innovated (*nithadesh*) in these our days to put on the top of the synagogues an image of the two Tables of the Covenant bearing the Ten Commandments. Following this, the new rabbis prepared emblems of the

55. [A tenth-century midrash of uncertain origin, first published in 1598.]

56. [Aramaic translation of the biblical books of the Prophets, attributed by the Talmud to Jonathan ben Uzziel (first century BCE to first century CE).]

Ten Commandments, and placed the Ten Commandments on the covers of all prayer books and religious books. This matter has emerged among the innovations and requires examination [as to its legitimacy]. I go as a talebearer (*holekh rakhil*), a discloser of their secret, their revealed root, leaves of heresy (*minut*). This matter is prohibited according to the Talmud and *Shulḥan Arukh*. I will [now] explain with the help of God.

In the Talmud (b. Berakhot 12[a]) it states, "Rabbi Nathan taught: Even outside the Temple they sought to [read the Ten Commandments along with the Shema],[57] but it had already been abolished on account of the insinuations of the heretics (*minim*)." And in the *Shulḥan Arukh* (Oraḥ Ḥayyim, section 1:5 [in the gloss of Rema]) [it says,] "it is permitted to recite the Ten Commandments specifically in private; however, it is forbidden to recite them in public." *Magen Avraham*[58] (*ad loc.* section 9) states: "'[it is forbidden to recite them] in public' because of the heretics who claim that [the Ten Commandments] alone are the Torah. [We should be careful to observe this prohibition] *especially in our times.* For this reason, we do not write the [Ten Commandments separately] in any pamphlet for the public." Now understand and observe what these [new rabbis] desire with the semblance of sanctifying us with the Ten Commandments—the actions of the early heretics are just like those of the later heretics.

You should know from this that there is nothing new beneath the sun[59] without a suspicion of a mixture of heresy, and how much one must distance oneself from all forms of their innovations.... [We must avoid transgression] even when we do not know the reason and source for the prohibition; how much the more so when we do know them. They raise their head concerning the Ten Commandments, but not concerning the mezuzot[60] on our doorposts or the phylacteries (tefillin)[61] on our heads?! [Certainly,] God gave us the Ten Commandments; but, for us, the nation of the Children of Israel, every law (din) of the *Shulḥan Arukh* is

57. [The central declaration of faith of the Jewish people: *Shema Yisrael Adonai Elohenu Adonai Eḥad* (Hear, Israel: The Lord our God, the Lord in One" (Deut. 6:4–9).]

58. [(Shield of Abraham), by Abraham Abele Gombiner (Poland, c. 1635–82), first published in 1692.]

59. [Eccl. 1:9.]

60. [A mezuzah is a scroll inscribed with specific verses of Torah, most often inside a decorative case, that is attached to the doorpost of a Jewish home.]

61. [Tefillin are small black leather boxes containing scrolls inscribed with verses of the Torah. Attached by leather straps, they are worn on the head and left arm by observant Jews during weekday morning prayers.]

equal to the Ten Commandments, and every custom (minhag) of Israel is equal to the Ten Commandments. They were given by one Shepherd.[62] . . .

Note: Someone raised the question, "If we must be careful regarding the customs of the fathers, why do we employ [the] useful innovations that are now invented by the wise of the world?" They replied to him, "Concerning the deeds of men (ma'ase benei adam) the new is certainly superior to the old, for all who innovate add goodness. This is not the case in the practice of religion (hanhagat ha-dat), the source of which is God in the bestowal of the Torah and [thus] in which we have to search for those who are closest to the source. . . ."

"The Manifesto of Ultra-Orthodoxy (1865): Rabbinical Decision of the Michalowce Assembly," in The Jew in the Modern World, edited by Paul Mendes Flohr and Judah Reinharz, translated by Dov Weiss (New York: Oxford University Press, 2010), 224–29.

. . . Due to our great sins, we see that these are the times, that those who know their Creator have breached and transgressed the law and intend to rebel against Him.

And they built and are building altars to uproot and to destroy, to replace and to change the form and image of the synagogue building. . . .

It undoubtedly appears that the intention of the evil inclination and its messengers, "a bat of deadly messengers" (Psalms 78:49), is only to imitate, join and intermingle with other religious practices of the nations of the world, and to weaken and uproot, God forbid, the Jewish religion. . . .

The Torah warns [us] against [these assimilatory ways], and commands us to become there (in the lands of the gentiles) "a great and populous nation" (Deuteronomy 26:5)—thus we learn that Israel maintained there its distinctiveness—and only this prevented them from not being lost amongst the nations in Egypt.

. . . We are, therefore, obligated to legislate with an iron and lead pen—as a memorial for future generations—the following:

> 1. It is forbidden to deliver sermons in a language of the nations of the world. It is also prohibited to listen to a sermon delivered in the language of the nations of the world. . . . And the preacher must preach in the Yiddish language, one that is spoken by kosher [sic] Jews of this country.

62. [See Eccl. 12:11 and t. Sotah 7:7.]

2. It is forbidden to enter and pray in a synagogue [that] does not have a [reader's stand] in the middle.

3. It is forbidden to construct a synagogue with a tower.

4. It is forbidden to make special clothes for the cantor and other singers in a manner that resembles the customs of other religions.

5. It is forbidden to make a [partition], which separates the women's and men's sections, in a way that enables the men to look at the women. . . .

6. It is forbidden to listen to the prayers of a choir. . . .

7. One is forbidden to enter so-called "choir synagogues," since they are houses of . . . *heresy*, for as it is stated in [b.] Shabbat 116a, "even if someone is in pursuit of him in order to kill him or a snake was running [after him] to bite him, he should enter a house of idolatry to save one's self rather than to enter the houses of these [Jewish heretics] etc."

8. It is forbidden to place a [wedding canopy] in a synagogue. Rather, it should be under the heavens.

9. It is forbidden to change any Jewish custom or practice in the synagogue, since it has already been accepted by our fathers and our fathers' fathers.

. . . .

[We enact this prohibition] in order to repair the breach in the Torah by the multitude of God's nation, [and] so that they will [now] know clearly that all of the customs and ordinances of Israel have their "foundation on the holy mountains" (Psalms 87:1) and stand at the pinnacle of the world.

. . . [Y]ou should know that everything they are doing to change the customs of Israel, to imitate [the gentiles]—"How did those nations worship their gods" (Deuteronomy 12:30)—transgresses a few "do not dos" (negative Torah commandments). It is worse than eating pork, both in terms of quantity and quality.

Quantitatively. Eating an olive-size piece of pork is but a [violation] of one negative commandment, while in changing and substituting customs in order to imitate [the gentiles], one violates many negative commandments.

And qualitatively: these prohibitions pertain to the [accoutrements] of idolatry and [thus] there is a question whether they fall within the category of "[rather] be killed than transgress [them]" ([b.] Sanhedrin 74a). . . .

Now, please know, that these [prohibitions] are the fundamentals of Torah and are included under the category of [accoutrements] of idolatry, and [the prohibition against] changing one's language is included in the "eighteen matters"[63] that were established with the sword ([y.] Shabbat 1:4), and even Elijah, if he would come to nullify them—we will not listen to him (see [b.] Avodah Zarah 36a).

And the great guide, the Rabbi of Israel in the last generation, the light of the Diaspora, our master and teacher, the author of the *Hatam Sofer*, of blessed memory—may he abide in paradise, commanded his congregation [in his last will and testament] "that they should not have a preacher who preaches in the language of the nations, but only in the manner as you have heard from me." ...

And all the aforementioned [regulations] keeping a distance, [that is], that one is forbidden to imitate [the gentiles] and to practice their customs and to walk in their ways, is only in relation to religion and issues of faith. Because the preservation of our Torah and our religion is very far from other religions and since our Torah beseeches only us with regard to the 613 ... commandments—unlike the other nations who are not so commanded. ...

This [ruling] emerged from us, the undersigned, at a conference where we conferred and deliberated on the matter according to religion (dat) and, moreover, these are matters that are patently clear according to our Holy Torah without any alteration.

And on this we have signed here in the holy community of Michalowce ... 5625 [28 November 1865].

63. [The reference is to eighteen abiding prohibitions (*gezerot*) legislated just after the destruction of the Second Jerusalem Temple. They were meant to reinforce Jews' social and cultural distance from the gentile world.]

21

Moshe Shemuel Glasner, *Fourth Generation*

Moshe Shemuel Glasner (1856–1924), the great-grandson of Moshe Sofer, was the chief rabbi of Klausenberg, part of the Austro-Hungarian Empire and then Romania. While Glasner continued his family's tradition of rabbinic erudition and leadership, he also deviated from it. Instead of conservatism, his view of Jewish law emphasizes human creativity. Glasner argues that just as technological invention draws on nature to serve human needs, rabbinic interpretation mines scripture to adapt Jewish law to changed circumstances. Indeed, similar to the view of Krochmal, Glasner argues that this flexibility is precisely the reason for the orality of the Oral Torah. Legal truth is not divine and absolute, but human and conventional. From Maimonides, Glasner draws an expansive view of the authority of rabbinical courts to overturn precedent. Yet he acknowledges that in practice this authority is limited. Due to the trials of oppression and exile, it was necessary to write down the Oral Torah, beginning with the Mishnah and Talmud. Not only has this rigidified Jewish law, it has also deformed Jewish legal interpretation, which has become sophistical. Glasner looks forward to a messianic age that will renew the Oral Torah. But, again breaking with the Hungarian Ultra-Orthodoxy centered on the image of Ḥatam Sofer, Glasner believes that human initiative is necessary for this, too: he was an advocate of Zionism and emigrated to Mandatory Palestine in 1922. This support for Zionism would bring him into direct conflict with the young leader of a nearby Hasidic community, Yoel Teitelbaum. But Glasner would be an influence on Eliezer Berkovits, who would rearticulate Glasner's views on the Oral Torah and Zionism after the establishment of the State of Israel.

Moshe Shemuel Glasner, *Sefer Dor Revi'i* (Klausenberg: Weinstein and Friedman, 1921), 1a–4b (translated by Jason Rubinstein).

[T]he light of truth will always be hidden from the righteous, who will search and seek it out. And they find their most vital delight and the very justification of their existence in ascending from the depths to the heights, in ardently aspiring to grasp what is ever higher and higher in this world of action,[64] "which God created to make."[65]

Rabbi Abraham ibn Ezra[66] of blessed memory understands th[e verse] "to make" as the genetic material that gives each species the ability to make [new beings] in its likeness.... In my insignificance, I think I can support Ibn Ezra's interpretation: ["To make"] refers ... specifically to humanity. It means that out of what God created, people will use their intellect to make new things, realizing and activating the possibilities inherent in the created world....

In light of this, it is very sweet to ground the Torah's conclusion in its beginning.[67] In the natural sciences, a person uses his intelligence and understanding to invent new things out of the unchanging elements; so too in the study of our holy Torah. Our sages of blessed memory said, "'If you hear'—the old, 'you will hear'—the new."[68] They meant that a person who gives his life to the study of the "old" Torah, which we currently possess, can invent something new from it, which never before existed. And in this vein our sages of blessed memory said that the Holy Blessed One showed Moses everything that a diligent student would ever innovate,[69] for everything that will ever be innovated in every generation was present in the Torah as potential [from the very beginning].

"Humanity was born to toil,"[70] and "to enjoy goodness ... [ellipsis in original] and our work,"[71] that is, in innovating and inventing to meet humanity's

64. [In Lurianic Kabbalah, the "world of action" is the lowest of the four emanated worlds. The word for "action" and "to make" in Gen. 2:3 derive from the same stem in Hebrew.]

65. [Gen. 2:3; New Jewish Publication Society (NJPS) Tanakh translation, modified.]

66. [Abraham ben Meir ibn Ezra (1089–1161).]

67. [Following the third-century CE Talmudic sage Rabbi Simlai (see b. Sotah 14a), Glasner interprets the beginning and end of the Torah as governed by the same theme.]

68. [b. Sukkah 46b, based on Deut. 30:17.]

69. [See y. Pe'ah 2:4 and Midrash Leviticus Rabbah 22:1.]

70. [Job 5:7; NJPS, modified.]

71. [See Ec. 5:17–18; NJPS, modified.]

physical needs, in turning dross into gold, in advancing knowledge, and in revealing what is hidden in the Torah, the secrets of the living God.

Our holy Torah hints at this in its closing words, "And for all the mighty deeds and awesome power"—as interpreted by Rashi[72] of blessed memory to mean the giving of the Torah—"which Moses made before the eyes of all Israel."[73] This means that Moses "made" a written text so that the community's "eyes"—those who devote themselves to the Torah—will continually study it, interpreting it with the methods they received. And this is precisely like "When God began to create heaven and earth,"[74] which God created and gave to humanity "to make," to perfect and improve them from generation to generation.

So too with the Torah which Moshe placed before the children of Israel: It was given to them to constantly improve and perfect it.[75]

The Torah was given complete, and one may neither add to it nor subtract from it.[76] Our sages understood the verse "these are the commandments,"[77] to mean that no prophet [after Moses] may add anything.[78] But this only means adding to or subtracting [from the Torah itself]. When it comes to interpreting and expounding [the Torah], every authorized rabbinical court may do so. And here too [the Torah] is like creation: humanity does not have the power to create ex nihilo, only to combine and rearrange its forces and disparate elements by manipulating their invisible bonds.

In this way the Torah and creation are identical. The only distinction between them is that creation was given to all of humanity, while our holy Torah was given to the chosen people, the children of Israel. It is ours, to cherish and to perfect, to give our lives to its study to grasp its light that it may reveal new lights to us, fulfilling our spiritual lives.

And this is the position of Maimonides of blessed memory in [*Mishneh Torah,*] "Laws of Rebels," 2[:1]: "If the high court, by employing one of the hermeneutical principles, deduced a ruling which in its judgment was in consonance with the law (din) and rendered a decision to that effect, and a later court finds a reason for setting aside the ruling, it may do so and act in accordance with its own opin-

72. [Shlomo Yitzḥaki (France, 1040–1105).]
73. [Deut. 34 12; NJPS, modified.]
74. [Gen. 1:1.]
75. [Text amended.]
76. [See Deut. 13:1.]
77. [Lev. 27:34]
78. [Sifra Beḥukotai 5:13 and b. Megillah 2b.]

ion, as it is said: '[and appear before] the magistrate in charge at the time,'"[79] that is, we are bound to follow the directions of the court of our own generation.[80] . . .

But *Kesef Mishneh*[81] asks, according to Maimonides' position, why the Talmud objects to the statement of a Talmudic sage (*amora*) based on a mishnah or an early tradition not incorporated in the *Mishnah* (*baraita*) such that either an [alternative] precedent for the statement must be found or it is rejected. Why not say that there is a dispute [between the Talmudic sage and the earlier texts] since the later generations are permitted to disagree with the earlier ones? And [*Kesef Mishneh*] suggests, "perhaps when the Mishnah was codified it was accepted that later generations could not disagree with earlier ones, and a similar process occurred with the codification of the Talmud, forbidding later generations from disagreeing with it." But if *Kesef Mishneh* is correct, how could such a great and awesome principle never have been mentioned once in either the Babylonian or the Jerusalem Talmud, given that it is the foundation of ruling (*hora'ah*)? It seems at first as if [later authorities'[82]] acceptance [of this principle] never to disagree with the Mishnah, and similarly afterward for the Talmud, is never mentioned, nor grounded.[83] . . .

In my humble opinion it seems that the resolution of this lofty and exalted matter is based on the statement in b. Gittin 6ob, "It was taught in the school of Rabbi Yishmael, 'How do we know that you may not write down oral teachings?[84] As it says, "Write *these* words for yourself"[85]—you are to write "these words" [the Written Torah], but you may not write rules (*halakhot*)."'[86] . . .

79. [Deut 17:9.]

80. [Adapted from Moses Maimonides, *The Code of Maimonides (Mishneh Torah), Book 14: The Book of Judges*, translated by Abraham M. Hershman (New Haven, CT: Yale University Press, 1949), Laws of Rebels, 2:1.]

81. [*Kesef Mishneh* (a play on words, the title means double silver, with an allusion to Maimonides' *Mishneh Torah*, on which it is a commentary), written by Yosef Karo (1488–1575) and first published in 1574–75.]

82. [The later authorities (*aharonim*) are leading rabbis and decision makers who were active since the mid-sixteenth century.]

83. [Glasner pursues a pair of questions: Why does the Talmud never mention its fundamental jurisprudential rule of precedence? And how can Maimonides' granting of intellectual freedom to later courts (and Glasner's own picture of creativity in Torah study) be reconciled with this rule?]

84. [Literally, "say oral words in writing."]

85. [Exod. 34:27; NJPS, modified.]

86. [b. Gittin 6ob.]

[M]any reasons have been offered for [this prohibition] against writing down the Oral Torah to teach to others. . . .

Know that the great, obvious distinction between Written Torah and Oral Torah is that the Written Torah was communicated to Moses word for word, from Genesis 1:1 through Deuteronomy 34:12, while the meaning of the Oral Torah was transmitted, but not in words. . . .

It is the nature of oral transmission to alter the sense of a message as it passes from person to person, since each person introduces some of his own personal perspective and sense into the message. . . .

At this point, anyone who does not want to pervert the truth will arrive at the conclusion that the Torah's interpretation was transmitted orally, and that it was forbidden to write it down, so that [the interpretation] should not endure from generation to generation. This was so as not to tie the hands of the scholars of each generation from interpreting the Written Torah according to their understanding. And only in this way can we understand the Torah's eternality, since the variation between generations—their ideas, their situations, and their physical and ethical stature—requires variations in their laws, enactments, and regulations. . . .

The truth is that one of the most wonderful aspects of the Torah's wisdom is that it delegated its interpretation to the sages of each generation, so that the Torah would live with the nation and develop with it: This is what it means for the Torah to be eternal. This idea elegantly explains the blessing on the conclusion of Torah reading [in the synagogue], "[Blessed are You, Lord our God,] Who has given us a true Torah, and implanted eternal life within us." See Tur[87] and Shulḥan Arukh, Oraḥ Ḥayyim, section 138, which interpret "a true Torah" as the Written Torah and "eternal life" as the Oral Torah. According to what they said, we can understand well that the Written Torah is called "true," absolute truth that admits neither addition nor subtraction, which is why it is written. . . . But [the Torah's] interpretation, which is the Oral Torah, is not called absolute truth but rather conventional truth, which depends on the understanding of contemporary judges. And for this very reason it is called "eternal life implanted within us" for through [the Oral Torah] the living spirit of each generation becomes human action, which is why it is called "eternal life." . . .

87. [Tur refers to both the book Arba'ah Turim (Four rows) written by Ya'akov ben Asher (1270–1340), and its author. The title alludes to the rows of jewels in the High Priest's breastplate, and the book is organized in four sections: Oraḥ Ḥayyim, Yoreh De'ah, Even Ha-Ezer, and Ḥoshen Mishpat.]

... [E]ven though the Oral Torah was given to Moses at Sinai, since it was given not as words but rather as ideas, which he was not allowed to write [down], this indicates that the will of the Blessed Commander was for the Torah's interpretation not to endure, so that life and the Torah will never be seen to contradict one another.... Each time requires the writing of a new interpretation, different from what preceded it to meet the needs of that time and place. For this reason, they called the Oral Torah "new,"[88] because the Oral Torah is not absolute truth but rather conventional, since the truth is nothing other than what the sages of a given generation agree upon. And when [the sages] contradict what had previously been true, their new interpretation becomes true, for the Blessed One commanded us not to stray from what the contemporary sages tell us,[89] even if they uproot what had been previously agreed on. And this is also a meaning of "These and these are words of the Living God."[90] ...

This is precisely the position of Maimonides quoted above: each generation's court, even if it is inferior to those of previous generations, can contradict [precedent], interpreting and expounding scripture from its own understanding and according to the principles that are accepted among the scholars as transmitted to Moses from Sinai....

Maimonides wrote what is true in principle ... as he often did. But this [freedom of contemporary courts] is really only a Messianic rule (hilkhata le-misheḥa].[91] For, may it come speedily, when the [Jerusalem] Temple will be rebuilt, the exiles returned, and the crown [of Torah] restored to its former glory, the Oral Torah will be only oral and never written. For the permission of each generation's courts to interpret the Torah without heeding the interpretations of prior courts depends on the Oral Torah's orality, on its not being made to endure with the iron pen. But from the moment that [Rabbi Yehudah the Prince] and the sages of his generation uprooted the prohibition against writing the Oral Torah [by composing the Mishnah], it clearly became forbidden to us to depart from what previous generations established in writing so that it may long endure. For their intent in permitting the writing [of the Oral Torah] was to block the path of future generations who might disagree with their predecessors.

88. [b. Eruvin 21b, based on Song 7:14.]
89. [Deut. 17:11.]
90. [See b. Eruvin 13b.]
91. [See b. Sanhedrin 51b).]

And only now can we appreciate the great tumult that accompanied this permission [to write the Oral Torah by composing the Mishnah], which led our sages of blessed memory to say (b. Temurah 14b), "Someone who writes rules (halakhot) is like a person who burns the Torah." And they justified the permission to write [the Oral Torah] by saying, "It is better that the Torah be uprooted than forgotten." . . . [For] by permitting its writing, the Oral Torah was made into Written Torah—that is, later courts were now forbidden to disagree with the expositions and decisions of earlier ones, and were allowed only to interpret the words of the earlier courts, as they interpret the Written Torah. We no longer need the tenuous explanation of Kesef Mishneh of blessed memory, for the act of writing itself implies the acceptance of a prohibition against contradicting or altering what earlier generations set in writing. . . .

. . . [Y]ou must know that [the written form of the Oral Torah] has, over millennia of exile and wandering, killed our capacity for right reason and critical evaluation, giving rise to a practice of sophistry that is as far from wisdom as east from west. The greatest rabbis of recent generations have bemoaned this, seeing in it the ruin of our poor people, to the point that anyone who can think straight views us with scorn and derision. . . .

. . . [Y]ou must know that straightforward thinking has always been a queen who cannot be deposed. . . .

22

Isaac Breuer, "The Philosophical Foundations
of Jewish and of Modern Law"

Isaac Breuer (1883–1946), grandson of Samson Raphael Hirsch, was a Jewish philosopher and communal activist. Breuer was born in Hungary, but his family moved
to Frankfurt am Main, Germany, when his father ascended to Hirsch's former position as the rabbi of the Orthodox community. Breuer studied philosophy at a
number of universities before receiving a doctorate in law from the University of
Strasbourg. His professional life was spent mainly in the service of Agudat Israel,
the main organization for Central and Eastern European Orthodoxy. He also authored many books in Jewish philosophy. Breuer rejects interpretations of Torah
as religious doctrine and Judaism as a confession, and instead views Torah as law,
which constitutes and preserves the Jewish nation. Because of this link between
law and nationality in Breuer's thought, he was attracted to the idea of Orthodox
settlement in Palestine to establish a Torah state. He immigrated there in 1936. Yet
due to its inherent secularity, he rejected Zionism as a perversion of true Jewish
nationalism, which he argued must be guided by Jewish law.[92] Moreover, as described in the selection below, Breuer argues that, while modern law and Jewish law
both acknowledge the equality of humanity, they have distinct conceptual structures and social ideals: Whereas for modern law the equality of humanity plays a
constitutive role, for Jewish law it is a presupposition. And whereas modern law is
divorced from ethics and the equality of humanity serves as a mere limit to free
action, Jewish is law is integrated with ethics and prescribes determinate duties.
Correspondingly, Breuer maintains that modern law must coercively eliminate all
distinctions of gender, status, and nationality, while Jewish law must retain those
distinctions and temper their abuses through free ethical action. Indeed, in contrast to other authors in this volume, Breuer views rabbinic enactments to enforce
morality as a symptom of the ethical deterioration of the Jewish community instead of its advancement.

92. [For a comprehensive study of Breuer's thought, see Alan L. Mittleman, *Between
Kant and Kabbalah: An Introduction to Isaac Breuer's Philosophy of Judaism* (Albany: State University of New York Press, 1990).]

Isaac Breuer, "The Philosophical Foundations of Jewish and of Modern Law," in *Concepts of Judaism*, edited by Jacob Levinger (Jerusalem: Israel Universities Press, 1974), 61–66, 68, and 70–81.

... Thus we see Jewish law surrounded by powerful barriers of an individual-sexual, social and national nature,[93] and at the same time we see that everywhere in modern law these barriers are being overcome to an increasing extent. . . . Jewish law appears to stand in irreconcilable contradiction to this whole process of legislative development. . . .

"Blessed be God, who has not made me a Gentile, not made me a slave, not made me a woman."[94] In these sentences from the daily liturgy we find expressed with surprising clarity the completely unique character of Jewish law and its barriers. In these sentences we find these barriers related to God himself, the eternal legislator, and for this reason equipped with eternal relevance for all persons subject to Jewish law. *To eradicate these sentences from the liturgy would be tantamount to rendering invalid the complete structure of Jewish law.* . . .

We shall not remove these sentences and in such a manner spread a tenuous veil over our divine law, but we shall attempt instead to show why modem law had of necessity to overcome the barriers of Jewish law, and why Jewish law did not need to overcome these selfsame barriers. . . .

The essence of modem law—disregarding, here and in the following, political and criminal law—consists, *objectively* seen, in the maintenance of a balance of social interest with the help of coercive regulations for maintaining order in society.[95] Viewed *subjectively*, it consists in granting power and the rights to exercise power to those who are authorized to wield it. The balance of interests among those subject to the law is achieved according to considerations of expedience. . . . The objective satisfaction of personal interests and the delegation of power, therefore, proceed hand in hand.

The law is intended to be expedient. It is with this perception that the law is made to suit the lawfulness of purposes. The legal maxim and, associated with

93. [Breuer is referring to the distinctions, discussed earlier in the essay that is excerpted here, between man and women, master and slave, and Jew and non-Jew, which he claims are basic to Jewish law.]

94. [An amalgamation of blessings from the morning service.]

95. The initiated will doubtless realize the connection between the following explanation with regard to modern law and the highly significant work *Economy and Law* by [Rudolf] Stammler. . . .

this, the power granted by it, is [*sic*] justified by its purpose. This purpose itself, however, needs first of all to be justified in its turn. The objectively authorized, i.e., correct, legal maxim can therefore be only one which still appears authorized when assessed on the highest scale of *all purposes*. That is the point at which law in the precise sense links up with ethics. For ethics are nothing more than the rules governing the aims of all men. . . .

Both the balancing of personal interests and the delegation of power, which is bound up with it, ought to be ethically approvable. . . .

Modern law sets out to be a *social* law. It attempts to settle a true *balance* of personal interest, not to further one-sided growth of power. The law wishes to be "correct."

In such a manner the basis of ethics has also become the basis of modern law. . . . The basis of ethics, however, its final, its sole concept, from which it is able, as applied science, solely and exclusively to deduce all its precepts, is the concept or rather the idea of the *human being as such*. . . .

From this ethical basis of the law there appears clearly its tendency towards the basic *equality* of the persons subjected to it. . . .

It is as members of an all-embracing human community, enjoying complete equality of rights, that the members of the nation on principle come together in modern law which is supported on ethics. In the face of the idea of humanity as such, the differences between man and woman disappear, slavery cannot exist, and even the partitions which have existed for thousands of years, set up by nations against one another, begin to totter more and more. The idea of the human community imprints upon modern law its universal character. . . .

What is the relationship between Mosaic law and the idea of the human community?

. . . *The concept of the human community is a Jewish concept.* It is not, however, the *sole* concept of Judaism. It is not even the basis of Judaism. It is its self-evident presumption.

. . . It is a Jewish concept, but obviously from the beginning not *only* destined for Jews. On the other hand, the *application* which this concept undergoes in Judaism, and by whose consequences Judaism also is completely affected, is a specifically Jewish one and separates Jewish and non-Jewish views immensely.

Autonomous ethics are based on humanity. They serve to partition from one another man's *spheres of power*. The idea of the human community is the prerequisite in Judaism for the service of God. In autonomous ethics it serves for the derivation of the rights of men towards one another; in Judaism for the derivation of *duties* to God. The idea of humanity is the final, most fundamental, absolute idea of autonomous ethics. The idea of the human community is not the final, not the absolute idea of Judaism.

It is *presumption, preface to the idea of the service of God which towers magnificently above it....*

Autonomous ethics knows no other standard for the correctness of an action than the will of the perpetrator. The attempt to regulate, in a generally valid way, the human-social relationships by typifying, as it were, actions and assessing them simply as mass phenomena, in short, the attempt to mold the relationships of men into legal relationships had therefore necessarily to lead to a *separation of ethics and law....* Therefore, autonomous ethics is the science of the *agent* and modern law the science of the *action.*

... What if there is an ethical doctrine which has never become autonomous, has never ceased, not merely to set up a formal principle and for the rest from case to case to have recourse to the intent, but demands actions, actions which are defined by their content? ...

This ... is precisely the case in Judaism. Mosaic law does not serve the balance of personal interests but the distribution of duties. Law and ethics are related to one another in Judaism just as pure and applied science....

Law is nothing profane in Israel. Just as over the idea of the human community, so likewise over the law it is the name of the Lord that is pronounced.... The Creator of ethics is at one and the same time Creator of the law in Israel....

Mosaic Law ... is nothing else but the delegation of duties by the Creator of man and Creator of all ethics. This delegation allots the one a greater measure than the other; defines for the man the lot of setting his own boundaries in free self-control, which his own individuality demands of him with regard to the human community, yet demands from the woman greater renunciation with regard to the family; bestows on the slave the lot of subjecting himself servilely with complete bending of his own will; and concludes by lifting an entire nation above the rest of the human community so that it may serve as an example and light the way as the noblest bearer of duties.... The Creator of nature is the Creator of Mosaic law; should it, then, cause surprise that, as everywhere in nature the *principium individuationis* rules supreme, so too in the law the spheres of duty are graduated according to age and sex, rank and nation? ...

Whoever approaches Jewish law with the concept of the separation of law and ethics exceedingly common and familiar to modern man, has from the very start robbed himself of absolutely every possibility of arriving at an understanding, no matter how superficial, of this law and of the aims it pursues.... [S]ince

Jewish law sets out to be a divine one, it can only be understood and judged as divine law.

... [T]he infinitely original nature of Jewish law displays itself most evidently as a doctrine of the distribution of *duties*, not as a doctrine of the distribution of *power*. According to the modern legal view, the law of slavery incumbent on the one party would have to correspond to the other's law of mastery, the helplessness of the slave to the sovereign, plenary power of the master. Valid Jewish law runs strictly contrary to this: ... "Treat him, yourself, like a brother, but he should bear himself like a slave."[96] ...

It is not under the coercion of the law but from the free moral resolve of those subject to the law that the divine legislator expects the forestalling of every abuse of power....

... It is a fact that is by no means sufficiently appreciated, that, as the heteronomy of modern law corresponds to the autonomy of modern ethics, so the *autonomy of Jewish law* corresponds to the heteronomy of Jewish ethics. Just as the first main governing principle of Jewish law is the disparity in the delegation of duties, so the second, whose scope equals that of the first, is the liberty of those subject to the law. And the liberty of those subject to the law is supposed to rectify the disparity in the delegation of duties. The disparity in the delegation of duties is handed over to the compulsion of the law, and the preservation of the *idea of the human community* is handed over to the *liberty of those subject to the law*....

... [O]ur sages, by reason of their divinely invested authority to make prescriptions, saw themselves many times constrained partly to ensure the preservation of the idea of the human community entrusted to the liberty of those subject to the law, by means of supplementary legal measures restricting this liberty by way of legal coercion. Far from being able to glimpse in these prescriptions the progress which gradually prevailed in Jewish law, we rather see them as documents of historical weakness, pedagogic measures dedicated to educating the Jewish nation to the bright heights of the divine law, which is not a law of constraint but one of liberty....

---

96. *Torat Kohanim, Behar*, Chapter 7, No. 1. [Torat Kohanim, a midrashic legal commentary to Leviticus, is also known as Sifra.]

23 | Selections from the Writings of Avraham Yeshayahu Karelitz

Avraham Yeshayahu Karelitz (1878–1953) was the major Jewish legal authority for Ultra-Orthodoxy in the State of Israel. Born in Lithuania, he immigrated to Mandatory Palestine in 1933. Although he never held an official rabbinic position in Palestine or Israel, he become known through his responsa and scholarship, which were printed under the title *Hazon Ish* (Vision of man), a term often used to refer to him. Karelitz's worldview is focused exclusively on the study and practice of Jewish law. Indeed, in his posthumously published theological work *Emunah u-Vitahon* (Faith and trust), portions of which are included below, he propounds a divine command ethics, in which Jewish law determines ethical obligations. Karelitz even criticizes, albeit obliquely, other Orthodox approaches to study and practice for deviating from the requisite focus on Jewish law in the spirit of modernity. He disapproves of contemporary manifestations of the Musar movement because they turn inward to develop ethical sensitivity. He censures the Brisker method for an overemphasis on interpretive creativity. For Karelitz, the ideal is submission to both the texts and practices of Jewish law. The Torah scholar who embodies this ideal becomes one with Jewish law and possesses *da'at torah* (knowledge of Torah). His opinion, even on issues that are not narrowly legal, is authoritative. In this role, Karelitz led the non-Zionist Ultra-Orthodox community in its confrontation with the Israeli government over its attempt to conscript Ultra-Orthodox girls for national service. Thus, somewhat counterintuitively, a "legal" conception of Jewish law provided the basis for a robustly political conception of Jewish legal authorities. The selections below show other features of the political in Karelitz's Jewish legal theory. In the second selection, he rejects the proposal put forward by Zionist rabbis, including Abraham Isaac Kook, to permit agricultural work in Israel during the sabbatical year (*shmitah*), when it is normally prohibited, through the mechanism of temporarily selling agricultural lands to non-Jews. Karelitz argues that there is an insurmountable biblical commandment against enabling non-Jews to settle in the Land of Israel. Though rejecting the project of establishing a Jewish nation-state, he expels, at least in his Jewish legal imaginary, non-Jews from the Jewish settlement in the Land of Israel. In the third selection, he develops a conception of Jewish public law based on the Talmud by delineating its differences from partnership law, explaining rules for voting and selecting an executive and describing the types of regulations that are allowed to be established. While this public law provides the authority for communal regulations that do not directly derive from biblical or rabbinic law, these regulations are unstable because they can always be vetoed by the standard sources of Jewish and their representative — the Torah scholar.[97]

Avraham Yeshayahu Karelitz, *Chazon Ish: Faith and Trust*, translated by Yaakov Goldstein (Jerusalem: Am Asefer, 2008), 58, 62, 76, 90, 94–95, 98, and 110 (translation adapted by the editors).

ETHICS AND JEWISH LAW (*MUSAR VE-HALAKHAH*)

Ethical obligations are sometimes as one with determinations of Jewish law (*piskei ha-halakhah*), and Jewish law (ha-halakhah) decides what is prohibited and what is permitted in ethical doctrine (*torat musar*). . . .

One of the obligations of ethics is that a person should try to instill in his heart this great principle: in any case in which one finds oneself in opposition to a fellow Jew, one has to weigh the matter in accordance with Jewish law (ha-halakhah), to define the persecutor and the persecuted. The study of perfecting one's character traits (musar) instills in one love and pity for the persecuted, and severe condemnation of the persecutor; how terrible is, then, the danger of misidentifying the persecutor as the persecuted and vice versa. The only way to know the truth is to study the books of the decisors — those books of rulings that we have received from the great rabbis of the past. . . .

Our sages extolled the virtues of true justice greatly, as far as to say (in the first chapter of b. Shabbat): "A judge who gives an absolutely true judgment even

97. See Benjamin Brown, *He-Ḥazon Ish: Ha-poseḳ, ha-ma'amin u-manhig ha-mahpekhah ha-Ḥaredit* [Ḥazon Ish: The decisor, the believer, and the leader of the Ultra-Orthodox revolution] (Jerusalem: Magnes, 2010). This work, as well as communication with its author, informed the choice of selections and the description of their significance. For other important studies on Karelitz in English, see Lawrence Kaplan, "The Ḥazon Ish: Ḥaredi Critique of Traditional Orthodoxy," in *The Uses of Tradition: Jewish Continuity in the Modern Era*, edited by Jack Wertheimer (New York: Jewish Theological Seminary Press, 1998), 145–73; Menachem Friedman, "The Lost *Kiddush Cup*: Changes in Ashkenazi Ḥaredi Culture — A Tradition in Crisis," in ibid., 175–87. For an overview of the concept of da'at torah, see Lawrence Kaplan, "*Daas Torah*: A Modern Conception of Rabbinic Authority," in *Rabbinic Authority and Personal Autonomy*, edited by Moshe Sokol (Northvale, NJ: Aronson, 1992), 1–60.

one time, it is as if he has become a partner to the Holy One, blessed be He, in Creation." For judgment [done according to Torah] ensures the existence of the world, as it says in the first chapter of m. Avot, "The world stands on three things, on justice, [and on truth and on peace]." And *Tur*, Ḥoshen Mishpat section 1 said: "This is what our sages meant when they said "A judge who judges" etc.: that the Holy One, blessed be He, created the world so that it should be perpetuated. The evil people who rob and steal destroy it with their actions. . . . From this we see that a judge who breaks the arms of the wicked, takes their loot from them and returns it to the rightful owners ensures the existence of the world and brings about the completion of the Creator's will. . . . It is, then, as if he becomes a partner to the Holy One, blessed be He, in Creation. . . ." . . . Tur put these principles at the beginning of Ḥoshen Mishpat [which concerns monetary laws] to teach us that the criteria of robbery and stealing are not set by human beings' opinions, but only by the laws of the Torah. . . .

One of the difficulties in accepting the results of a judicial proceeding is that the absolute verdict is not an axiom, nor is it a simple notion: it comes about only through the labor of the judge and his constant study. . . . Only those who devote themselves totally to understanding its truth will find it after much perseverance and deep study, so much so that the judge and the verdict are really one and the same. . . .

It is necessary to elaborate on the obligation to study Jewish law because of the decrease in the number of students in our generation. . . . [T]here is great neglect within the study hall, which causes the students to be lax about studying Jewish law thoroughly; instead, the time is wasted on fabricated ideas and notions, on innovations that have nothing in them of what Moses our Teacher heard from Sinai. Even though the topic of study is . . . perfection of one's character traits, or some external examination of Jewish law, this kind of study does not fulfill the desired goal of man on this earth, as long as it is not accompanied by practical knowledge of the legal Torah (*ha-torah ha-dinit*). . . .

The Great Sanhedrin, the supreme authority according to the Torah, sat in the Chamber of Hewn Stone. Whoever disobeyed their decrees was to be punished by death, and it is they who decided whether or not to go to war, and whom to appoint king. What was demanded of them? Full command of Jewish law—the laws of permitted and forbidden foods, laws pertaining to monetary issues, and other rules—as mentioned by Maimonides in [*Mishneh Torah*,] "Laws of the Sanhedrin," 4:8. . . .

In b. Bava Kamma 41b it says that Shimon Ha'amsuni . . . would extrapolate [rules] from every "*et*"[98] in the Torah. When he reached the verse "[et] the Lord, your God, you shall fear," he took back his words, until Rabbi Akiva came and taught that the "et" there comes to add Torah scholars (*talmedei ḥakhamim*), who should also be revered.

We learn from this that the most desired and excellent personality according to the Torah is the personality that deserves the title of Torah scholar. Rabbi Akiva allowed himself to compare the reverence that should be felt toward this highly valued person to the reverence that is due to God. . . .

Avraham Yeshayahu Karelitz, *Sefer Ḥazon Ish: Zera'im* [Vision of man: Seeds], (Bnei Brak, Israel, 1993), 297–98 (translated by Noah Bickart).

SHEVI'IT SECTION 24

With regard to selling land in Israel to a non-Jew (*nokhri*):

(1) There are two biblical negative commandments with regard to giving idolaters a place in the Land [of Israel]: [The first is] "They shall not remain in your land, lest they cause you to sin [against Me; for you will serve their gods] . . ." (Exod. 23:33), [which is explained by] Maimonides [in his work] *Sefer ha-Mitzvot*, Negative Commandment no. 31. . . . [The second is]: "[(When) the Lord your God delivers them to you and you defeat them, you must doom them to destruction: grant them no terms and] give them no quarter (*tiḥanem*)" (Deut. 7:2), [which is] mentioned [by] Maimonides [in his work] *Sefer ha-Mitzvot* (ibid.), with regard to a foothold (*ḥaneyah*) in the land. . . .

The logic (din) of the prohibition of allowing [idolaters to] settle [in the Land of Israel] is because we are commanded to expel them from our land, and this is incumbent upon every Israelite. All the more so one who sells [an idolater] a house or rents it to him transgresses this negative commandment. . . .

That the law "Give them no quarter," according to all opinions, refers to allowing all idolaters a foothold in the Land [of Israel] is taught in a mishnah [cited at] b. Avodah Zarah 19b: "One should not sell to idolaters [an object which is attached to the soil]." The Talmud asks, "Whence do we derive this rule? . . . [and answers with the scriptural words], "Give them no quarter (*tiḥanem*)" [which may be rendered] 'Do not allow them a foothold (*ḥaneyah*) in the Land.'" . . .

. . . [T]his law encompasses the will that the Land [of Israel] should be inhabited by Israel, and that the Land [of Israel] should not be given over to idolaters. Since

98. [A word that usually marks a direct object.]

the Land of Israel retains [its status as the Land of Israel] even during our exile, we are [nonetheless] obligated in its settlement, to live in it, even in our exile. . . .

This is stated explicitly by Maimonides in [*Mishneh Torah*,] "Laws of Idolatry" 10:3, where he writes, "It is permitted to sell them houses and fields outside the Land of Israel, because it is not our Land." If indeed the issue were to have been contingent upon the sanctity of the Land [of Israel], it would not be relevant to give a reason for this allowance [on selling houses and fields] outside the Land of Israel. Rather, since the prohibition granting them a foothold in the Land is one of the details of the commandment of destroying idolatry, it would have made sense to prohibit [selling houses and fields to non-Jews] even outside the Land [of Israel]! However, owing to the impracticality of being warned [about this] for the whole world, we are warned only with regard to our Land. But this [commandment] to destroy idolatry from our Land [obtains] at all times. . . .

There is no distinction between whether the idolater already has land in the Land [of Israel] or not, for with each house and field that one gives them, one gives a foothold for idolaters in this Land. Even if one were to doubt this, the categorical language of the Mishnah, Talmud, and the decisors is decisive [evidence] that there is no distinction. . . .

(2) Now, despite the fact that the Torah warns us neither to allow [idolaters] to dwell nor to grant them a foothold [in the Land of Israel], with regard to a "resident alien" [these things are] permitted, as it is written (Deut. 23:17), "He shall live with you. . . . [ellipsis in original]" . . . As Maimonides writes in [*Mishneh Torah*,] "Laws of Forbidden Sexual Relations," 14:7, the reason why he is called a "resident alien" is that he is permitted to dwell with us, and therefore it is permitted to allow him a foothold in the Land. For from the verse, "Give them no quarter," [a prohibition on giving] gifts without remuneration is also derived. But it is permitted to give gifts without remuneration to a resident alien as it is written, "[You shall not eat anything that has died a natural death;] give it to the stranger in your community . . . [ellipsis in original]"[99] as is explicated at b. Avodah Zarah 20a.

With regard to the resident alien, we follow the position of the sages [found] at b. Avodah Zarah 64b that "Any [gentile] who takes upon himself the seven [Noahide] commandments,"[100] [is a resident alien]. And this means that he

99. [Deut. 14:21.]

100. [According to the Talmud, there are seven "Noahide commandments" incumbent upon all "descendants of Noah," that is, all human beings. Six are negative (not to deny

must accept [these laws] upon himself in the presence of a rabbinical court of three [judges]. . . . Acceptance of resident aliens is dependent upon the ongoing observance of the Jubilee, as it is stated in b. Arakhin 29a, and as Maimonides decides in [*Mishneh Torah*,] "Laws of Forbidden Sexual Relations," 14 and in "Laws of Idolatry." . . .

(3) The opinion of Maimonides [is thus] that because we are unable to accept [a resident alien], his dwelling in the Land is not permitted, despite being punctilious in the [performance] of the seven [Noahide] commandments. For without [formal] acceptance [by a rabbinical court], we are not certain about his punctiliousness [in fulfilling them] and we are not experts with regard to [resident aliens]. . . .

(4) Even though when it comes to the prohibition against showing them mercy (*lo titen lahem ḥen*], anything that is done for the benefit of Israel is allowed, as Ran[101] writes [in his commentary to b. Gittin Ch. 4] . . .; here, with regard to a foothold in the Land there is no [such] distinction. For [the prohibition of] showing them mercy is only when there is a feeling of mercy [on the part of the Jew], but not when [the Jew] pursues his own gain. However, [with regard] to a foothold in the Land, the [simple fact of] the existence of idolaters on the Land of Israel, by means of purchase, is hateful to God, for any [gentile] who buys land, such that it is his, that idolater dwells on the Land. . . .

Therefore, there is no reason to allow the sale of the land to a gentile to suspend the holiness of the sabbatical year. To the contrary, the prohibitions of the sabbatical year are of rabbinic [authority] at this time, but selling [land in the Land of Israel] to [gentiles] is a biblical [prohibition]. . . .

Avraham Yeshayahu Karelitz, *Sefer Ḥazon Ish: Ḥoshen Mishpat* [Vision of man: Breastplate of Judgment] (Bnei Brak, Israel, 1994), 301–2 and 307–8 (translated by Noah Bickart).

BAVA BATRA SECTION 4

. . . .

(8) [At b. Bava Batra 9a the Talmud introduces the following case: There are two butchers who made an agreement with each other to divide up the days of

---

God, blaspheme God, commit murder, engage in illicit sexual relations, steal, or eat from a living animal) and one positive (to establish courts to uphold the rule of law).]

101. [Nissim ben Reuven of Girona (Spain, 1310–76).]

the week for business. If either encroached on the other's day by slaughtering on it, the skin of the animal that was slaughtered should be torn up, which would yield a financial loss, as a penalty. One of the butchers did slaughter on the other's day, and the other went and tore up the skin of the animal. The one who did so was then summoned before Rava,[102] and he obligated him to make restitution to the first butcher. Rabbi Yemar b. Shelemiah then called Rava's attention to the rabbinic dictum that the people of a city may inflict penalties on individuals for breach of their regulations. Rava did not answer him. Rabbi Papa said: Rava was quite right not to answer him], for "this [rule] holds good only where there is no distinguished man (adam ḥashuv) in the town, but where there [is such a man]. . . . [ellipsis in original]"

In Naḥmanides' commentary it is explained that there are two issues:

> 1. A guild (ba'alei umanot) has authority (koḥ) like the people of the city do. Just as the people of a city have the authority of a rabbinical court [over its members], so too every guild has the authority of a rabbinical court over its own artisans (bnei umaniyot). . . .
>
> 2. Individuals may agree among themselves with regard to partnership. For example, they might agree that any profit must be shared [among them].

There are many differences between the laws [of guilds and individual partnerships]. [For example:] If all [the artisans of a trade] agree, an issue is resolved verbally without an act of acquisition; none of them are able to [unilaterally] withdraw; their agreement is in effect both for profits gained through physical labor and for [profits] from discounted purchases that arise for them. However, individuals who make an agreement require an act of acquisition [to effect the agreement]; and [even] after the act of acquisition, they may withdraw [from the agreement]; and the [agreement by means of the] act of acquisition is only in effect on their labor and not on discounted purchases that they buy. . . .

Now, [with regard to a case in which] all the people of the city or all the artisans stipulated [some agreement], this must refer to a [city in which] there was no local scholar (ḥaver ha-ir).[103] However, where there is a local scholar, then they do not have the authority of a rabbinical court without [the agreement of] the local scholar. Naḥmanides writes that the reason [for this is] that we are con-

---

102. [Rabbi Abba ben Joseph ben Ḥama, a fourth-century CE Talmudic sage.]
103. [See b. Megillah 30a-b.]

cerned that they have acted improperly to raise prices. And even if we find that they have acted properly, their stipulation is nonetheless invalid, since there was a local scholar. However, if truly they stipulated improperly, their agreement is not effective even where there is no local scholar. . . .

BAVA BATRA SECTION 5

(1) *Darkhei Moshe*[104] to [*Tur*, Ḥoshen Mishpat] section 163 cites a responsum of Maharam[105] [that states that] in a matter in which a majority [of a community] has the authority to compel a minority (see above section 4 [which details that] this is regarding [rabbinic decrees] to prevent sin (*le-migdar milta*) [literally, "to hedge a situation" of breach] or [rabbinic enactments] for the betterment of society) the whole community is invited [to come together]; and if anyone refuses to share his opinion, his opinion is not taken under consideration; and they follow the [opinion] of the assembled majority. [Maharam] adds that they count only those who pay taxes. A reason must be given for why the poor, who do not pay taxes, are not considered to be part . . . of the community. It would seem that Maharam's claim obtains only with regard to monetary issues. Since the matter under discussion does not concern [the poor individual], for he will neither lose out if others do not pay nor benefit if others pay more, thus he is not considered part of the community. Now, a guild is equivalent to the people of a city, and the people of a city, when it comes to the needs of the city, are like partners in that matter. However, this [poor] one who is not in partnership with them, it is not right (*ba-din*) that he should judge them. As such, if the matter under discussion is [a decree] to prevent sin with regard to heavenly concerns, it is right that the poor should be counted among them.

[*Darkhei Moshe*] also quotes Terumat ha-Deshen[106] who states that if there are two rich powerful men in the city, and the opinion of the community is that five people should be chosen to assess the taxes, and the two rich men wish to choose two [of the persons] among the five, because these two have connec-

104. [(Ways of Moses), a commentary by Moshe Isserles (Poland, 1520–72) on the *Arba'ah Turim*.]

105. [Meir ben Baruch, rabbi of Rothenberg, Germany (c. 1215–93).]

106. [Terumat ha-Deshen (Offering of the ashes) refers to Yisrael Isserlin ben Petachia —also known as Israel of Neustadt, Israel of Marpurk, and Maharai—(Slovenia, 1390–1460) as well as his work by that name.]

tions to them, . . . the law is with them. [Terumat ha-Deshen's] intention is not that these two rich men may choose two [persons] against [the wishes of] the majority of the community, for certainly a majority of the community must agree with the appointment of each and every one of [the five]. Rather, . . . it is good form (*midat ha-yosher*) that the majority of the community agrees with the two persons who the rich men chose, so long as the community does not find fault with their selections. Further, these two [persons selected by the rich men] do not constitute a majority of the court, for five are chosen. It will be like the law of "this one chooses one [judge], and this one chooses one [judge]" in the Mishnah.[107] And this is the path of peace and justice, as Rashi explains at the beginning of [chapter 3] of b. Sanhedrin.

However, this is not exactly the same as "this one chooses one [judge], and this one chooses one [judge]," for in our case it is impossible that those chosen will enact the underlying law (*omek ha-din*), for it is impossible to be fully precise in this [forum]; however, those chosen from the community have the authority of the court. . . . On such [authority] we require the agreement of a majority of the community. Also [it is unlike the case of the Mishnah because] there is no back and forth between the rich men and the rest of the city, rather the back and forth is between each and every individual. Those chosen, who become as judges between each and every individual, need the consent of the community. The consent of the two rich men is not enough. . . .

. . . .

(3) . . . [T]he community may coerce the individual:

A. To build a wall and similar matters, for which there is no need for the agreement of the community; rather, the individual may force the community. And the agreement of the community is not effective to nullify [the individual's claim]. For this is not preventing sin or bettering society. And it is possible that even if all of them agree not to build a wall, each individual can withdraw from [such an agreement and coerce the rest to build the wall], for this is a bad custom and [building the wall] does not nullify a rule (*halakhah*). . . .

B. A matter that does not derive from the law, but the majority of the community agreed upon it and there is an element of the betterment

107. [m. Sanhedrin 3:1. This mishnah discusses the formation of an ad hoc court of three individuals by having each party to a dispute select one judge, and these two judges then agreeing on a third.]

of society in it. Here too [the community] possess the authority of the rabbinical court and their enactment stands. . . .

C. A matter that does not entirely benefit the city and the majority of the community cannot coerce the minority, but if they all agree, their agreement stands. . . .

Moshe Feinstein, *Epistles of Moshe*

Moshe Feinstein (1895–1986) was among the major Jewish legal authorities for Orthodox Jews in the United States. Born near Minsk in Russia, he held a rabbinic position in the town of Luban until 1936, when he immigrated to the United States due to pressure from the Communist government. From 1938 until the end of his life, he served as the head of Mesivta Teferet Jerusalem on the Lower East Side of Manhattan. He was the president of the Union of American Orthodox Rabbis of the United States and Canada as well as the chairman of the Council of Torah Sages for Agudat Israel of America. In his multivolume work of responsa, *Iggerot Moshe* (Epistles of Moshe), Feinstein addressed many of the most important issues of the day for American Orthodoxy. The first selection below is from the introduction to the first volume of that work. Feinstein distinguishes between the absolute truth of God, which is unattainable, and the legal truth of the rabbinic decisor, which emerges from his best efforts to interpret the Jewish legal tradition. He also develops a corresponding interpretive theory that is akin to textualism: Feinstein claims that it is the text of the Torah, and not its authors or interpreters, that is sovereign. Yet he acknowledges that, in practice, this empowers its rabbinic interpreters, according to whose consensus the meaning of the text is established. In closing the introduction, Feinstein suggests that his responsa lack any authority independent from the persuasiveness of their arguments. This view of rabbinic authority as expertise can be compared to the political conception of Avraham Yeshayahu Karelitz. The second set of selections, which concern the permissibility of in vitro fertilization with a donor, exhibits Feinstein's approach to decision making. In ruling that this procedure is permissible, Feinstein deems few sources to merit consultation. He fixes on a central legal source, which initially seems to argue in favor of prohibiting the procedure, and, by adding further considerations, is able to derive a lenient ruling. This is especially remarkable since, as Feinstein acknowledges at the beginning of the second responsum, permitting a woman to give birth through in vitro fertilization, does not enable her to fulfill the commandment to procreate because she is not obligated by that commandment, and also risks the legal consequences of adultery, unclear paternity, and illegitimacy of the resulting child. The daring of Feinstein's arguments is evident when compared with the response to them by Yoel Teitelbaum, which are included in selection 25, along with Feinstein's rejoinder to a supporter of Teitelbaum.

Moshe Feinstein, *Iggerot Moshe* (Brooklyn, NY: Noble Book, 1959), 1:3–4 (translated by Ezra Blumenthal).

INTRODUCTION

The content of this book mostly consists of what I replied to those who sought to know my opinion, what seemed to me, in my humble opinion, [to be appropriate] to teach as practical rule (*le-horot halakhah le-ma'aseh*).

… There is certainly a concern that perhaps we have not arrived at the [very] truth of the law as [it] is [recognized as] true by heaven; however, [it has been established] already that the truth [in the context] of ruling is "not in heaven."[108] Rather, truth [in the context] of ruling is what appears to the scholar to be the legal decision (pesak din) after he has appropriately studied to clarify the rule (ha-halakhah) in the Talmud and responsa as best as he can with seriousness and fear of God, blessed be He. [The scholar] is obligated to rule [according to his opinion] even if in essence it is revealed before heaven that the interpretation is not [like his view]. It is of such an instance that it is said that even his words are the "words of the living God,"[109] since the interpretation seemed to him to be as he decided and nothing contradicted it. He will receive [heavenly] reward for his ruling, even though the truth is not according to his interpretation.

… The truth [in the context] of ruling, which one is obligated to rule and for which one receives reward, is thus as the scholar reasons after he studies as best as he can, even though it does not correspond to the truth itself. …

It is explicitly so in b. Sanhedrin 6b: "Judges must be cognizant of who they judge, before whom they judge, and who in the future will punish them … and lest the judge say, 'What good is this burden,' (Rashi explains, 'For if he makes a mistake [in judgment], he is punished'), scripture says, 'He is with you when you pass judgment.'[110] The judge has only what his eyes see." Rashi interprets: The judge should not be afraid and refrain from judgment but should [decide] according to what seems to him [proper] to judge; he should intend to bring [the judgment] to its justice and truth, and then he will not be punished. See [Rashi's comments] there. Rashi means that this is the truth [in the context] of ruling: that one is obligated to refine oneself, to rule, and to judge, even though [one's judgment] is not the truth itself.

108. [Deut. 30:12.]
109. [b. Eruvin 13b.]
110. [2 Chron. 19:6.]

I have thereby explained what is found in b. Menaḥot 29b: "Rabbi Yehudah said in the name of Rav:[111] When Moses ascended to heaven he found the Holy One, blessed be He, sitting and tying crowns (*ketarim*) on the letters [of the Torah]. He asked him, 'Master of the Universe, who stays your hand?' He replied to him, 'There is a man by the name of Akiva ben Yosef[112] who in the future will expound from each and every embellishment (*kotz*) piles and piles of rules.'" However, it appears that the use of the word "crowns (ketarim)" is not clear. Additionally, what Moses intends with his question, "Who stays your hand?" is difficult. . . .

However, based on what I have previously explained, the word "crowns" is precise. For God crowned the letters of the Torah as kings. That is, the scholar should go, compare a case to another case, and decide the law according to his understanding of the meaning of the letters of the Torah. And when there is a dispute, [the scholar] should follow the understanding of majority of Torah scholars, even if it is possible that they do not correspond with the truth, and the opinion of the Blessed One was not thus. For the Holy One, blessed be He, gave the Torah to Israel so that they should do according to their understanding of the verses and what was transmitted orally at Sinai, according to their understanding. God, bless Him, will not interpret nor will He decide anything more concerning the laws of the Torah, for it is "not in heaven"; rather, He agreed from the outset to the understanding and interpretation of the Torah scholars. The letters of the Torah are thus kings, for we act according to what is understood from the [letters of the] Torah by the scholars of the Torah, even if this [understanding] was not like the understanding of God.

. . . This is the interpretation of "who stays": Moses asks, "Why does the Holy One, blessed be He, crown the letters king so that we should act according to the understanding of the scholars of the language in scripture and tradition? For who prevents You from writing in a manner that would only make it possible to understand [the Torah] in one way, [that is,] according to Your true interpretation? Why did you give kingly power to the letters so that sometimes we act against your intention?" God replies: "Because on account of this, Rabbi Akiva and all the other scholars will expound numerous rules (halakhot) that are the expansion of the Torah from the minimum that was written and transmitted. [Furthermore,] to write much—each thing in detail—would be endless, for the

111. [Abba Akiva (Babylonia, third century CE).]
112. [Rabbi Akiva (Eretz Israel, c. 40–c. 137 CE).]

Torah is without end or limit. See b. Eruvin 21. Since it has been clarified that the truth [in the context] of ruling is that which seems to the scholar appropriate to rule in practice and obligatory to rule after he works and toils to clarify the rule (ha-halakhah) in the Talmud and responsa as best as he can with seriousness and fear of God, the scholars in this generation should also be considered fit to rule and obligated to rule because their rulings are considered true law (din emet). . . .

And this is what I have relied on to rule and also to reply with what seems, in my humble opinion, [to be the rule] to those that wish to know my opinion after I clarified the rule with great effort, especially since I have written out the reasons [for my rulings]. [For in regard to] anything that is clarified in this manner, I am merely like a teacher of the rule (ke-melamed ha-halakhah) so that the inquirer can investigate on his own, check [my response], and choose [a ruling]. . . .

Moshe Feinstein, "Even Ha-Ezer #71 (1959): On the Recently Developed Techniques of Artificial Insemination" and "Even Ha-Ezer #10 (1961): Whether a Woman Who Has Been Artificially Inseminated with the Sperm of a Donor Is Forbidden to Her Husband and Whether There Is Any Taint on the Child," in *Jewish Law (Mishpat Ivri): Cases and Materials*, edited by Menachem Elon, Bernard Auerbach, Daniel D. Chazin, and Melvin J. Sykes (New York: M. Bender, 1999), 629–31.

EVEN HA-EZER #71 (1959)
ON THE RECENTLY DEVELOPED TECHNIQUES
OF ARTIFICIAL INSEMINATION

[In his commentary on the *Shulḥan Arukh*,] Taz[113] . . . clearly rules that artificial insemination from a donor is prohibited.[114] He quotes Rabbeinu Perez, who states in *Haggahot Semak*[115] that a woman should be careful not to lie on sheets upon which a man other than her husband has slept, lest she become impregnated by that other man's sperm. From this statement, we see that it is forbidden for a woman to become pregnant from another man's sperm even without intercourse, [still] in which case the resulting child is not [illegitimate (a *mamzer*)].[116]

113. [David ha-Levi Segal (Poland, c. 1586–1667), also known as Turei Zahav (Rows of gold).]

114. *Turei Zahav (Taz)* to [*Shulḥan Arukh, Yoreh De'ah* section] 195, subpar[agraph] 7.

115. [(Notes on the *Sefer Mitzvot Katan* [Concise book of commandments]), by Perez ben Eliyahu of Corbeil (France, 2nd half of the thirteenth century).]

116. [A mamzer (one who is illegitimate) is an individual who results from prohibited

However, inasmuch as the reason [for the prohibition] is stated to be the concern that the child might marry his sister born of his father . . . , it is permissible to use the sperm of a non-Jew. The child is Jewish because his mother is Jewish; and there is no concern about any adverse consequences, inasmuch as the child's status does not derive from the non-Jewish father, especially when there has been sexual intercourse, and certainly [this is so] when there has been no sexual intercourse. . . .

The fact that the sperm is taken from a non-Jew will solve the problem for those who argue that a child born from the sperm of anyone other than the husband, even without sexual intercourse, is [illegitimate]. . . . A child born from the sperm of a non-Jew . . . even as a result of sexual intercourse, is not [illegitimate].

Therefore, in a case of extreme urgency, when the parents are suffering from intense distress in their desire for a child, there is ground to permit artificial insemination, but only with the sperm of a non-Jew. It is reasonable to assume that any contributed sperm is that of a non-Jew. . . .

The opinion cited in *Otzar ha-Posekim*[117] . . . that Jewish women should not, God forbid, prostitute themselves by submitting to the recently developed technique of artificial insemination is baseless. The prohibition has nothing to do with promiscuity; it is based on the concern that the child might marry his sister born of his father. . . .

EVEN HA-EZER #10 (1961)
WHETHER A WOMAN WHO HAS BEEN ARTIFICIALLY
INSEMINATED WITH THE SPERM OF A DONOR IS
FORBIDDEN TO HER HUSBAND AND WHETHER
THERE IS ANY TAINT ON THE CHILD

This matter involves a woman who was childless for ten years. The medical opinion was that this condition was attributable to her husband. Desiring to give birth like all women—and as is found in b. Yebamot 65, though women are not subject to the commandment of procreation, we force a husband to divorce [his wife] and give her the dower [if they cannot have children together] on the

---

sexual intercourse, such as adultery or incest. A mamzer is prohibited from marrying a
legitimate Jew.]

117. [A multivolume compendium of responsa keyed to the organization of the *Shulḥan
Arukh*. Feinstein refers to *Otzar ha-Posekim*, edited by Isaac Halevi Herzog and Isser Zalman
Meltzer (Jerusalem: Ha-Mesorah, 1955), vol. 1, section 6, subsection 42.]

strength of [her] claim, "what will become of a woman like this when she is old" and "does not a women like this need a staff to lean on and a hoe to dig a grave," and even without this [claim] we know that the holy matriarchs wanted to give birth and all women do[118]—she was artificially inseminated with the sperm of another man. . . . The husband now asks whether his wife may continue to live with him and what the status of the child is.

It is settled law that a woman is not forbidden to her husband unless she had sexual intercourse with another man. . . . If she receives another man's seed not by way of intercourse but in a bath, as mentioned in the Talmud, there is no promiscuity and she is not forbidden to her husband.

The child is also legitimate, as the status of [illegitimacy] is created only by intercourse. . . . This is explained . . . by Joel Sirkes . . . in his commentary Baḥ,[119] quoting from Haggahot Semak by Rabbeinu Perez. . . .

If the identity of the donor is known, and he is Jewish, the child may not marry any offspring of the donor. . . . However, inasmuch as [in the case at hand] his identity is not known, the child may marry any woman, because most women are permissible to him. . . .

118. [The material in the dashes was restored from the original by the editors.]
119. Bayit Ḥadash 10 [Shulḥan Arukh, Yoreh De'ah section] 195.

Yoel Teitelbaum (1887–1979) was the founder of the Satmar Hasidic dynasty and an ardent opponent of Zionism. He became the rabbi of the Romanian town of Szatmár in 1934. In 1944 he escaped the Holocaust and went to Mandatory Palestine, reaching the United States in 1947. There he reestablished his Hasidic court in the Williamsburg section of Brooklyn, New York. Though Satmar was a small Hasidic sect before World War II, in the United States it absorbed many other small sects that had been nearly destroyed. Satmar is now the largest Hasidic sect and has even developed its own incorporated village in Monroe Township, New York.[120] Teitelbaum is known for his extremism but also for his erudition. The selections below from his writings demonstrate both of these characteristics. The first selection includes portions of two responsa that are criticisms of Feinstein's responsa about in vitro fertilization with a donor and Feinstein's rejoinder to a supporter of Teitelbaum. From a narrowly legal perspective, Teitelbaum argues that Feinstein has neglected to consider both in-principle and practical problems entailed by children with unclear paternity. But Teitelbaum does not restrict himself to this perspective. He offers novel arguments drawn from biblical commentaries to claim that the prohibition of adultery is violated even when there is no sexual intercourse. Additionally, in response to Feinstein's attempt to circumvent problems of unclear paternity by assuming that the sperm donor is not Jewish, Teitelbaum mobilizes rabbinic narrative to condemn such supposed adulteration of the genetic purity of the Jewish people. If Teitelbaum's response highlights the minimalism of Feinstein's decision making, Feinstein's rejoinder underlines Teitelbaum's maximalism in his responsa. Feinstein describes Teitelbaum's perspective as contaminated by extralegal considerations, in contrast to Feinstein's sticking to Jewish law. The second selection is from Teitelbaum's most famous work, *Vayoel Moshe* (And Moses consented). It is an exhaustive analysis of the three oaths mentioned in the Talmud, which Teitelbaum argues prohibit attempts to immigrate en masse to the Land of Israel and to establish a Jewish state before the coming of the Messiah. Again Teitelbaum's expansive view of Jewish law, which includes biblical commentary and rabbinic narrative as well as — in this case — theology and sacred history, is evident.

His view stands in marked contrast to the Zionist writings presented in the next part of this volume.[121]

Yoel Teitelbaum, *She'elot u-Teshuvot Divrei Yoel* (Brooklyn, NY: Sander Deutsch, 1983), 2:401–4, 407–8, and 416 (translated by Shlomo Zuckier).

EVEN HA-EZER NO. 107

Regarding the question concerning artificial insemination that they have now invented that can place in the womb of a married woman sperm from other men [that is, not her husband] without sexual intercourse, which was permitted as a practical rule (*le-halakhah le-ma'aseh*) in the book *Iggerot Moshe* [of Rabbi Moshe Feinstein][122] ...: When I saw this [responsum], I was bewildered at its sight, and the idea is shocking, may God save us....

A.

What [Feinstein] wrote to compare this case of artificial insemination to the case of Rabbeinu Perez regarding [a woman] sleeping in sheets [on which a man not her husband had slept] and the case of becoming impregnated while in a bathtub is a complete and absolute error, as I will explain clearly below. But ... even according to his errant comparison of our case to that of Rabbeinu Perez [Feinstein's argument is invalid]. Rabbeinu Perez prohibited [entering such a scenario] due to [the issue of] "distinction," while [Feinstein] made the novel claim that when the sperm of a non-Jew [is used] it is not subject to this reason that [the resulting child of unclear paternity] might marry his paternal sister.

But it is clear in b. Yebamot ... 42a regarding the mishnah that [a woman] must wait three months [before remarrying]:

Rabbi Naḥman said Shmuel said, since the verse said "to be God to you and to your offspring to come"[123] — [it teaches us] to distinguish between children of a first and second [husband].

Rashi [*ad loc., s.v. le-zarekha aḥarekha*] explains that "the Divine Presence only

---

120. The education system of the village, which like the village itself was designed to serve the Satmar community, was the subject of a Supreme Court case, *Board of Education of Kiryas Joel Village School District v. Grumet.*

121. For more on Satmar anti-Zionism, see Aviezer Ravitsky, *Messianism, Zionism, and Jewish Religious Radicalism* (Chicago: University of Chicago Press, 1996).

122. [See the previous selection, by Feinstein.]

123. [Gen. 17:7.]

rests on those who are of certain lineage, and we also establish this in b. Nedarim: "'I will remove from you those who rebel and transgress"[124]—these are 'children of mixture' [that is, unclear lineage].'" [Continuing in b. Yebamot 42a]:

Rava asked: On that basis, why must a male and female convert [who were previously married to each other] wait three months [before getting remarried as Jews]? What distinction is there to be made? [An answer:] Here also there is a distinction to be made between one who was conceived in holiness [that is, after his parents' conversion] and one who was conceived not in holiness [that is, before his parents' conversion]. Rava said: It is a rabbinic decree, based on the concerns that [the child in cases of unclear paternity] might [accidentally] marry his paternal sister [which is forbidden]; contract levirate marriage with his [deceased] maternal brother's wife [which is forbidden]; allow his mother to remarry anyone [literally, "to (allow her to) the market"] [when she should have to contract levirate marriage]; or allow his sister-in-law to remarry anyone [when she should have to contract levirate marriage].

And it is explained in Rashi [ad loc. s.v. ve-yiftor et yebamato la-shuk] that there is a total of four concerns [in cases of unclear paternity], and for the case of a male and female convert [who marry] there is concern only for one, that [the child] might contract levirate marriage with his maternal brother's wife, which is one of the four concerning cases, see [Rashi's comment] there.[125]

If so, it is clear that in Rava's opinion, even in a case where there is no concern that he might marry his paternal sister—a case where only one of the four usual concerns apply, it is still prohibited. For he diverged from the words of Rabbi Naḥman in the name of Shmuel [who derives the prohibition of "distinction" from a biblical verse] and offered the novel reason for these rabbinic decrees [of "distinction"] because of the question from the case of the male and female converts, a case in which there is only one concern. If so, how does the fact that in

---

124. [Ezek. 20:38]

125. [The child is erroneously assumed to have been conceived after his parents' conversion, when in fact he was conceived before it. Since he was thus conceived by a non-Jewish father, he does not have a legal relationship to him. In this case, the parents subsequently have another son, who was conceived after their conversion. This second son marries but dies before having children. Because the first son is (erroneously) assumed to have also been conceived after his parents' conversion, he is considered the second son's full brother and thus engages in levirate marriage with his wife. But he is actually only his maternal half-brother and is thus forbidden to marry her.]

the case of sperm from a non-Jew there is no concern that [the child] marry his paternal sister help, since, among the other concerns, two concerns [still] apply even with the sperm of a non-Jew. For even if he has no [legal] relation with [his] non-Jewish [father], he is still not the son of this [Jewish husband of his birth mother], and the concerns relating to levirate marriage . . . would apply.[126] . . .

. . . .

C.

And, concerning the principle of the law of "distinction," two reasons are given in the Talmud, those of Shmuel and Rava. . . .[127]

. . . [I]t is certain that most early authorities and major later authorities[128] hold that the words of Shmuel are the rule. If so, in our case, presuming that the sperm is from a non-Jew accomplishes nothing, because, in any event, we do not know who the father is, and this is the prohibition according to Shmuel. . . .

And one might further say the following: Radbaz[129] in his responsa no. 264 wrote on the topic of "distinction" [as follows:] "The opinion of Maimonides is that it is of biblical authority, as it says 'to be God to you and to your offspring to come.' But the opinion of Tosafot is that [the verse] is a mere 'scriptural support (asmakhta)'" and that the prohibition [related to] "distinction" is of rabbinic authority. . . . In truth, if it is a rabbinic [commandment] the language in the derivation of the sages of blessed memory—"'to be God to you [and to your offspring to come],' [teaching that] that the divine presence only rests on those of certain lineage"—does not really make sense. For if so, then the reason for

126. [That is, since he is not actually the son of the Jewish husband but might be thought to be so, his mother might erroneously be permitted to marry anyone she likes if her husband dies, or the son might erroneously engage in levirate marriage with his maternal half-brother's widow.]

127. [Shmuel claims that the three-month waiting period before remarriage stems from an in-principle interest, based on a scriptural verse, in establishing paternity. In the case of converts, he holds that it stems from distinguishing offspring conceived in holiness from those who were not. In contrast, Rava understands the waiting period, as well as the interest in establishing paternity, as deriving from a rabbinic decree to prevent prohibited marriages by the offspring. In the case of converts, while Rava admits that some of those possibilities do not apply, some of them still do.]

128. [The later authorities (aḥaronim) are leading rabbis and legal decision makers who were active since the mid-sixteenth century; the early authorities (rishonim) were those who preceded them, from about the eleventh century.]

129. [David ben Zimra (active in Spain and Safed; 1480–1574).]

[the commandment] is to facilitate the resting of the divine presence, and for this purpose it says about these children "I will remove from you those who rebel and transgress against Me," but we do not find rabbinic decrees on this sort of matter [that is, the dwelling of the divine presence]. . . .

And it appears that the primary exegesis that the sages of blessed memory derived—that the divine presence does not dwell on those who are of doubtful lineage, namely those "children of mixture"—is a full derivation from the Torah. . . .

. . . .

E.

In *Benei Ahuvah*[130] ["Marriage," chapter 15] . . . [the author] wrote concerning the law [prohibiting a woman] to sleep in the sheets [of a man other than her husband] that we cannot infer from the prohibition of [intercourse] with a menstruating woman (niddah) to the prohibition of adultery. Because in [the former case] we only find the prohibition against sexual intercourse in the Torah and there is no mention of the word "seed," whereas [in the latter case] "a laying for seed" is mentioned,[131] which excludes [and prohibits] seed from another man. I originally thought that he said this based on independent reasoning, but I later saw that this is made clear in several early authorities of blessed memory. This is the language of Naḥmanides . . . on the verse "Do not have carnal relations (*shikhavtkha le-zara*) [literally, "your laying for seed")] with your neighbor's wife":[132] "And it is possible that it says 'for seed' to mention the reason for the prohibition. For [if one were to have this forbidden intercourse] one would not know whose seed it is, and great and evil abominations will result for both [parties]. And it does not mention this [reason] in the description of the punishment [in the Torah], because even if [the male] . . . did not release seed, he will still be guilty [and liable for punishment]. Therefore it says in the context of the woman accused of adultery (sotah): 'A man has had carnal relations (*shikhvat zera*) [literally, "laying for seed"] with her,'[133] because [the husband's] indignation is on account of the seed. . . ." It is thus clear that the principle of the prohibition is the seed that he inserts into her and not the intercourse. Even though [Benei Ahuvah] himself cites the fact that

130. [(Children of the beloved), by Jonathan Eybeschütz (Poland, 1690–1764).]
131. [See Lev. 18:20 and Num. 5:13.]
132. [Lev. 18:20.]
133. [Num. 5:13.]

with mere intercourse without releasing seed [the adulterous couple] is liable for punishment, this is not an objection. Since the overwhelming majority of cases of intercourse lead to the release of seed, scripture did not distinguish [between cases when there is release of seed and when there is not], and it prohibited all cases of intercourse that could lead to release of seed [inside the woman]. . . .

In this manner Ra'ah of blessed memory in [*Sefer ha-*]*Ḥinnukh*,[134] commandment no. 35, on the prohibition "You shall not commit adultery"[135] writes: "Among the roots for this commandment: In order that the world be settled in accordance with God's will, and God, blessed be He, wanted that His entire world create their progeny, each among its own type, and that they not mix one type with another, and similarly he wanted that it be known to whom a person's 'seed of men'[136] belongs, and that they not mix one with the other." . . . And he wrote later that the prohibition against [sexual intercourse with] relatives that the Torah establishes is "entirely undermined by adultery, for people will not recognize their relatives [and will have intercourse with them]." Lastly he wrote, "Aside from the fact that the prohibition of adultery . . . has an aspect of stealing [from the husband], it is also cause for loss of life, because it is well known about human nature that [men] are jealous about their spouses' adultery with others and make attempts on the adulterer's life." The last reason is also a reason for the prohibition of intercourse without insemination. However, it is clear from his words that the primary reason is that people will not know whose offspring it is. . . .

However, in any case, it is certainly clear that the opinion of Naḥmanides and Ra'ah is that one is liable for insertion of seed even without sexual intercourse. For if they thought that there is no prohibition regarding the insertion of seed without intercourse, they would not have written a reason that is extremely laughable. How is it possible to say that the prohibition of intercourse is because of the seed if inserting the seed itself has no prohibition at all? It is clear, then, that their view is that the principle of the prohibition (*ikkar ha-issur*) is due to the seed and not due to the intercourse. If so, even if it was clear from the words of Rabbeinu Perez to permit in this case, it would not be in our power to decide against Naḥmanides and Ra'ah. . . .

134. [The anonymous medieval work *Sefer ha-Ḥinnukh* (Book of [mitzvah] education), is commonly misattributed to the Ra'ah, Aharon ben Yosef of Barcelona (thirteenth century).]

135. [Exod. 20:13.]

136. [1 Sam. 1:11.]

Thus, according to the law, those who bring the seed of another man [that is, the individuals who physically insert the semen] into a married woman violate the prohibitions of sexual promiscuity, which carry with them the punishment of [spiritual] excision (*karet*), may God save us, the woman becomes prohibited to her husband, and the [resulting] child is illegitimate (mamzer).[137] May blessed God have mercy on His people Israel that the matter should be forgotten and no one among Israel should consider this depraved act, to increase impurity, illegitimacy (*mamzerut*), and mixture to such a degree in Israel. . . .

EVEN HA-EZER NO. 108

. . . "No wisdom, no prudence, and no counsel can prevail against the Lord"[138] so as to allow the carrying out of such a debauched act. [Feinstein], who permitted it, predicated his error on [the presumption that the sperm donor was] a gentile, for this is the basis of his permission—to assume that [the child] is the seed of gentiles. . . . [E]ven if there was a way to know for certain that [the child] is of gentile seed and from which gentile he descends, nevertheless, it would doubtlessly be a debauched act and an abomination. . . .

. . . [O]n the verse "There came out among the Israelites one whose mother was Israelite and whose father was Egyptian . . . [The son of the Israelite woman pronounced the Name (of God) in blasphemy.],"[139] Naḥmanides' opinion (*ad loc.*) is that [the Israelites in the desert] had the status of Jews even prior to the giving of the Torah [on Mount Sinai]. Thus, perforce [the verse] writes there that the child, even though he was the son of an Egyptian, was still legitimate to marry in the community. For this accorded with the rule that if a gentile or slave has sexual intercourse with an Israelite woman, the child is legitimate. And he wrote further that although he is legitimate to marry in the community, he is still tainted (*mezuham*) and is not an Israelite in name, see [Naḥmanides' comment] there. And we see that the verse calls him the son of an Egyptian man. Sforno[140] comments on this "and thus he dared to curse (*levarekh*) God, as an Israelite would not be so rebellious." And that was a case of rape, as it is [presented] in [Midrash] Exodus Rabbah [1:28]. . . . But even so, since the child was of Egyptian seed, look and see what he ended up doing [that is, cursing God]!

137. [These are the general consequences of adultery.]
138. [Prov. 21:30.]
139. [Lev. 24:10–11.]
140. [Ovadia ben Ya'akov Sforno (Italy, c. 1475–1550).]

... Rashi writes on the verse "the clan of the Enochites [*ha-ḥanokhi*]"[141]: "Since the nations were ridiculing [the Israelites] by saying, '[Look] how these [Israelites] attribute their lineage to their tribes, as if the Egyptians did not have their way with their mothers! If they controlled the bodies [of the Israelite men], certainly [they controlled] their wives!' Therefore, the verse placed [God's] Name on them, [adding] a *heh* on this side and a *yod* on the other, to say, 'I testify about them that they are the sons of their fathers.'[142] And this was made explicit by David, [when he writes,] 'the tribes of the Lord (*Yod-Heh*)—a testament for Israel'[143]: This name [Yod-Heh] testifies for them about their tribe. . . .'" Note that it does not mention in the claim of the nations that they suspected the Israelite women of intentional promiscuity, heaven forbid, with the Egyptians. . . . Thus, even according to the [nations'] claim, they were forced in the matter (*anusim ba-davar*) and have no guilt. For God forgives one who is coerced.[144] . . . The children are also therefore legitimate, as it is in the rule that if a gentile or a slave has sexual intercourse with an Israelite woman, the child is legitimate. Nevertheless, the ridicule of the nations, that they say the seed of gentiles is mixed into Israel, was massive, . . . until the verse went out of its way to include [the yod and the heh] in the names next to all of the tribes to testify about them and save them from this embarrassment. And in truth by natural means [alone] this would be a very strong a fortiori argument—if [the Egyptians] controlled the [Israelite men's] bodies, they certainly controlled their wives! But there was a miracle of miracles from the Holy One, blessed be He, to save them, to improve their end. Like our sages said (Yalkut Shimoni, Num. 684) that if gentile seed had been mixed among them, they would not have been fit to receive the Torah. [Therefore h]ow could it possibly be considered to allow and to give oneself up willfully and with disdain to receive gentile seed and to mix it with Jewish seed!? . . . [T]he basis of the permission of [Feinstein] who permitted [it], that he presumes the [sperm donor] is a gentile—the presumption on the gentile itself is an abomination, and a horrible and criminal sin. . . .

141. [Num. 26:5.]

142. [In Numbers 26, clan names of the Israelites are listed after the name of their founder, with a slight modification: the letters *yod* and *heh*, which spell one of the names of God, were added to them.]

143. [Ps. 122:4; NJPS, modified.]

144. [See, for example, b. Nedarim 27a.]

Moshe Feinstein, "Even Ha-Ezer II No. 11 (1962): Concerning My Responsa #10 and #71 of Resp. Iggerot Moshe on EH," in *Jewish Law (Mishpat Ivri): Cases and Materials*, edited by Menachem Elon, Bernard Auerbach, Daniel D. Chazin, and Melvin J. Sykes (New York: M. Bender, 1999), 632–33.

EVEN HA-EZER II NO. 11 (1962)

CONCERNING MY RESPONSA #10 AND #71

OF RESP. IGGEROT MOSHE ON EH

... I have received your very lengthy letter exhaustively setting forth your vehement contentions that [my responsa concerning artificial insemination] will cause an impairment of the purity and sanctity of the genealogy of the Jewish people. . . . [I]n truth, there is nothing in what I wrote or decided that will, God forbid, cause any profanation in the purity and sanctity of the Jewish people. What I wrote is true Torah, based on the statements of the rishonim.

Your objections arise out of foreign concepts that influence even great scholars without their being aware of it. The result is that they understand God's commandments in our holy Torah according to those false concepts. Thus, what is prohibited becomes permitted and what is permitted becomes prohibited, and the Torah is interpreted erroneously. . . . I, thank God, am not among them. My entire outlook rests on study of the Torah without any admixture of foreign concepts. Its laws are true, whether restrictive or permissive. Arguments based on foreign concepts and baseless reasoning are of no significance, even if they tend to restrictiveness and purport to lead to greater purity and sanctity.

. . . The basic rule is clear and simple—the laws against illicit sexual unions prohibit actual intercourse, not the introduction of seed for the purpose of procreation. For this reason, for example, the law makes no distinction between fertile women and barren women. Also, sexual intercourse in a manner that will not result in pregnancy is equally prohibited. . . .

Inasmuch as it is sexual intercourse that is proscribed, the prohibition does not apply to artificial insemination where there is no intercourse; [such insemination] is neither incest nor adultery. It follows that a child born from this procedure is not [illegitimate (mamzer)]; that status can result only if there has been sexual intercourse. . . . It is also clear that the woman is not forbidden to her husband, inasmuch as there has been no illicit sexual intercourse. . . .

It is established law that if a child's father is not Jewish, the child's status does not follow the status of the father but rather that of the mother; it is considered that the child has no father at all. Therefore, the argument that the Divine Spirit will not rest on such a child is misplaced. The verse "[to be a God to you] and your offspring to come" signifies that the Divine Spirit rests only on those whose genealogy is certain. And, in our case, the child's genealogy is not doubtful but certain, for it is certain that he is considered to have no father. The verse applies only to the situation where a child's genealogy follows the father, but the identity of the father is unknown. . . .

It is thus manifest that what I have written is correct and accurate, in accordance with the Torah, and satisfies our responsibility to Heaven. The purity and sanctity of the people of Israel remains intact. . . .

Moshe Feinstein

Yoel Teitelbaum, *Vayoel Moshe* [And Moshe consented] (Brooklyn, NY: Jerusalem, 2005), 5–11 (translated by Shaul Magid).

In these past years because of our many sins we have suffered bitterly in ways that Israel has not suffered since it became a nation (*goy*). . . . But with the mercy of God, bless His Name, some of us have survived, albeit few in number. Not a few from a multitude but a few from a few, all because of an oath that the Holy One, blessed be He, made with our ancestors not to annihilate us completely, God forbid.[145] . . .

Whereas previously among Israel, in every generation when a time of travail beset Jacob, we searched for reasons why this happened to us, what sin caused this to come about, to be able to rectify it and return to the Holy One, blessed be He. . . .

Now in our generation we do not even need to seek among the concealed and to search out the sins that brought about this suffering because it is clear from the words of the sages of blessed memory.[146] For they tell us in no uncertain terms, reading it from scripture[147] that because we transgressed the oath not to ascend en masse (*ba-ḥomah*) [literally, "as a wall"][148] [to the land of Israel] and not to "force the end," heaven forbid, [God fulfilled his threat:] "I permit

145. [See Midrash Exodus Rabbah 44:10.]

146. [b. Ketubot 111a.]

147. [Song 2:7: "I adjure you, O maidens of Jerusalem, by gazelles or by hinds of the field: Do not wake or rouse love until it please!"]

148. [The interpretation of *ba-ḥomah* is disputed, however, Teitelbaum argues (section 10) that it means en masse.]

your flesh like [the flesh] of gazelles and hinds of the field." And due to our great many sins, so it was! Heretics (minim) and apostates (apikorsim) acted in many ways to transgress these oaths, to ascend [to the Land of Israel] en masse and to take upon themselves sovereignty (memshalah) and [collective] freedom (ḥerut) before the proper time.[149] This is the meaning of "forcing the end" and most of the hearts of the Children of Israel were drawn by this defiled idea....

... [The Zionists] performed many and terrible deeds for this bitter action, with different ruses and techniques, so as to transgress these oaths. It is clear that every action that was done [by the Zionists] was a transgression of these oaths. We see this in Maimonides' "Epistle to Yemen" regarding one who said of himself that he was a messiah and gathered some people around him. Maimonides warned [his readers] that this is very dangerous and when the authorities discover this it will be the cause of great pains, God forbid. He also warned them against transgressing the oaths, and wrote that the reason for the oaths is that King Solomon knew with divine foresight (ruaḥ ha-kodesh) that the nation will plead to move toward [the land of Israel] before the appointed time and that they will suffer losses because of this and experience suffering.[150] ...

It is explained in b. Shavuot (39[a]): "For all transgressions of the Torah the sinner himself is punished, while in the case of oaths he, his family, and the whole world is punished." ... It is for this reason that this tragedy [the Holocaust] has come upon us,[151] fulfilling what our sages said since [our flesh] was permitted like "gazelles and hinds of the field," God forbid.[152] [And we know that] bad tidings only come through evildoers but begin with the righteous.[153] ...

We do not find in scripture any punishment as evil, bitter, terrible, and threatening like the punishment of "I will permit your flesh—totally ownerless—like gazelles and hinds of the field," except [as punishment] for the sin of transgress-

---

149. [In general when Teitelbaum mentions "heretics and apostates," he refers to Zionists.]

150. [For an English translation of and commentary on the "Epistle to Yemen," see David Hartman and Abraham Halkin, Epistles of Maimonides: Crisis in Leadership (Philadelphia: Jewish Publication Society, 2009).]

151. [The connection between Zionism and the Holocaust was explicitly stated by Teitelbaum in other places. See, for example, Yoel Teitelbaum, "Le-Ma'an Shalom Eretz ha-Kodesh" (For the sake of the peace of the Holy Land), Ha-Me'or 9, no. 8 (Tammuz 1958): 3–9.]

152. [b. Ketubot 111a.]

153. [See b. Baba Kamma 60a.]

ing "forcing the end" and the oath [concerning going up en masse to the land of Israel], as we read in scripture, "I adjure you, O maidens of Jerusalem[, by gazelles or by hinds of the field],"[154] and as the sages interpret [it]. Israel has not suffered like this from the time it has become a people, except in our generation because of our great many sins. . . .

In the Torah portion of Ki Tisa[155] Naḥmanides discusses [the sin of the golden calf] in a number of passages [and claims] that the number [of Israelites] who prostrated [themselves] and sacrificed to the calf was small, but most of the people sinned in thought, and that is why God was enraged to destroy them, heaven forbid. . . . We see from this that [God's] anger over the calf was not because of the few who served the calf in action, with sacrifices and prostrations; but rather, because of the multitude who aided in its creation, whether by gathering with them or by giving their gold, and the like. For they thought this was a good thing, that [the calf] would be a leader and a guide in place of Moses, and [was done] in God's Name. . . .

So too is the bitter calf of creating a polity (melukhah) [literally, "kingdom"] before the coming of the messiah. This defiled idea was [proffered] for many years by the Zionists, who performed aggressive actions in many ways to transgress these oaths [of forcing the end and ascending to the land of Israel en masse]. But because of our great many sins, most of the people of all sects were instruments in helping [to create this polity]. Even those righteous among Israel (mukhsharim be-yisrael), even from among those who greatly fought the Zionists because of their actions to undermine religion (dat), heresy, and blasphemy, heaven forbid, were captured by the essence of their defiled idea, that is, attaining political autonomy and creating a polity before the coming of the messiah, which is a fundamental act of rebellion (poreh ro'sh vele'anah) [literally, "a stock sprouting poison weed and wormwood"].[156] . . .

. . . [T]he essential idea of Israel taking upon itself political autonomy (memshalah) before the coming of the messiah is [an act of] heresy and denial of the ways of God, bless His Name. Since He, bless His Name, is the only one who exiles and who redeems, there is none but Him, bless His Name, our Redeemer in the days of the messiah. An idea of heresy and rebellion, heaven forfend, certainly damages even in thought [and not only in action]. For heresy is a more

154. [Song 2:7.]
155. [Exod. 31–34.]
156. [Deut. 29:17.]

grievous sin than idolatry, as is explained in the Talmud and Maimonides, as is known.[157] How much the more so when many [transgressive] actions were done in Israel, in our great many sins!

Even more so, these sects that continue with this defiled idea to establish a sovereign state (*medinah*) before its proper time [and, in addition, one] not based in Torah, draw Israel to terrible heresy and apostasy the likes of which has never existed since the foundation of the world. For even the nations of the world, idolaters, believe that God, blessed be His Name, is the first cause. But these evil ones [Zionists] deny th[is] principle. At first, they draw the hearts [of the Jewish people] after earthly desires, to be like the [other] nations—a people and a government—like the [other] nations. [The Jewish people] are, then, drawn after them also concerning the principle, the idea that there is "no judge or justice," God forbid, but rather everything is dependent on human power and weaponry.[158] . . . Literally many millions of Israel have fallen into the trap of this heresy, heaven forbid, because of [the Zionists] and because sects joined [the Zionists] that said that they did so to rectify [Zionism] and to bring the way of Torah to the heretics. . . .

It is clear that this same despicable idea actually prevents redemption and the salvation of our souls. . . .

I see that the root of the error that has spread in this world [is caused by a few conditions]: The first condition is that they have not fully understood this rule (halakhah) of the three oaths.[159] That is, how [a complete transgression of the law results from the transgression of] the awesome prohibition of creating a polity (memshalah) before its proper time. They, therefore, did not resist their temptation to become "like all the other nations"—a people and polity against the law (dat).[160] They also found excuses to join [the Zionists] even though they are heretics and blasphemers (*kofrim*), tempters and inciters. . . .

The principle of the foundation of the prohibition of the three oaths is not

157. [See b. Shabbat 117a, b. Avodah Zarah 26a, and Maimonides, *Mishneh Torah*, "Laws of the Foundations of the Torah" 8, "Laws of Witnesses" 11:10, and *Guide for the Perplexed* 1:36.]

158. [This is the classic expression of Jewish heresy in rabbinic literature.]

159. ["They" seems to refer to the Torah-observant community that has colluded with the Zionists.]

160. [The notion of being like the other nations is a major precept of Zionism. Teitelbaum uses it here to point how it is almost always used as a negative in Torah. See, for example, Deut. 17:14.]

explained in detail among decisors (poskim) like other rules that are applicable at all times and in every generation. . . .

. . . [M]any hundreds of years have passed during which it never occurred to anyone to transgress these oaths, and they did not think about them at all. In any event, it was not possible [to transgress the oaths], and so the decisors in all those generations saw no need to explain [the prohibition of transgressing them] in their time, and thus it is not explained in depth in the [works of] the decisors. However, all those who pay attention to the early authorities and the great ones among the later authorities who did indeed deal with [the oaths] will find clear statements, which are unmistakable.

It is clear and there is no argument that these oaths are established law (ha-lakhot kavu'ot), about which no one disputes. For at the end of b. Ketubot, Rabbi Yehudah, who introduces the rule that even an individual is prohibited to ascend [to the Land of Israel], derives it from the oaths. Rabbi Zeira [does] dispute Rabbi Yehudah on this rule [concerning the individual], [yet the sages] of the Talmud try to explain the oaths according to his opinion [as well]. Consequently, one cannot say that there is any dispute regarding the [status] of these oaths [themselves]. Rather, everyone admits that they are important rules (hilkhata rabata), [the violation of which incurs] a harsh and bitter punishment, God preserve us.

IV | Jewish Law and the State of Israel

The nine thinkers included in part 4 all grapple with the question of what role Jewish law could or should have within a modern Jewish state. With the exception of Yeshayahu Leibowitz, who insists on absolute separation between Jewish law and the laws of the state, all of the thinkers included in this part contend that Jewish law ought to be, in one form or another, the law that governs the Jewish state.

Nevertheless, despite this general agreement (again, with the exception of Leibowitz), a number of daunting theological, political, and philosophical problems immediately arise when considering how Jewish law could become the law of a modern nation-state. How can a legal system developed in exile apply to a sovereign state? What relationship, if any, is there between the establishment of the State of Israel and the messianic era, which has traditionally been understood as the end of Jewish exile? Is it possible to reconcile Jewish law with a modern, internationally recognized, democratic state in which women and, indeed, all citizens regardless of religion are entitled to equal rights and treatment? What about the commandments in Exodus and Deuteronomy about not allowing non-Jews to dwell in the Land of Israel? How can Jewish law apply to nonreligious Jews who do not accept its authority? And can Jewish law be adapted to new economic conditions that may demand new solutions to old problems, such as the commandments in Exodus and Leviticus to neither grow nor harvest anything in the Land of Israel during the sabbatical year?

In attempting to answer some of these questions, the thinkers included in part 4 offer different accounts of what Jewish law is. Abraham Isaac Kook, Shlomo Goren, and Isaac Halevi Herzog, all of whom served as chief Ashkenazic rabbis of either Mandatory Palestine or the State of Israel, argue that Jewish law is able to accommodate the full participation of non-Jews and nonobservant Jews. Nonetheless, despite this position, Kook maintains that Jewish law cannot endorse a woman's right to vote or hold public office. In contrast, Ben-Zion Meir Hai Uziel, who served as Israel's chief Sephardic rabbi from 1938 until his death in 1953, and the Jewish philosopher and theologian Eliezer Berkovits find no conflict between Jewish law and the modern quest for social justice in the Jewish state. From an internal, Jewish perspective, Ovadiah Yosef, who served as Israel's chief Sephardic rabbi from 1973 to 1983, argues for the legitimacy and relevance of the Sephardic legal tradition in modern Israeli life. Finally, some of the thinkers included here, such as Eliezer Waldenberg, reflect on the relationship between Jewish law and the laws of the state in ideal terms, while others, such as Shaul Yisraeli, take a far more realist position and consider the relationship in terms of coalition politics.

| # Selections from the Writings
of Abraham Isaac Kook

Abraham Isaac Kook (1865–1935) — also known as Ra'ayah (for Rabbi Avraham Yitzchak HaCohen), or Ha-Rav — was born in Latvia and studied at the Etz Ḥayyim Yeshiva in Volozhin.[1] In 1904 he immigrated to Palestine, and in 1924 the British appointed him chief rabbi of Mandatory Palestine, a position he held until his death, after the establishment of the State of Israel. Often considered the father of religious Zionism, Kook sought to reconcile secular Zionism's goal of working and settling on the land with traditional Judaism's messianic hope and focus on observing the commandments. In keeping with his attempt to balance both innovation and traditionalism, Kook's legal arguments appear flexible at times and inflexible at other times. His flexibility is apparent in the first text included here, from *Shabbat ha-Aretz* (The land's sabbath). Kook establishes the basis for his argument that it is permissible to nominally sell land in Israel to a non-Jew during the sabbatical year, so that the land can be planted and harvested. He then argues that such a sale to a non-Jew does not violate the prohibition of allowing non-Jews to dwell in the Land of Israel (described in part 3 by Avraham Yeshayahu Karelitz). In the second text, from *Li-Nevukhei ha-Dor* (For the perplexed of the generation), Kook reflects explicitly on the relationship between faith in Torah and religious reform. He explains that the Sanhedrin has the authority to determine Jewish law according to what is necessary at a given time. However, this interpretive freedom, which reformers argue is permitted to everyone at any time, is not suited for the period of exile, which needs the stabilizing force of the unsurpassable authority of the Talmud. When the nation is redeemed, in contrast, the Sanhedrin's full authority will be restored. Finally, the third text is a letter in which Kook rejects the claim that women should be allowed to vote or be elected to public office. Among his arguments are that the claims for women's right to vote and serve in public office reflect non-Jewish values and that the acceptance of such values undermines not only specific articles of Jewish law but also the integrity of the Jewish nation as a whole.

---

1. See the selection in part 2 by Ḥayyim of Volozhin.

Abraham Isaac Kook, *Shabbat ha-Aretz* [The land's sabbath] (Jerusalem, 1909), xii–1b, 26b–27a, 31a–33a, and 35a–39a (translated by Julian [Yedidya] Sinclair).

NOTICE OF INTENT

All the matters that I set out in this "Introduction" to recommend concerning our brothers dwelling in our Holy Land, may it be built and established, who rely on the leniency (*heter*) that has been practiced in recent sabbatical years (*shime-tot*),[2] according to the teaching of scholars who saw fit to teach it as a practical rule and temporary ruling (*le-horot bo halakhah le-ma'aseh le-hora'at sha'ah*), are intended to show that there is no comparison whatsoever between these workers —who act according to an established ruling—and those who simply break the statute (*ḥok*) of our Holy Torah, God forbid. They are also meant to strengthen our brethren who are scattered in the diaspora and yearn to come and to take their place in this precious Land [of Israel] if they could only see a way to make a living here by the labor of their hands.[3] They are afraid of the interruption to their work in the sabbatical year when God's full blessing remains concealed until the time of our redemption, may it come speedily in our days. In particular, there are those who wish to invest large sums to establish orchards, vineyards, fields, and gardens but are very concerned that the cessation of trade during the sabbatical year could impede their ability to plan properly for the other years. Therefore, both groups are withdrawing their efforts from the Holy Land and investing in foreign countries; the holy delight to settle the Holy Land and develop it has left them. So I felt obliged to clarify the nature of the leniency that people customarily follow that works by temporarily suspending (*hafka'ah*) [the ownership and thus the holiness of the land] when necessary. One may thus know that if the necessity of settling the Holy Land requires him to avail himself of this leniency, it is sound and grounded on reliable foundations. . . .

2. [This refers to the leniency granted to selling the land to non-Jews for the duration of the sabbatical year, the justification of which is the subject of this text. This leniency was invoked as an expedient to permit struggling Jewish farmers to continue working during the sabbatical years of 1888–89, 1895–96, and 1902–3. However, it became increasingly controversial and was attacked as a legal fiction. In this work, Kook endeavors to place the leniency on firm foundations.]

3. [This text was written on the eve of the 1909–10 sabbatical year, in the midst of a wave of Jewish immigration to Ottoman-ruled Palestine that began in 1904 and ended with the outbreak of World War I in 1914.]

1. The meaning of the passage in the Talmud, that the rule is decided like Rabbi[4] that the sabbatical year at this time is of rabbinic authority.

The plain meaning of the passage in b. Mo'ed Katan (2b) teaches that there is no dispute regarding the following statement of Rabbi: "Scripture speaks of two kinds of release (shimetah): release of land[5] and release of loans.[6] In a period when land is released (mishameit kark'ah), so too loans are released (mishameit kesafim). In a period when land is not released, neither are loans released."[7] [Rabbi's] intention in saying, "neither are loans released" is that [all] the laws of the sabbatical year, which include the remission of loans, are now not in effect....

... We find ... that the rule is decided according to Rabbi: The sabbatical year, [including the remission of loans] as well as agricultural work, in our times is only of rabbinic authority....

This is also the opinion of Tosafot.[8] ...

....

11. The foundation for the leniency to sell the Land [of Israel]: whether the acquisition of a non-Jew suspends [the obligation of the sabbatical year on that land] or not; the dispute between *Bet Yosef*[9] and Mabit[10] over the holiness of the sabbatical year [of land in Israel that is owned] by non-Jews (nokrim).

The foundation for the leniency of selling [land in Israel] is fundamentally,

4. [Rabbi Yehudah the Prince (ha-Nasi) (Eretz Israel, 135–c. 217), also referred to as simply Rabbi and Rabbeinu (ha-Kadosh)]

5. [See Lev. 25.]

6. [See Deut. 15:1–10.]

7. [Rabbi infers from Deut. 15:2 that the two major areas of the sabbatical year, the sabbatical for agriculture and that for debt relief, are interdependent in their application. See Rashi, *ad. loc. s.v. be-zman.*]

8. [Gittin 36a *s.v. mi ikah.* Tosafot are medieval commentaries on the Talmud, composed from the twelfth to the mid-fifteenth centuries by numerous rabbis known as the Tosafists. The commentaries were additions (*tosafot*, in Hebrew) to the commentary of Rashi (Shlomo Yitzhaki, France, 1040–1105.]

9. [(House of Joseph), commentary by Yosef Karo on the *Arba'ah Turim*, by Ya'akov ben Asher (1270–c. 1340).]

10. [Moses ben Yosef di Trani (Safed, 1505–85). Though his arguments are not presented in this excerpt, he—in contrast to Karo—holds that laws of the sabbatical year apply even to land owned by non-Jews.]

according to most of the earlier and later authorities,[11] that the sabbatical year in our time is of rabbinic authority. This is the basis for Rashi's[12] statement (b. Sanhedrin 26a, *s.v. agiston*) that [a Jew] may plow and do all sorts of agricultural work [during the sabbatical year] on the land of a non-Jew. This is also the opinion of Rabbeinu Ḥananel[13] in his commentary (*ad loc.*) . . .; it is also the opinion of Tosafot and *Arukh*,[14] and those [rabbinic] decisors (poskim) who believe that the sabbatical year in our times is of rabbinic authority. . . .

But if the holiness of the sabbatical year *in general* is a rabbinic commandment, then the foundation of the [Land's] holiness is of rabbinic authority, and holiness by rabbinic authority is suspended when the land is purchased by a non-Jew. . . .

. . . .

12. The prohibition of "Give them no quarter (tiḥanem) . . . [ellipsis in original]"[15] in selling land to a non-Jew.

Regarding the issue of "Give them no quarter . . . [ellipsis in original],"[16] that it is prohibited to sell land to a non-Jew in the Land of Israel, one of the rabbinical court, the great Rabbi Z. Schakh[17] . . . correctly commented, that one might say that in the case of a non-Jew who would anyway have a dwelling place (ḥaneyah) in Israel [even without one's selling him more land], the addition—what one is adding [to his holding] now [through the sale]—is not prohibited by the Torah. According to this view, it is therefore preferable to choose [to sell to] a non-Jew who already owns land in the Land of Israel. Even though one could say that if a Jew were to buy his original piece of land, then the non-Jew's foothold in Israel would be removed, and the land that one would currently sell him would restore it to him; nevertheless, one could answer that we follow the current situation. Right now, [the sale of land] does not give [the non-Jew] a foothold in the Land

11. [The early authorities (rishonim) were leading rabbis and legal decision makers who were active from about the eleventh to the mid-sixteenth century; the later authorities (aharonim) were those who followed them.]

12. [Shlomo Yitzḥaki (France, 1040–1105).]

13. [Ḥananel b. Ḥushiel (North Africa, eleventh century).]

14. [A Talmudic dictionary complied by Nathan ben Yehiel (1035–1106).]

15. [Deut. 7:2.]

16. [b. Avodah Zarah 20a derives a prohibition to sell land in the Land of Israel to non-Jews from this verse. On this issue, see also the selection in part 3 by Avraham Yeshayahu Karelitz.]

17. [Zalman Schakh (d. 1929), a judge on the Jaffa rabbinical court that Kook headed.]

because he already has one; he is connected to the Land of Israel without [the current sale] through his original land holding. . . .

. . . In the end, there is no suspicion of a prohibition in the essential [act] and we may say that increasing the quantity [of land in the non-Jew's hands] is, according to all opinions, only prohibited by rabbinic authority. If this is indeed so, then when we need to act thus in order to rectify (le-taken) the settlement of the Land of Israel, it is like the category of telling a non-Jew to do work on Shabbat, which the rabbis did not decree [to be prohibited concerning actions that are biblically permitted and only rabbinically prohibited]. . . .

In general, we may say that in the case of a biblical prohibition even though the purpose of selling the land is to suspend the [sabbatical] restrictions against working the land and the land will not ultimately remain in the non-Jew's hand, still, we do not make fine distinctions to get around a decree of the Torah because the act of selling is itself also forbidden. However, the rabbinic prohibition was instituted only [for cases] where the principle of the prohibition is actually relevant, that is, when it is a real sale and the land is to remain owned by the non-Jew. But when the sale is to suspend the prohibitions [against agricultural work], the rabbis did not legislate any objection at all. What is more, when the purpose is to allow the settlement of Israel in the Land of Israel, it is certain that the [rabbinic] decree does not apply. . . .

It seems then, that since the prohibition "'Give them no quarter,' a foothold in the land," applies only to the Land of Israel, then according to the opinion that the holiness of the Land [of Israel] related to the obligation to observe the [agricultural] commandments dependent on the Land [of Israel] is canceled (batlah) in this time, it would follow that this is also the case with respect to the issue of [giving non-Jews] a foothold in the land. Consequently, [this latter commandment] would only be of rabbinic authority.

However, Maimonides'[18] view seems to imply that this is not the case. He writes ([Mishneh Torah,] "Laws of Idolatry," 10:6), "It is forbidden to allow idolaters [to dwell] among us, and they must not pass through our land, until they accept upon themselves the seven commandments which were commanded to Noahides,[19] as it says 'They shall not remain in your land,'[20] even temporarily. If they accept the seven [Noahide] commandments, then they have the status of a

18. [Moses ben Maimon, known as Rambam (Morocco, Egypt; 1135 or 1138–1204).]

19. [According to the Talmud, there are seven "Noahide commandments" that apply to all "descendants of Noah"—that is, all human beings. Six are negative (not to deny

resident foreigner (*ger toshav*). However, we only accept resident foreigners in an era when the Jubilee is practiced, but when the Jubilee is not [practiced], we only accept righteous converts (*gerei tzedek*)."[21] . . .

Maimonides' view requires further discussion. . . . One may say that on rabbinic authority it is still forbidden [to allow resident foreigners to remain in the Land of Israel]. Concerning this, Maimonides wrote that in a time when the Jubilee is not practiced, one may not accept foreign residents—that is, on rabbinic authority. This is also Maimonides' position in [*Mishneh Torah,*] "Laws of the Temple" (6:15–16). . . .

. . . .

14. The changed situation between the earlier and later generations as regards the leniency to sell the land.

Whereas today we rely on the leniency of selling the land during the sabbatical year, which has never been found [to have been used previously] and it does not seem that the earliest sages (*kadmonim*) of blessed memory relied on it during the Second Temple period, or in the era of the sages of the Jerusalem Talmud, or in the settlement in Israel that persisted afterward during the days of the early authorities; this is not surprising, and there are three reasons for it.

First, since in former times the custom was to forbid even [the use of] produce grown by non-Jews during the sabbatical year because of the decree that one might come to eat from the majority of lands that were owned by Jews (see *Kuntrus Aḥaron* 84:2).[22] It was therefore not possible to act in this way. Today, on the other hand, there is no such obstacle, because only a minority of a minority of the lands in Israel are owned by Jews. The necessity of the situation compels us to follow the leniency of selling the land, once there are grounds to rely on it.

Second, in those days, the sabbatical year was then fixed and fell at its proper time; there was no doubt then about the correct count of the years with respect to the sabbatical year. Today, however there is doubt about when the sabbatical year occurs, which was a point of contention between Maimonides and the

---

God, blaspheme God, commit murder, engage in illicit sexual relations, steal, or eat from a living animal), and one is positive (to establish courts to uphold the rule of law).]

20. [Exod. 23:33.]

21. [That is, full converts to Judaism.]

22. [*Kuntrus Aḥaron* is a collection of detailed notes appended to the end of *Shabbat ha-Aretz*].

Geonim.[23] One may join this doubt together with the previous reason. . . . Since the sabbatical year in our time is of rabbinic authority, [we deploy the principle that] where there is a doubt over a rabbinic commandment, we may be lenient. . . .

[Third,] apart from all this, the basic reason for the change in custom is that in the earlier generations, when the need was not so great, [the sages] did not involve themselves much with leniencies through legal fictions (*ha'aramah*). Afterward, in later generations, when the need increased, they began to permit [use of the land in Israel during the sabbatical year] through this [leniency] and to propound it publicly. . . . [I]f there was no great necessity, the sages did not want to publicize a leniency based on a legal fiction. This falls under the rubric: "It is the glory of God to conceal a matter."[24] . . . [W]hen necessity requires us to act, due to distress, according to [such leniencies] then obviously it is a commandment to teach [such leniencies], to remove stumbling blocks from before those who are prone to stumble and to relieve the great distress of that particular time. . . . In former times when the [economic] status of Jewish settlement in Israel was based on working the land to subsist, it was possible to observe the sabbatical year according to the law (*ki-dat*) without the leniency of [selling the land] to suspend [its sabbatical holiness], for, in any case, produce was rendered ownerless in the sabbatical year and the poor benefited, and it was close to the intention of the Torah: "[In the seventh year you shall let it rest and lie fallow.] Let the needy among your people eat of it."[25] Consequently, they did not publicize the leniency to suspend [the land's holiness] through sale [to a non-Jew]. However, in our times, when the settlement [of the Land of Israel] is based on trade of its agricultural produce, and preventing the flow of trade will also destroy its livelihood and economic viability in the future, there is a clear obligation to follow the leniency of suspending [the land's holiness] through sale, with the sages' agreement each year, until God has mercy on his people and his land, and brings back the good times so that it will be possible from an economic point of view as well to observe the holiness of the sabbatical year in the fullness of its laws, without any suspension.

23. [See Maimonides, *Mishneh Torah*, "Laws of the Sabbatical Year and Jubilee," 10:2–6. The Geonim were the heads of the rabbinical academies in Babylonia from end of the sixth to the middle of the eleventh centuries CE. They are thus the rabbinic authorites who followed the sages of the Mishnah and Talmud but who preceded the rishonim.]

24. [Prov. 25:2.]

25. [Exod. 23:11.]

15. The holiness of the Land of Israel and the holiness of the commandments.

... There is no level higher than the study of subjects of the Torah that have no connection to practice; it is higher than everything. That said, the capacity of the study of Torah to lead to practice is a part of its greatness. The same is true of the holiness of the Land of Israel. Even though its holiness, despite its state of devastation, still enables us to fulfill certain commandments that we cannot perform outside of Israel ... ; nevertheless, this is not the principle of its exalted status. One cannot say that the value of its holiness or the preciousness of the commandment to settle it would be diminished, if the obligation of certain commandments were canceled or, due to some external constraint that prevents us from fulfilling certain commandments, we were forced to find a way to exempt ourselves from our obligation to perform them. It is not so! Even if out of duress, one of the commandments that are dependent on the Land [of Israel] had to be suspended, this would not, heaven forbid, break the spirit of those who are privileged to dwell ... in this precious Land, "on which the Lord your God always keeps His eye, from year's beginning to year's end";[26] "How lovely is Your dwelling-place, O Lord of hosts. I long, I yearn for the courts of the Lord; my body and soul shout for joy to the living God."[27] The very act of living in the Land of Israel is equal in weight to all of the commandments in the Torah, within which the commandments that depend on the Land are included. ... The heart, spirit, and soul of every single member of Israel should yearn and desire to come and take hold of this precious Land, the eternal home for the life of God's people. ...

[Living in the Land] is, in itself, even in its details, considered to be equal to all of the commandments of the Torah, and it is not a mere enabling condition for the fulfillment of commandments. ...

If it is true of every individual that he is certainly obligated to try with all his strength and might to bring his obligation of love of the Land from potentiality to actuality and to come and take his share in it and not to settle permanently in the lands of the nations—where "there is no Torah among the nations,"[28] "he is like one who has no God,"[29] and "Israel outside the Land of Israel inadvertently worship idols"[30]—then how many more, innumerable times over is this true of this great commandment as it applies to the collective! ... Moreover, the con-

26. [Deut. 11:12.]
27. [Ps.84:2–3.]
28. [Sifre, Ekev.]
29. [b. Ketubot 110b.]
30. [Ibid.]

tinuation of Israel's coming to the Land of Israel is the fundamental cause of all salvations and holy things, which will in any case lead, through the complete salvation of Israel, to the fulfillment of all the commandments in the Torah and the commandments that are dependent on the Land [of Israel] in particular, on a very holy level, to which nothing comparable can be imagined amid the impurity of the lands of the gentiles. . . .

Abraham Isaac Kook, *Li-Nevukhei ha-Dor: Ha-Mekhuneh Moreh Nevukhim he-Ḥadash* [For the perplexed of the generation: Called the new guide of the perplexed] edited by Shaḥar Raḥmani (Tel Aviv: Yedi'ot Aḥaronot, 2014), (translated by Aryeh Sklar).

. . . There is no doubt in the world that the foundation of holding together the Oral Torah with the Written Torah is so that the Torah can be expounded in the rabbinical court (*bet din*) of every generation. Rulings, even though they are accepted [from tradition] in their principles, have many fine and innumerable details. . . . The perfect faith is [the belief] that any rabbinical court that arises among Israel and interprets the Torah according to the general consensus, concerning any matter of doubt, is itself the foundation of the Torah. However, the rabbinical court needs to be in "the place that God will choose."[31] . . .

The sealing of the Talmud was a preparation for the needs of the exile and was very necessary, taking the place of the living center that was nullified due to our sins. Therefore, one who wants to destroy the centrality of the Talmud by denigrating the laws that are practiced on its authority in the nation, because, according to his personal vision, he feels that [this practice] is burdensome and unnecessary, damages the soul of the nation and its center, and, on his part, severs the chain of the great mission of our Torah.

However, do not doubt for a moment that when we merit the true Oral Torah, for example the great rabbinical court in the Chamber of Hewn Stone [in the Jerusalem Temple], in "the place that God will choose," with fortified and secure national authority, [its members] will [then] no longer be subservient to the sealing of the Talmud [but] will interpret the Torah and decide as they see fit. . . .

. . . [W]hen we possess national strength . . . the living Oral Torah, which will return to its strength, certainly will have directly involvement with the Written Torah. Scripture, which writes, "You must not deviate from the verdict that they announce to you either to the right or to the left. Should a man act

31. [Deut. 12:14.]

presumptuously and disregard the priest ... [that man shall die]"[32] and "the magistrate in charge at the time,"[33] will be fulfilled in its fullest sense. The people will then no longer be able to complain that it suffers from enactments that are not appropriate to its time and from teachings that are not relevant to the generation. For only the judges of that generation will be the leaders of the Torah, and [only] to them [will the people] be obligated to listen.

But one who wants to "force the end"[34] by acting according to interpretations that we are only obligated and able to uphold when we are in "our life's home" while [we are] still in our dispersion and weakness, and thus breaches the boundary of the lofty national center—the Talmud and its sealing—for momentary pleasure and the aesthetic demands of the times, he exchanges the everlasting world for a passing world in the context of the nation and brings catastrophe to the world. . . .

There is nothing that limits the authority of the great rabbinical court to act and to enact for the sake of Heaven, according to all the needs of the generation, in all the details of the commandments. Aside from whatever results from [the sages being permitted to allow] passive abstention (*shav ve-al ta'aseh*) [from a commandment], it is the law (*dina*) that the sages [also] possess the authority to uproot something from the Torah (*le-akor davar min ha-Torah*), obviously when there is a need and a necessary collective goal, even through [urging] a positive action (*kum va'aseh*). Even though the conclusion of the Talmud (b. Yebamot 90a) is that [the sages] do not have the authority to uproot something from the Torah; nevertheless, the Great Sanhedrin in the Chamber of Hewn Stone, when it [was] on its foundation, will not be subservient to this detail. For Rabbi Hisda[35] and some other Talmudic sages (*amoraim*) hold that a rabbinical court does [indeed] have the authority to uproot something from the Torah, even through [urging] a positive action.[36] And if the great rabbinical court were to decide [this debate] according to them, then [the sages] would certainly have permission [to uproot something from the Torah]. For there is no reason that they should be subservient to the decisions of the post-Talmudic decisors. There were also early

32. [Deut. 17:11–12.]

33. [Deut. 17:9.]

34. [By "forcing the end," Kook means attempting to bring about the messianic age before its time, which is forbidden by the three oaths mentioned in b. Ketubot 111a. On "the three oaths," see the selection in part 3 by Yoel Teitelbaum.]

35. [Rabbi Hisda (Babylonia, c. 217–309 CE).]

36. [b. Yebamot 89b.]

authorities of blessed memory who decided according to [the view of] Rabbi Hisda.[37] Tosafot has already written that when there is a need and a proper reason, [the sages] have the authority to uproot something from the Torah, even through [urging] a positive action,[38] specifically if [the sages] can arrive at it through expounding scripture. . . . Any [ruling] for which evidence is brought from scripture by means of interpretation and from the agreement of the great rabbinical court involves no uprooting from the Torah at all. . . .

Obviously, just as the great rabbinical court will have the authority to be lenient at times regarding things which are [currently] treated strictly when they have found sufficient reason and evidence from the Torah for it, so too will it certainly be allowed and obligated to be strict at times when the circumstances require it, [that is,] to erect a fence around the Torah to strengthen and bolster it. Thus, whenever the nation is fastidious in keeping the commandments, the rabbinical court will then be able to be more lenient at times regarding some safeguards and fences. Contrariwise, whenever there is immorality and weakening of religious feeling prevalent in the nation, it will then be obligated to be stricter and make safeguards for the Torah.

Therefore, one of the preconditions for the improvement of the life of our people in the future is that we should be accustomed in general to go in an upright path and to observe the ways of the Torah and its commandments. There is then hope that when we merit national life in all of its details, among them also a living center for the Oral Torah, that all [those of] right reason will agree how it is appropriate to recognize and observe everything that comes from [this center] with all strength and might. . . . Our ethical training in observing the Torah and the commandments according to the accepted center in the exile—the center of the Talmud and of the decisors who build on it—will then be useful, for [because of it] the great rabbinical court will be able to establish more of the national life without the pressure of fences and decrees. However, should immorality be more prevalent and religious feeling, which is the life of the nation, weaker, then it will be forced to lay on fences and stringencies. Obviously, [these measures] will shorten the stride of the nation in its development. But it will be necessary. For ethical status and full religious feeling is the foundation of the life of the nation and its blossoming. Therefore, any hearty person, who truly loves his nation and who wholeheartedly desires its advancement, will lovingly raise

37. [*Tosafot*, b. Yebamot 110a *s.v. lefikakh, Tosafot* b. Ketubot 11a, *s.v. matvilin.*]
38. [b. Nazir 43b, *s.v. ve-hai met mitzvah.*]

up his shoulder to bear the yoke of Torah and its commandments, along with every stringency among them, according to the way that it was always practiced in Israel and according to the center of the Talmud, which stands for us in place of the great rabbinical court until that happy time when our judges will be returned to us as [it was] originally. Then, from Zion will Torah and light come forth to all of Israel, even to all of humanity. . . .

Therefore, we should love as well all the ways that prepare us and aid us to maintain our national life in our exile and dispersion, and that unify us and exhibit us as a living nation, so that we may be fit to receive the seal of perfect nationality when our turn comes to live true national life. This will come to us through preserving, with honor and love, the spiritual center of the people, [that is,] conducting our life according to the Talmud, which has already impressed its seal on the nation for two thousand years. . . .

The accepted principle in the Talmud that a rabbinical court cannot nullify a fellow rabbinical court's ruling unless it is greater than it in wisdom and number[39] cannot possibly be an obstacle for the perfect great rabbinical court to judge matters accepted in the Talmud, to decide on them just as we judge any matter accepted by the decisors according to reason and from the Talmud. [This can be understood] from many angles:

First, in general did not the sealing of the Talmud come from the acceptance of the entire nation of the Talmud as statute book, so as to judge according to it for all ways of the Torah? This acceptance, however, was because of exile and dispersion. If so, it is *ipso facto* understood that when a full and secure national revival comes to us, we will not [continue to] abandon the root of the Oral Torah, which the Torah said explicitly, from "the place that God will choose," [that is,] a living center, for a seal that was only due to the necessity of the exile. Certainly, the entire nation only accepted [the Talmud] on itself until the time that our national powers fully return to us. Furthermore, that [principle] was only about matters under the rubric of enactments and decrees [of the rabbinical court]. But [concerning rulings] that derive from reason and exegesis, the underlying law (omek ha-din) is that you only have the judge in your days [to rely on]: "Jephthah in his generation like Samuel in his generation."[40] . . . [W]hen the settlement of [the people of] Israel will burst forth and flower in the land of the forefathers, our previous strengths will return, with more intensity and might,

39. [b. Gittin 36b.]
40. [b. Rosh Hashanah 25b.]

and God will save us from those who rise up against us. For even the talent for prophecy, which our nation possessed in the past, will return to us. And it will no longer be said of our children that they are a rabbinical court that is smaller in wisdom and number in comparison to the earlier authorities, but rather that [they will] "be exalted and rise to great heights."[41] . . .

I know, though, that this lofty idea can be a hazard to the simple-minded who want to "force the end" and who chase after the distant future when it is not its proper time. They are the "damaging foxes,"[42] for even though their feelings are lofty and high, their spirit is not the calm spirit that is appropriate for any upright individual who knows what is in front of him. . . .

. . . [N]ow that [our] generation has come to the realization . . . that we are not at all separated from the rest of humanity on the face of the earth in what concerns the good of human life, a radical extremism has also come to a conclusion that must be completely denied: that even our relationship to faith and religion should be the same as the relationship of all the peoples to their religion. In truth, in this [relationship], we are separated.

It is completely impossible for all other religions in the world to be essentially national. Some of them are entirely cosmopolitan, and they have no relationship at all to the formation of their nation. Those that are national, cannot be essentially national, that is, that all of their religious matters would be necessary conditions for the nation—to preserve it—since never has there been a[nother] religion that has come to establish a nation from the start of its creation to its development. For such a thing could only happen with divine power: "Or has any god ventured to go and take for himself one nation from the midst of another [ellipsis in original] . . . [as the Lord your God did for you in Egypt before your very eyes]?"[43] Therefore, when the power of nationalism strengthens among the peoples, religious feeling in the cosmopolitan religions weakens, because [such religions] are not really needed for the national unit, and natural ethics can already maintain itself among any cultured people with the help of the sciences and rational morality. Nationalist religions also are not really needed anymore to preserve their nation, since the nationalist feeling has already come to take what had been their place. For even the nationalism of all [other] religions is only contingent nationalism.

41. [Isaiah 52:13.]
42. [Song 2:15.]
43. [Deut. 4:34.]

However, [in] our religion . . . only as result of the Torah and the tradition have we received our invigorated national strengths. . . . And the religious spirit has worked on us to such an extent that our whole life and all our ways are distinguished through religious marks, which maintain us as one unit. We possess nothing else in the world that has so much binding power, to bind all the scattered of our people into one organic body, except the religious unity that is constantly practiced in life. And we have nothing that disperses the strength of our people to the wind and shatters it to pieces like the nullification of that religious unity. . . .

Therefore, besides all the great value of the splendor and glory of the divine holiness that is in our holy Torah, which is the light of the world and life for those who hold fast to it, it is incumbent on us to recognize religious observance as primary among the instruments of nationality. And among all of the national instruments that we must be concerned about how to acquire and develop, it is proper that the top priority should be the inquiry into how to make all of our people disciplined to follow in the way of the Torah and to live according to faith and religion in all of its ways.

Abraham Isaac Kook, "On the Election of Women," translated by Zvi Zohar, in *Edah* 1, no. 2 (2001): 3–4.

AN OPEN LETTER!

. . . It seems to me that the issue can be analyzed under three headings:

(a) Regarding the law (din), whether the matter is permitted or forbidden

(b) Regarding the general good, whether good for Israel will result from an affirmative answer or from a negative one

(c) Regarding the ideal, whether our moral consciousness opposes the prospect or supports it . . .

Regarding the law, I have nothing to add to the words of the rabbis who came before me. In the Torah, in the Prophets, and in the Writings, in the [law (ha-lakhah)] and in the [narrative (aggadah)], we hear a single voice: that the duty of fixed public service falls upon men, for "It is a man's manner to dominate and not a woman's manner to dominate" ([b.] Yebamot 65b), and that roles of office, of judgment, and of testimony are not for her, for "all her honor is within" (Ps. 45:14). Striving to prevent the mixing of sexes in gatherings is a theme that runs through the entire Torah. Thus, any innovation in public leadership that necessarily brings about mixing of the sexes in a multitude, in the same group and gathering, in the routine course of the people's life, is certainly against the law.

Next to be discussed is the aspect of the general good. . . .

. . . [O]ur holy duty is to see to it that the inception of our movement towards a measure of [autonomy based on] our own political-social character be properly marked by the sign of biblical integrity and purity with which our life has been imbued from time immemorial. This will be so only if we avoid the European novelty—alien to the biblical spirit and to the national tradition deriving from it—of women's involvement in elections and public life, which is tumultuous and noisy and involves multitudes. . . .

Finally, as to the ideal: Deeply imprinted in our soul is the ideal of being unblemished by any sin. When this ideal is realized, the world will be purified, and proper and safe ways will be found for the delicate and holy participation of Woman, the mother in Israel, in public life, both generally and particularly, with wholesome influence and in accordance with her special inner worth, thus fulfilling the vision: "Every woman of worth is a crown unto her husband" (Prov. 12:4). But this future vision is as yet not even glimpsed in temporal cultural life, which, though outwardly well groomed, is rotten within. So any step we take in the course of our public life that carelessly disregards our outlook concerning Woman's present and future worth—something that is deeply imprinted in our spirit—merely impedes this ideal course. Only Israel's return to its land, to its setting and its kingdom, and to its holy spirit, its prophecy and its Temple, will eventually bring into the world that sublime light, for which all noble souls of all humanity yearn.

Ben-Zion Meir Hai Uziel (1880–1953) was born and raised in Jerusalem. Descended from a renowned Sephardic rabbinical family, Uziel served as Israel's chief Sephardic rabbi from 1938 until his death in 1953. While the Modern Orthodox and Ultra-Orthodox traditionalist movements that developed in Europe defined themselves as opposed to what they regarded as Reform Judaism's false equation of Judaism with universal justice, modern Sephardic rabbis and decisors felt no tension between traditionalism and the modern quest for social justice. This perspective is represented in the selection included here. Uziel's arguments about whether women are permitted to vote or to hold elected office are a direct response to Kook's position, although Uziel does not specifically refer to Kook. Uziel argues that it is permissible for women to vote and run for office. His general approach is to argue independently for the justice of these positions and then to criticize the Jewish legal arguments against them.

Ben-Zion Meir Hai Uziel, "Misphatei Uziel 44," translated by Zvi Zohar, in *Edah* 1, no. 2 (2001): 8–14.

I wrote this responsum originally to clarify the [rule (halakhah)] for myself, not wishing to publicize and teach this responsum and this [rule] for implementation. However, now since this question has been resolved by itself, I deem it good to publicize it for the purposes of enhancing Torah.

A. WOMEN'S RIGHT TO VOTE

This issue became a central controversy in [the Land of Israel], and the whole Land of Israel rocked with the debate.

Posters and warnings, pamphlets and newspaper articles appeared anew every morning, absolutely prohibiting women's participation in the elections. Some based their argument on "Torah Law," some on the need to preserve the boundaries of modesty and morals, and others on the wish to ensure the peace of the family home. All leaned upon the saying "The new is prohibited by the Torah (*ḥadash asur min ha-torah*)."[44]

44. [On this claim, see part 3, especially the selections by Moshe Sofer.]

I regret to say that I do not have available now before me all the literature that has accumulated on this issue. I am very grateful to my friend, a virtual repository of Torah, the great Rabbi Ḥayyim Hirschensohn, who in . . . [*Sefer*] *Malki ba-Kodesh*,[45] part 2, summed up all the relevant material. Thus I have the opportunity to hear all the opinions of those who prohibit [women's suffrage], and to discuss them to the best of my limited capacity.

The issue can be subdivided into two headings: (a) the right to vote, and (b) the right to be elected.

Regarding the first [heading], we find no clear ground to prohibit this, and it is inconceivable that women should be denied this personal right. . . .

If anyone should tell us that women should be excluded from the voting public because "their minds are flighty (*da'atan kalot*)" (b. Shabbat 33b and b. Kiddushin 80b) and they know not how to choose who is worthy of leading the people, we reply: Well, then, let us exclude from the electorate also those men who are "of flighty minds" (and such are never lacking). However, reality confronts us clearly with the fact that, both in the past and in our times, women are equal to men in knowledge and wisdom, dealing in commerce and trade and conducting all personal matters in the best possible way. Has it ever been known that a guardian is appointed to conduct the affairs of an adult woman, against her will? . . .

Or, perhaps, it should be prohibited for the sake of preserving peace in the home (*shalom bayit*)? The author, being a great rabbi, has answered this well: If so, we must also deny the right to vote of adult sons and daughters still living at their fathers' home[s]. For in all cases where our rabbis concerned themselves with ensuring tranquility, they gave equal treatment to the wife and to adult sons living at home (see b. Bava Metzia 12b). It might still be objected, that denying this right to adult children should indeed have been proposed, but since it wasn't, let us at least not increase friction even more by allowing women to vote! But the truth is that differences of political opinions and attitudes will surface in some form or another, for no one can suppress completely his outlook and opinions. . . .

B. MAY WOMEN BE ELECTED?

The second issue is whether a woman can be elected to public office. Now, it seems prima facie that we have come up against an explicit prohibition. For

45. [(My king, in the sanctuary), by Ḥayyim Hirschensohn (1857–1935), who was born in Mandatory Palestine and became the chief rabbi of Hoboken, New Jersey.]

in the Sifre[46] on Deut. 29:16 it is written: "Thou shall appoint—and if he dies, another is appointed in his stead, [that is,] a king and not a queen."

From this source Maimonides derived the rule:

> A woman may not be appointed to the throne, as it is written: "'A king'—and not a queen." And likewise, all public appointments in Israel are to be made from amongst the men and not the women. Therefore a woman should not be appointed as head of a community ([*Mishneh Torah*, "Laws of Kings and Their Wars,"] 1:5).

. . . .

Our method will be to investigate whether the position of the Sifre and Maimonides' decree are binding or whether proofs can be adduced to contradict their actual applicability. On its face, it would seem that since this opinion was not mentioned in the Talmud, neither in the Mishnah nor the [Gemara], and since the [rule] of not appointing a woman as a community leader, despite having practical applicability in the present time, was not mentioned by the [decisors (poskim)], it therefore has been rejected as a [normative Jewish legal] position. . . .

C. APPOINTMENT OF WOMEN TO
POSITIONS OF POLITICAL POWER . . .

Despite our having clarified the fact that on Talmudic grounds there is no source for denying women the possibility of authoritative appointments, an adversary could still take issue with us and say that the ["]absence of proof is no proof["] ("*Lo ra'inu aino re'ayah*"). Therefore, I shall now present a positive proof for my position. Tosafot (b. Niddah 50a, s.v. *kol ha-kasher*), when discussing women's capacity to serve as judges, offer two opinions. According to one opinion, a woman is legally fit to serve as a judge, since the injunction: "These are the judgments which thou shall set before them" (Exod. 21:1) relates to the judges and also teaches that Scripture views women and men equally with respect to all Torah laws. Clearly, this entails a rejection of the idea that "All appointments you appoint . . . [ellipsis in original]." Otherwise, how would it be possible to appoint a woman as judge and obligate the public to be judged in her court? Is this not an appointment involving authority?

46. [Sifre is a midrashic legal commentary to Numbers and Deuteronomy.]

The other opinion that appears in Tosafot is that women are basically unfit to judge. But even this position justifies Deborah's function by suggesting that she served as a public teacher and mentor. Accordingly, this opinion must be understood as holding that the verse "And the children of Israel came up to her for judgment" (Judg. 10:5) means that they were in need of her judicial teachings. Thus, a woman's ineligibility relates only to her not being authorized to hear pleas or take evidence, but she is eligible to judge in the sense of deciding law and legislating. Now, is this not deemed authoritative office? Both opinions presented by Tosafot prove, then, that the position advocated by the Sifre is not accepted as definitive [rule].

And if one's *heart* still hesitates—and it should be so, rather than to reject outright the Sifre's and Maimonides' position by sharp conjectures and purely logical operations and analyses without any positive indication of the existence of an alternate [Jewish legal] position—then women's eligibility to be elected [to office] can be . . . justified [by Jewish law] on other grounds: the prohibition relates only to an appointment made by the Sanhedrin, but in our situation, the issue is not one of appointment but rather one of acceptance. Through the election process, the majority of the public expresses its acceptance of, and confidence in, certain persons as their representatives, and designates them to be their agents in supervising all its public affairs. Now, regarding such a case even Maimonides acknowledges that there is not the slightest prohibition. And also Ran,[47] of blessed memory (on b. Shevu'ot, beginning of Chapter 3) writes that what we find written regarding Deborah, that she judged Israel (Judg. 4:4), should not be understood in the sense of judging but rather that she led Israel. And although the Sifre says, "'Thou shalt appoint a king'—and not a queen," Deborah was not appointed; rather they followed her leadership (or, possibly, she did judge them and held court sessions for them, but on the basis of their voluntary acceptance, just as one can accept a relative as judge). . . .

In conclusion, it is clear that even according to the Sifre she may be accepted as judge, that is, leader, and she may make decisions just as one can accept a relative [as judge]. Therefore, in appointment by election, which is the public's acceptance of those elected as their representatives and leaders, the law is that they can also elect women, even according to the positions of the Sifre and Maimonides. And in the writings of the [early authorities] in general no dissenting opinion has been found.

47. [Nissim ben Reuven of Girona (Spain, 1320–76).]

Nevertheless, there is still basis for doubt—namely, that even though from a legal standpoint the acceptance [of an elected woman] is valid and people may elect her on the grounds that they have accepted her over them, from the standpoint of morality and conventions of modesty there might be a prohibition....

Logic dictates that in no serious assembly or worthy discussion is there licentiousness. Daily, men meet and negotiate with women in commercial transactions, and yet all is peace and quiet. Even those inclined to sexual licentiousness will not contemplate the forbidden while seriously transacting business....

Further proof can be brought from the teaching (b. Megillah 23a): "All may ascend to reading of the Torah [to the quorum of seven], even a child, even a woman, but the sages ruled that a woman should not read the Torah in public out of respect for the community" (*kevod ha-tzibbur*), that is in order to preclude the inference that there are no men in the community who can read from the Torah. But they did not rule in this way out of concern over licentiousness....

Finally, I have seen a newly contrived basis for not giving women the right to participate in elections (even to vote)—namely, out of consideration for the prohibition of flattery, lest a woman insincerely cast her vote for the individual or party that her husband favors. *Sefer Malki Ba-Kodesh* wrote correctly that such is not flattery but the upright nurturing of love. To which I would add: Would that this would be the case that every woman would esteem her husband to the extent of suppressing her will on account of his. One might even voice this reason in favor of giving [women] the right to vote, so that a wife might thereby show love and esteem to her husband, and peace thereby abound in the house of Israel.

If we have come to suspect as much, the opposite actually makes sense—namely, to worry that she in fact be opposed to her husband's opinion and flatter him by saying that she agreed with it, for the sake of peace or out of fear. Yet if so, we would need to institute open, non-secret elections; for this suspicion holds true for children, relatives, lovers, and friends. Such, however, is not deceitful flattery but comes under the rubric of (b. Yebamot 85a) "One may distort the truth for the sake of peace."

E. CONCLUSIONS:

(1) A woman has an absolute right of participation in elections so that she be bound by the collective obligation to obey the elected officials who govern the nation.

(2) A woman may also be elected to public office by the consent and ordinance of the community.

28

Shlomo Goren, "Is a Torah Constitution Possible?"

Born in Poland, Shlomo Goren (formerly Grontchik; 1918–94) immigrated to Palestine in 1925. He fought for the Haganah, the Jewish paramilitary force in Mandatory Palestine, beginning in 1936, in the War of Independence in 1948, and for the Israeli Defense Forces in the Six-Day War in 1967 — during which he was among the soldiers who liberated the Western Wall in Jerusalem. Goren headed the Rabbinate for the Israeli Defense Forces from 1948 to 1968, and he served as chief Ashkenazic rabbi of Israel from 1972 to 1983. The selections included here are taken from a series of articles Goren wrote in early 1948 on the eve of the establishment of the State of Israel. Goren aims to reconcile the obligation to establish a constitution for the new state according to the Torah and the requirements of the United Nations that it respect the equality of rights among its inhabitants. Focusing on the court system as the site for this resolution, he argues that though the ultimate goal is for life to be governed by the laws of the Torah, to establish a proper political order, which is also a divine command, it might be necessary to construct an alternative court system on the basis of the acceptance of the people, which would allow the state to comply with its international obligations. Goren explores the status of non-Jewish minorities in Israel and concludes (in contrast to Avraham Yeshayahu Karelitz) that they are allowed to live in the Land of Israel.

Shlomo Gorontchik (later Goren), "*Ḥukah Toranit Keytzad?*" [Is a Torah Constitution Possible?], in *Teḥukah le-Yisrael al-pi ha-Torah*, edited by Itamar Warhaftig (Jerusalem: Mosad ha-Rav Kook, 1989), 1:146–56 (translated by Daniel Tabak).

IS A TORAH CONSITUTION POSSIBLE?

[1]

With the declaration of the Jewish people's political independence in the Land of Israel, religious Judaism faces a serious challenge. It must decide how to fight for the infusion of the Torah's spirit (*ruaḥ*) and its laws (*ḥukeha*) in the state, to the point where it is seen as paving the way for the ultimate redemption. It is not enough to demand that the state be based on the statutes of the Torah; specific legislation must be prepared so that every single problem has a fitting solution. The solutions need to be both acceptable to all segments of the population and viable. Framers of the legislation will have to take into account the U[nited] N[ations] Charter and make sure that the legislation will not contravene international law, which requires equal rights for the entire population.

One of the most significant challenges requiring a comprehensive solution is the organization of the courts in the Jewish state. It is the courts that by and large determine the nature of every state and the character of every people. If we can ensure that this vital artery in the life of the state will run according to the statutes of the Torah, we can hope for success in every remaining area, too. . . .

The accepted opinion in the religious community (*ha-tzibbur ha-dati*) is to make existing statutes of the Torah the foundation for the new courts' body of law. In practice, this cannot be implemented easily. The laws regarding judges and witnesses would infringe on the rights of minorities and women. Moreover, they would arouse strong opposition from both the secular (*ḥilloni*) element of the Yishuv[48] and the United Nations. The legislation of the Torah disqualifies Torah violators—not to mention non-Jews (*she-einam benei brit*)—from being judges and witnesses. It bars women from testifying, excepting certain cases. . . .

By means of Torah-based ingenuity, however, it may be possible to establish arbitration courts in which even transgressors and non-Jews can serve as judges and witnesses. . . . In [Moshe Isserles's gloss[49] on *Shulḥan Arukh*,[50] Ḥoshen Mishpat] section 8:1 we find: "Any community may assent to a court that the Torah considers unfit." We see, then, that communal power includes accepting judges unfit for judging, and once the residents of a city have agreed to them, no one else can disqualify them. . . ." . . .

On this authority, we can also authorize those disqualified from testifying by using predetermined communal ordinances. If the consent of an individual qualifies the disqualified for serving as judge or witness (as explained . . . in [ibid., Ḥoshen Mishpat] section 22:1), and we find no distinction between individual and communal consent for judging, then certainly the same is true for testifying. . . .

On the basis of such a [method of] appointment we can also put on the bench

48. [The Jewish settlement in the Land of Israel.]

49. [Moshe Isserles (Poland, 1520–72), *Ha-Mapah* (The tablecloth).]

50. [(The set table), a comprehensive Jewish legal code by Yosef Karo (1488–1575) and published in 1565. Its principal sections—Oraḥ Ḥayyim, Yoreh De'ah, Even Ha-Ezer, and Ḥoshen Mishpat—correspond to the sections in the earlier code, *Arba'ah Turim*, also known as the *Tur*, by Ya'akov ben Asher (1270–c. 1340).]

those who will focus specifically on civil cases (*dinei mamonot*), given their appointment by communal consent. We should emphasize especially that courts of this type would not have the title "bet din,"[51] seeing as their authorization to adjudicate derives not from the Torah but from the public.

Criminal cases pose no great difficulty. . . . *Shulḥan Arukh* in Ḥoshen Mishpat section 2 states outright that the good men of the city[52] possess the authority of the great rabbinical court when operating within their own city and can thus mete out all manner of punishment, even where no absolute proof is available. "Witnesses and warning are only required to judge according to Torah law (din torah), but one who violates the statutes of the state can be dealt with according to the needs of the hour." (This is the language of Naḥmanides in a responsum.[53]) On the force of this authority, the community can make laws and set punishments for criminal offenses that include imprisonment and the like, in line with what the judges or legislators see fit for maintaining public order (*ha-seder ha-tzibburi*).

This entire approach is predicated on a great number of sources that cannot be elaborated on here, but it holds promise only for Jews disqualified from serving as witnesses or judges—not for non-Jews. In [*Shulḥan Arukh,*] Ḥoshen Mishpat, section 26:1 we find: "One may not try one's case before idolatrous[54] judges or in their courts. Even if they will apply Jewish law (*dinei yisrael*), and even if the litigants have agreed to have their case tried by them, it is forbidden. . . .

One can resolve this difficulty through the opinion of *Shakh*[55] in [Ḥoshen

51. [A bet din is a duly authorized rabbinical court. Goren contrasts this with a *bet mishpat*, a civil, nonrabbinical court.]

52. [A committee chosen from among the populace to make halakhic decisions in medieval and early modern Jewish communities. See *Jewish Political Tradition*, edited by Michael Walzer, Menachem Lorberbaum, Noam J. Zohar, and Yair Lorberbaum (New Haven, CT: Yale University Press, 2000), vol. 1: *Authority*.]

53. [It is, in fact, the language of Rashba (Shlomo ben Aderet, Spain, 1235–1310), as the responsum is included in a collection of responsa authored by him and misattributed to Naḥmanides (Moses ben Naḥman, 1194–1270), also known as Ramban), no. 279. See also Rashba's responsum 4:311.]

54. [AKU'M (*ovdei kokhavim u-mazalot*)—literally, "worshippers of stars and constellations."]

55. [Shabbatai ben Meir ha-Kohen (Eastern Europe, 1621–62), referred to by the acronym for his major work, *Siftei Kohen* (Lips of the priest), a commentary on portions of the *Shulḥan Arukh.*]

Mishpat] section 22:15, who distinguishes] . . . "between accepting upon oneself the laws of idolaters, which would be prohibited, and accepting adjudication by a specific idolater, which would mean only that they consider the idolater trustworthy and would not be considered supporting their religion (*datam*)." Using this line of thinking, it goes without saying that should the non-Jewish judges be appointed by us and adjudicate based on Jewish law (dinei yisrael) it would be permissible, as we would not be lending support to their religion. Furthermore, one could not claim that bringing one's case to them would be considered "putting aside Jewish judges (*dayyanei yisrael*) and going to idolaters" or "making our enemies judges," which constitute the main reasons behind [the law that one must bring court cases] "'before them'—and not before idolaters" (as is written in Midrash Tanḥuma,[56] Mishpatim). The non-Jews would apply our laws and the courts would be Jewish ones because they would be appointed judges by means of communal consent only due to minority rights.

As regards the appointment of non-Jewish judges or officials, . . . they will be formally appointed to serve the minorities. No prohibition, therefore, governs the appointment of non-Jewish judges, just as none pertains to their appointment to other government positions.

We have learned that, notwithstanding many difficulties, it is possible to set up new courts (*battei mishpat*) that will rule based on the laws of the Torah without infringing on civil rights and without making racial, religious, or gender distinctions. . . .

[2]

. . . [S]ince a large portion of the rules of the Torah governing testimony and adjudication will not be in practical force in these courts, should we take this path or attempt to find another way to preserve the purity of Torah law (*ha-mishpat ha-torani*), even if not everyone will be satisfied?

. . . These courts will not bear the title "torah bet din" since their Torah authority is indirect in coming from the public, and it is on this selfsame authority that those disqualified from adjudication and testimony become qualified. In which case, we must investigate two fundamental issues:

56. [Midrash Tanḥuma is a collection of narrative homilies to the Pentateuch, first published in 1522. The standard edition, published in 1563, includes portions taken from earlier versions of this collection that are no longer complete.]

(1) Does this communal authority, which lends judicial power to courts of this type, limit the courts solely to the set body of Torah law (*mishpetei ha-torah*), by means of which they must adjudicate? Or, since the very essence of these courts' authority flows from the power of the community, perhaps this communal power even works to establish and introduce unique statutes by which they will try civil suits and criminal cases, punishing both corporally and pecuniarily? If it turns out that the power of these courts works for the latter as well, so that they can deviate completely from the fixed body of Torah law and introduce special statutes and laws, then in those instances the entire applicable force of the Torah's laws in the life of the Jewish state will be undermined, God forbid, "and what will become of the Torah"?

(2) Have there been precedents for courts of this type in the life of this nation over the course of its history . . . ?

In b. Sanhedrin 23a, there is a dispute between Rabbi Meir and the sages. Rabbi Meir says, "This [litigant] can disqualify that one's judge, and that [litigant] can disqualify this one's judge." The sages say, "Neither one can disqualify the other's judge." About Rabbi Meir's statement the Talmud asks: "Is it really within his power to disqualify judges?" Rabbi Johanan answers, "This was taught regarding the courts[57] of Syria,[58] not experts." . . .

The explicit statements of Rashi and Rashba, brought into sharper focus and expanded upon by Ran, clearly demonstrate that the "courts of Syria" were permanent Jewish courts for monetary cases and the like, whose authority stemmed from the general assent of the community, and which handed down rulings based on "their own judgment" and not on Torah law, seeing as they were not "learned in Torah." The Vilna Gaon[59] also inclines toward the line of reasoning given by Rashi, Rashba, and Ran. . . .

---

57. [*Arka'ot*, which historically meant "court" or "archive." See Daniel Sperber, *A Dictionary of Greek and Latin Legal Terms in Rabbinic Literature* (Jerusalem: Bar-Ilan University Press, 1984), 62–65. Given the word's common collocation with a modifying noun phrase identifying it as a non-Jewish court, the question commentators face is whether the court and its laws are Jewish or non-Jewish when such an accompanying description is absent. No such doubt would have been entertained had *battei din* been used instead of *arka'ot*.]

58. [The reference is to an area located to the north and east of Israel, which is not coextensive with the modern state of Syria.]

59. [Eliyahu of Vilna (1720–1797). See the selections by him in part 2.]

At this point, the two aforementioned fundamental queries have been answered.

(1) Courts of this type have no connection to the laws of the Torah; they may set their own standards by which they will adjudicate "using their reasoned judgment and making use of statutes and mores."

(2) There was precedent in Syria for this type of court, and setting them up on a national and political basis is possible and legal "were all the citizens of the state to accept them in a general manner." . . .

Now the original question stands before us. If these courts can deviate from the established framework of the statutes of the Torah, operating with their own set of "statutes and mores" rooted in "reasoned judgment," would that not undermine the entire foundation of our approach to organizing the court system in the Jewish state, and if so, "what will become of the Torah"? "The Torah is rendered no honor except through acting in accord with its statutes and laws" (Maimonides, [*Mishneh Torah,*] "Laws of the Sanhedrin," 24:10).

However, it is worth discussing whether the insistent and exacting imposition of every statute of the Torah in the life of the state, with respect to corporal and pecuniary punishment for criminal violations and the like, could hold together the particular and general order of the state without any additional statutes, mores, and special enactments by communal consent. Rashba considered this extensively in his responsa (3:393), writing:

> It is my opinion that if the executive body (*berurim*)[60] believe the witnesses, then they can fine or corporally punish, all in accord with what they see fit. This is necessary for the world to keep running. For if you use only the Torah's set laws and punish only as the Torah does with regard to causing injury and the like, the world would be destroyed, because we would require witnesses and warning. As the sages of blessed memory have said, "Jerusalem was destroyed only because they judged in accord with Torah law."[61] . . . The shallow-minded would upend the natural order of things,[62] rendering the world desolate.

60. [Berurim were "members of the executive body in the Jewish communities in the Iberian Peninsula." Yom Tov Assis, *The Golden Age of Aragonese Jewry* (Oxford: Littman Library of Jewish Civilization, 1997), 338, *s.v. baror.*]

61. [b. Bava Metzia 30b.]

62. [Literally, "breach the wall of the world," based on b. Bava Batra 15b.]

Ran writes in a similar vein in one of his sermons (no. 11). . . .

We have reached, then, the following conclusions:

(1) The central goal is the implementation of all statutes of the Torah in the life of the state, both in the life of the individual and that of the collective.

(2) To preserve religion (dat) and to keep the political order intact (which God has likewise commanded us to do to keep the world inhabited), we must of necessity invoke our sovereign authority, which flows from the assent of "the entire state," to set up additional specialized "statutes and conventions"[63] in civil and criminal matters, and to ease legal procedure with respect to witnesses, warning, and so on.

(3) Seeing that national and international considerations are decisive, we are under an obligation to recognize the full rights of all segments of the population. The appointment of judges also should require us to use our sovereign authority, through the power of the entire state's assent, to accept all judges appointed by the state who will be obligated to rule according to the Torah. . . .

[3]

A new approach to the organization of the court system in the Jewish state, which on the one hand will preserve the full Torah character of the courts, and on the other hand will satisfy the general aspiration for equal rights for all segments of the population as required by international law, can be proposed via a fundamental Torah-based inquiry into the problem presented by minorities in the Jewish state.

The issue of minorities in the Jewish state also deserves a comprehensive Torah solution. We need to establish their constitutional status and their legal and societal rights, while bearing in mind international laws on minority rights. The nature of every state and the ethics of every people are established and measured by their relation to the minorities among them. The Jewish people, who have suffered for the duration of their exile as the perpetual minority, must serve as an example to the world in their tolerant relationship to the other peoples in their midst.

International lawmakers struggle with delimiting the exact boundaries be-

63. [Although translated as "mores" above, that word does not fit Goren's choice of verb here. The Hebrew is more flexible, as the phrase covers obligations of various kinds that fall outside the strict purview of law.]

tween the national majority of citizens and those appropriately termed the national minority. From a Torah point of view, there is no difficulty. Religious affiliation assigns responsibilities and also establishes the various national boundaries. In the Jewish state, then, those affiliated with the Jewish religion constitute the majority and those affiliated with other religions perforce constitute the minority.

The Torah splits this minority into two types: those with rights within the state, called "resident aliens (gerei toshav)" or "foreigners at the [city] gate," and those with no rights, called "idolaters." . . .

In [*Mishneh Torah*] "Laws of Idolatry" 10:6, Maimonides writes briefly, "And if he accepted the seven commandments, he is a resident alien." We learn, therefore, that the first condition for being accepted as a resident alien is observing the seven Noahide laws. It can be said reasonably that every contemporary nation has a general desire to keep five of these commandments, that is, the prohibitions on cursing God, murder, illicit sexual relations, theft, and eating a limb from a living animal, and that they have been accepted already by every people and religion. The two remaining commands, the prohibition on idolatry and the requirement of *dinim*,[64] require clarification as to what extent they are currently observed by the nations of the world and by the minorities documented to be living in the Land of Israel more specifically.

As for Muslims, Maimonides has ruled in his responsa to Rabbi Obadiah the Proselyte (edition *Mekize Nirdamim*) no. 369: "These Ishmaelites are not idolaters at all; [idolatry] has already been excised from their mouths and hearts. They ascribe a unity to the elevated God that is appropriate and faultless . . . [ellipsis in original]." . . .

As for Christians, most of the sources have been muddled by censorship. In old printings of Maimonides' "Laws of Idolatry," 9:4, it is clear that "Christians are idolaters." . . . *Shulḥan Arukh* implies as much in many places, as do many other earlier authorities. Still, there is room to rely to Meiri's[65] comments . . . , wherein he writes: "It seems to me that all of these statements were made only about idol worshippers and their images and idols, but nowadays it is completely permissible. . . ." . . .

One also finds support in the position of *Tosafot* to b. Sanhedrin 63b and

---

64. [Literally, "laws," although the precise meaning of the term here is subject to dispute.]

65. [Menaḥem ben Solomon Meiri (Spain, 1249–1306).]

b. Bekhorot 2b that Noahides were not prohibited from association (shittuf),[66] contrary to *Noda bi-Yehudah*[67] (second edition), Yoreh De'ah, no. 148, but in line with the citation in *Pithei Teshuvah*,[68] Yoreh De'ah 148:2 in the name of *Darkhei Moshe*,[69] *Shakh*, and so on that association was not prohibited for Noahides at all.

With respect to the last of the seven Noahide laws, it will become clear further on that the organization of courts and establishment of civil statutes for monetary and criminal matters constitute the minorities' observance of this commandment.

We can, prima facie, grant resident alien status with all its attendant rights to minorities in the Jewish state. Many obstacles, however, still obstruct that path:

(1) Maimonides, in his [*Mishneh Torah*] "Laws of Idolatry" and "Laws of Forbidden Foods," writes that we only receive resident aliens when the Jubilee is observed, and today even were he to accept the entire Torah except for one detail, we would not receive him.

(2) In [*Mishneh Torah*,] "Laws of Kings" 8:11 we find: "He must accept [the seven commandments] for himself in front of three learned Jews (*haverim*)," and observance of the seven Noahide laws without acceptance in the presence of three such Jews is ineffective.

(3) Ibid.: "Anyone who accepts the seven commandments and takes care to observe them is among the pious of the nations of the world and has a portion in the world to come. This is if he accepts them and observes them because the Holy One, blessed be He, commanded them in the Torah and informed us, via our teacher Moses, that even before [the giving of the Torah] Noahides had been commanded to fulfill them. But if he accepts them because of rational determination, he is neither a resident alien nor from among the pious and wise of the nations of the world." In responsum no. 364, Maimonides rules that Muslims, unlike Christians, believe that the Torah is not divine. Thus, even if they keep the seven Noahide laws, they are unfit to be received as resident aliens.

---

66. [The association of the biblical God with something else, such as Jesus, the saints, or the Holy Spirit. See David Berger, *The Rebbe, The Messiah, and the Scandal of Orthodox Indifference* (London: Littman Library of Jewish Civilization, 2001), 175–77.]

67. [(Known in Judah), by Yeḥezkel Landau (Poland, 1713–93).]

68. [(Openings for repentance), by Avraham Tzvi Eisenstadt (Poland, 1813–68).]

69. [(Ways of Moses), a commentary Moshe Isserles (Poland, 1520–72) on *Arba'ah Turim*.]

An egress from this thicket of difficulties presents itself in Raavad's[70] comment on [Maimonides'] "Laws of Idolaters," 10:6 and "Laws of Forbidden Sexual Relations," 14:8, as explained by Meiri on b. Yebamot 48b: "Their statement that we do not accept resident aliens except when the Jubilee is observed means that the person does not have the status of a resident alien, creating stringencies in some matters and leniencies in others." Kesef Mishneh[71] in "Laws of Idolatry" *ad loc.* writes: "Although we do not accept a resident alien at a time when the Jubilee is not observed, were someone to accept the seven [Noahide] commandments, why would we prevent him from settling [on] the Land [of Israel]? There is no concern that 'they will lead astray.'" *Minḥat Ḥinnukh*[72] says in commandment 93: "It appears that even when the Jubilee is not observed, as long as they accept the seven commandments it is permitted to make a treaty with them, because the main concern of the negative commandment is idolatry. Even today there is a command to sustain him, but the court does not receive [him]," as Kesef Mishneh also wrote. *Kaftor va-Ferah*,[73] chapter 10, reads: "When it says that 'the [legal status of the] resident alien is not in force,' it means not to sustain him except when the Jubilee is in force, when sovereignty is ours, but we would receive him even today to bring him under the wings of the Divine Presence."

We thus find a special law that applies to resident aliens, who even without formal acceptance and "as long as they keep the seven commandments are considered religious practitioners (ba'alei dat)" (Meiri on b. Sanhedrin 56b). . . . Based on the foregoing, one can say that even if they do not punctiliously adhere to all of the seven commandments, as long as they do not practice idolatry they have the status of resident aliens for the purpose of civil rights in the state, in which case they may be granted the very same rights as a true resident alien. With this the aforementioned difficulties dissipate. In addition, Maimonides' requirement that they perform the commandments "because God commanded them, etc." seems to apply only to a true resident alien, one considered "among the pious and wise of the nations of the world," and would not negate his rights as a citizen with respect to the prohibition on settling in the Land [of Israel] and the like. "The chief concern is idolatry." . . .

70. [Abraham ben David of Posquières (Provence, c. 1125–98).]

71. [*Kesef Mishneh* (a play on words, the title means double silver, with an allusion to Maimonides' *Mishneh Torah*, on which it is a commentary), by Yosef Karo (1488–1575)].

72. [(An offering of eduction) by Yosef Babad (Poland, 1801–1874).]

73. [(Button and flower), by Isaac ha-Kohen ben Moses, known as Eshtori ha-Parḥi (active in France, Spain, and Eretz Israel; 1280–1355).]

With the establishment of the Jewish state, the obligation will devolve on us to provide minorities with their civil rights. Included in these rights is the right to form a system of special courts that will judge them in accord with their laws....

. . . [D]o Noahides have the right to adjudicate using a body of special law set up for them? We find an answer in y. Bava Kamma 4:3: "Rabbi Hiyya taught: An idolater's ox that gores another idolater's ox—although [the idolater] agreed to be judged according to Jewish law, he pays damages in full whether it was deemed harmless or a repeat offender. Regarding this Rabbi Abbahu said in the name of Rabbi Johanan, 'It is in accord with their laws.'"

What is more, we find that Maimonides writes in "Laws of Kings and their Wars" 10:12, "Jews and idolaters who bring a case before us, if the Jew has an advantage according to their laws we judge according to those laws; if the Jew has an advantage in our laws, we judge according to Torah law and tell him, 'So it is in our laws.' It seems to me that we do not do this for a resident alien but always judge him according to their laws."

We conclude from this that in cases between gentiles, and even in cases between resident aliens and Jews, we rule in accordance with their laws. This applies when they bring their case before us, and it need not be said that in their network of courts they may judge according to their own constitution.

In the Jewish state about to be established with God's help, we are obligated, then, to create a dual system of courts. The one will include a network of courts (*battei din*) in the full Torah sense, in which the statutes of the Torah will be enforced as they are. Jurisdiction over criminal cases must be granted to these courts via the assent of "the entire state," which is based on our sovereign power....

The second court system will include civil courts that will apply a uniform civil constitution in compliance with international law, and will take pains not to contravene the statutes of the Torah. The goal in establishing these courts will be to clarify laws pertaining to the minorities, but they will also have the authority to try cases between Jews. This duality of the court system will leave in its wake many jurisdictional problems that will require a comprehensive Torah solution. What is set forth here constitutes but the general outlines of jurisdiction....

In conclusion, two paths have emerged for navigating the question of how to organize the courts in the Jewish state. One is predicated on a uniform constitution, according to which a single system of courts will be established that will embody Torah law, receive additional authority based on the assent of the entire state to try civil and criminal cases, and relax the legal requirements for being a witness or judge. The second path suggested in this article has greater strength in preserving the purity of Torah law so that it will not be tarnished by compromises and dispensations.

Religious Judaism has the great and sacred charge right now to work out a detailed Torah constitution for the nascent State of Israel. This will pave the way for returning the Torah's crown to its former glory, the establishment of the Sanhedrin, and the ultimate redemption.

29

Isaac Halevi Herzog, *Constitution and Law in a Jewish State According to the Torah*

Born in Poland, Isaac Halevi Herzog (1886–1959) was educated in London and Paris. He served as chief rabbi of Ireland from 1922 to 1935. After the death of Abraham Isaac Kook, Herzog immigrated to Palestine. There he became the second chief Ashkenazic rabbi of Mandatory Palestine and then, in 1948, the first chief Ashkenazic rabbi of Israel, a post he held until his death in 1959. In the first selection included here, Herzog discusses the relation between Torah law and the law of the state. He maintains that the State of Israel must be governed by Torah law, but he also recognizes the infeasibility of such an approach since Jewish law discriminates against women, nonobservant Jews, and non-Jews. He thus concludes that religious Jews should merely insist on the right of observant Jews to use religious courts and the exclusive jurisdiction of such courts on questions of personal status — that is, marriage, divorce, child custody, and inheritance. In the second selection, Herzog describes the relationship between law and ethics in Judaism. While he notes that there is always a gap between what the law can command and what morality demands in any legal system, he also argues that, as religious law, the Torah always attempts to narrow that gap. He also notes that what was once only a moral obligation often becomes a law with the passage of time. This is not because there is a development in the Torah itself, but because the development of the character of the people allows more of the Torah's revealed morality to be translated into enforceable laws. Herzog's claim that Jewish law strives to narrow the gap between morality and legality stands in striking opposition to Isaac Breuer's view (see part 3) that the narrowing of such a gap is a symptom of the Jewish community's moral deterioration, rather than its advancement.

Isaac Halevi Herzog, "*Al ha-Mishpat Bikhlal*" [On the law in general], in *Teḥukah le-Yisrael al-pi ha-Torah*, edited by Itamar Warhaftig (Jerusalem: Mosad ha-Rav Kook, 1989), 1:215–220 (translated by Alexander Kaye).

ON THE LAW (HA-MISHPAT) IN GENERAL

After an investigation, I have come to the following conclusion: Since unfortunately the time has not yet come for the fulfilment of the divine promise "I will restore your magistrates as of old, and your counselors as of yore,"[74] as a matter of principle we must request the introduction of a clause into the constitution of the state that will establish that the law (ha-mishpat) will be according to the laws (dinei) of the holy Torah. However, it is almost certain that even if we [the religious Zionist community] will merit, with the help of God, a substantial representation in parliament, we will not succeed to pass the proposed clause. The most decisive reason [for this] is that the laws of the Torah include also the laws of judges and witnesses.

[Judges who do not observe the Torah.]

1.... [T]he government has already appointed judges and it is not reasonable for them to agree to remove those they have already appointed. The large majority are not knowledgeable in the laws of the Torah, even though they are honorable and honest men who are expert in the laws of the gentiles (mishpetei ha-goyim).[75] ...

[Testimony of women.]

2. Similarly, we encounter the great difficulty of those who are unqualified to testify for the aforementioned reasons, and we encounter the difficulty, no less great, regarding the acceptance of the testimony of women, in cases in which they are not qualified by law or the enactment of the earlier [sages] of blessed memory, to testify. Regarding the acceptance of testimony in criminal cases, to punish wrongdoers, the difficulty is not so great. ... But regarding civil law, which is not included in the framework of criminal law, the difficulty is genuinely great. ...

[Testimony of strangers (nokhrim).]

3. We also have before us the great difficulty regarding the acceptance of testimony, (in matters that do not pertain to religion [dat],) of non-Jews (einam bnei brit). It is impossible to ignore the fact that acting according to the strict law

74. [Isa. 1:26.]

75. [Throughout this essay, Herzog uses a variety of terms to refer to non-Jews, including nokhrim (strangers), goyim (gentiles), and einnam bnei brit (literally, "not members of the covenant"). The translation has generally striven to capture these different usages, though when that would result in confusion "non-Jew" or "gentile" has been substituted for a more literal translation.]

would create the danger of inviting hatred (*evah*)[76] from the nations,[77] for in the courts of cultured countries, the testimony of a Jew is accepted, even against a non-Jew. . . . Perhaps it is possible to distinguish between the gentiles (goyim) of the past and the strangers (nokhrim) of today especially as they are citizens of the State of Israel. This helps somewhat, but it is not the opinion of the majority of decisors and the matter is not simple.

[Stranger (nokhri) judges.]

4. The same is true regarding the appointment of judges who are non-Jewish (she-einam bnei brit).

Certainly there is nothing that prevents the appointment of non-Jews as judges over other non-Jews. . . . But what is the basis to permit them to judge a Jew? There is room to explore this question regarding the State of Israel. Three reasons are given for the established law of "before them and not before gentiles,"[78] which prohibits Jews from bringing cases before judges like these, even with the agreement of both parties: (a) they honor idols there; (b) they show a preference for their laws; (c) they show a preference for their judges over Jewish judges, as if Jewish judges are not, God forbid, as honest and intelligent as them. Regarding reason (a), it is possible to say that even if stranger judges do not judge by our law books, but by their codices, that since the codices of the stranger, secular (ḥilloni) judges are not dependent on their religious sources, but on secular law books which do not relate to superhuman sources (according to their faith), then reason (a) falls. . . . In circumstances like these, reason (b) also falls. Regarding reason (c), it is possible to say that regarding the parties to the

76. Not all hatreds are equal. There is a hatred that falls into the category of danger to the entire [people], and we are lenient [to prevent] this even with a biblical prohibition. And in my book [*Main Institutions of Jewish Law*] I wrote at length about this. Although this regards the category of an ongoing removal of a prohibition [literally, "uprooting for the generations"], we should nevertheless deal with this, because strengthening the power of antisemitism brings with it danger for all of [the people of] Israel who are outside the Land of Israel, which is most of the nation. And accursed antisemitism begins with the removal of the rights of the citizen and causes pogroms and expulsions, may God protect us.

77. [The hatred discussed here is a category with legal consequences. Some rabbinic laws, for example, are overridden in Jewish law if keeping them would incur the hatred of non-Jews. See, for example, *Shulḥan Arukh*, Yoreh De'ah section 148:5, which is based on b. Avodah Zarah 6b.]

78. [See Midrash Tanḥuma, Mishpatim.]

case, since the government of [the State of] Israel has appointed foreign judges in a certain place, the Jews who come before them are not showing a preference for gentile judges over Jewish judges, because in that place only the gentile judge has the power to judge, so the Jews have no choice and this would not constitute showing a preference for non-Jewish judges.... Therefore, in principle, the government could exempt Jews from the prohibition of being judged in the courts of gentiles.

In any case, this is relevant only when the parties agree [to be judged by a non-Jew]. But forcibly to appoint a judge who is disqualified from judging ... it is clear that this is prohibited even without the reasons mentioned above. This is prohibited because of [the dictum] "All the appointments that you make should be only from among your brothers."[79] ... In this matter it is as if we are under duress (ke-anusim)....

... [B]ecause of [the resolution of the United Nations], it is not we who are appointing [unqualified judges] but in fact it is the nations who are appointing them over us.... Perhaps it is also possible to deal with the earlier problems in such a way that we raised above, and also with regard to the testimony of women and the testimony of those who are unqualified because they have transgressed commandments between man and God. Because it is presumably a condition of the nations that we not discriminate for religious reasons except in the framework of purely religious matters (devarim datiim tehorim), like marriage, divorce, and so on. Nevertheless, the matter is complicated and very difficult and needs investigation and clarification by scholars of the Torah. And who would dare qualify all the unqualified through the expropriatory power of the court[80] and entirely to annul in practice the principles of the laws of judges and testimony?

[Permitting the unqualified.]

5. The proposal of a wholesale acceptance (kabbalah)[81] for future generations to permit, in relation to civil law, all the unqualified judges and witnesses who

79. [b Kiddushin 6b. Deut. 16:15 says "from among your brothers shall you appoint a king over you." The Talmudic exegesis extrapolates from this that Jews may appoint only other Jews to positions of authority over themselves.]

80. [In civil cases, through the mechanism of "expropriation by the court" (hefker bet din), rabbinic law permits the court to dispose of private property at its discretion, in the interests of reaching a just outcome. See, for example, Maimonides, Mishneh Torah, "Laws of Sanhedrin," 24:6.]

81. ["Acceptance" here is a technical term. People who are unqualified to serve as

are not "evil and violent" is a very dubious and complicated matter, even from a practical perspective, for how would one bring about such an acceptance? . . . If the government would agree to accept in principle the aforementioned clause [that the law of the State of Israel would be the law of the Torah] and would turn to the Torah scholars to find ways and proposals, then we would find ourselves standing before difficult and tremendous problems. But it seems likely to me that even if they would agree to this, and even if we were able to find proposals and ways, we would lose as much as we would gain. Among Israel the law has always been under the authority of the rabbis, scholars of Torah who deeply fear God. It would now, with our approval, be placed under the authority of people who, most of them, perhaps the large majority, are not religious! And they would have the authority to interpret our laws and to use their interpretations in practice. . . .

Ultimately, I am very afraid of the destruction, God forbid, of the rabbinate in Israel and the institutions of the holy yeshivot, from which the Torah goes out to all of Israel and, may God prevent it, of a terrible ethical reform in the wake of this arrangement, even if it will be accepted—and even if we find means and devices, which I believe is even more dubious.

[Expansion of the authority of the rabbinical courts.]

6. In my opinion, together with the maximal claim that all the law (mishpat) in the State of Israel should be based on the laws of Israel (dinei yisrael), including the rules (halakhot) of judges and witnesses, we must make a second claim as an alternative. That is: to expand the authority of the courts of Torah that encompass personal status law so that they should have exclusive authority in [personal status law], and with regard to the rest of civil law, the choice should be given to every Jewish defendant to respond: "I am going to the court of Torah." . . .

[Decisive authority in matters of personal status.]

7. . . . As an absolute minimum the court of Torah should be given exclusive authority in the entire realm of personal status law, and the power of the author-

---

witnesses or judges in a case may nevertheless serve in that capacity if they are accepted by the parties involved. See, for example, Maimonides, *Mishneh Torah*, "Laws of Sanhedrin," 7:2.]

ity of the holy Torah should not be less than—not to equate them—the power of the authority of the laws of the Muslim community in that area.[82] . . .

Isaac Halevi Herzog, *"Ha-Mishpat ve-ha-Musar bi-Yahadut"* [Law and ethics in Judaism], in *Teḥukah le-Yisrael al-pi ha-Torah*, edited by Itamar Warhaftig (Jerusalem: Mosad ha-Rav Kook, 1989), 1:218–25 (translated by Alexander Kaye).

LAW (MISHPAT) AND ETHICS (MUSAR) IN JUDAISM

[The gap between law and ethics]

In every cultured society subject to a certain approach to law (mishpat), there is . . . a certain gap, more or less wide, that is sometimes found between the law (din) applied in the courts and the general or categorical imperative (tzav) of ethical obligation. The most advanced approaches to law (ḥok) and to constitutions or legislation always strive to fill that gap, but it does not always turn out to be possible—or, more accurately, practical—to fill it entirely. . . . But in general, legal codes and legal rules pass in silence over the ethical perspective, even when there is a possibility of introducing it as a supplement to the law as it is applied in the courts. . . . But here the Jewish law (ha-ḥok ha-yehudi) or, more accurately, the law of the holy Torah (mishpat ha-torah ha-kedoshah), is exceptional. In return for its observance of the laws, the Torah of Moses has already assured the Jews not great conquests or a global empire but the recognition, flowing from the conscience of the gentile nations, of the ethical superiority of the laws of Israel (mishpetei yisrael).

. . . This unique phenomenon of the law of the Torah derives without a doubt from its religious (dati) character, and from the religion (dat) of Israel's being what it is, namely the Torah from heaven. Therefore, what is called in most cultures civil law (ha-mishpat ha-ezraḥi) is an organic part of the Torah that is from heaven. . . . The law books of other cultured peoples are specifically for the judge

---

82. [Under the British Mandate for Palestine, Muslim religious courts had greater powers than Jewish religious courts. Essentially the jurisdiction of Muslim courts extended to all Muslims, irrespective of citizenship, whereas Jewish courts had jurisdiction only over citizens of Palestine over eighteen years of age who were officially registered as part of the Jewish community. Furthermore, Muslim courts had exclusive jurisdiction in aspects of law that the Jewish courts did not, such as guardianship and adoption.]

or the lawyer, whereas Jewish law is intended as much for the regular Jew as for the judge. . . . So its scope is not limited by whether the courts do or do not apply it, for one reason or another, but by whether it is right or wrong in itself. . . .

[*Main categories of ethical rights and duties*
that are emphasized in Torah law]

A general survey of the entire background of Torah law (*ha-mishpat ha-torati*) offers a scale of the ethical categories that appear in it as a complement to law proper (*din gamur*). . . . The closer it is to actual law, the lower it is on the scale with regard to high ethics. Clearly, we will look at the matter from a positive perspective, that is, from the perspective of the benefit in the spiritual sense that the fulfillment of an ethical obligation provides to its performer. From this perspective, I count as the lowest category on the scale of high ethics those obligations included in the general category of "laws of heaven (*dinei shamayyim*)." Cases of this kind are exemplified in the law of the Torah in actions or inaction by which the claim of the plaintiff is dismissed by the rabbinical court, but along with its dismissal, the court issues a warning to the defendant that he is obligated by the higher law (*din ha-elyon*) to pay the plaintiff. . . .

Similar to this category are certain unjust acts that the law of the Torah (mishpat ha-torah) does not make liable under law (ba-din) but considers them to be wicked acts. . . .

A lighter measure [from the perspective of the law], and therefore a higher level of ethical obligation than that of the category of laws of heaven, is an ethical obligation that the law dictates in order to "fulfill a duty to Heaven (*kedei la-tzet yedei shamayaim*)" (b. Bava Metzia 37a, [*Shulḥan Arukh,*] Ḥoshen Mishpat section 365, compare. ibid., sections 75:9 and 76:1). Needless to say, we do not enforce "to fulfill a duty to Heaven," but sometimes we enforce "beyond the letter of the law (*lifnim mishurat ha-din*)."[83] . . .

[*Is there ethical development in Jewish law (halakhah)?*]

. . . I am convinced that there was not, God forbid, any ethical development of Jewish law (halakhah) in the normal sense. That is, I am convinced that the Torah of Moses together with the Oral Torah that was transmitted to Moses on Sinai is at the very peak of both law and ethics. Where development did take place was in the nation, meaning in the great masses. . . . The highest standards

83. [Literally, "within the line of the law."]

of ethics were already present in the two Torahs as they were given at Sinai, but the two Torahs, taking into consideration the spiritual state of the masses of the house of Israel, did not immediately establish all the levels as law (ḥok) because this would have been too much for the masses, and the two Torahs, the Written and the Oral, were intended primarily to educate the masses. . . .

30

Yeshayahu Leibowitz, "The Religious
Significance of the State of Israel"

Born in Riga, Yeshayahu Leibowitz (1903–94) studied chemistry and philosophy in
Berlin and then medicine in Basel. He immigrated to Palestine in 1934. For almost
sixty years, Leibowitz taught courses in biochemistry, the history of science, and
philosophy at the Hebrew University of Jerusalem. Although he continually af-
firmed his commitment to Zionism, Leibowitz became a harsh critic of the way in
which Judaism was used as a political tool in the Israeli state. His criticism intensi-
fied in 1967 after Israel gained control of the Gaza Strip and the West Bank as the
result of the Six-Day War. In the excerpts included here, Leibowitz emphatically
insists that while it has political significance, the State of Israel has no religious
significance. The claim that the Israeli state has religious significance, he warns, is
the greatest danger to the future of Judaism, which he defines solely in terms of
the religious values of Torah and commandments.

Yeshayahu Leibowitz, "The Religious Significance of the State of Israel,"
in *Judaism, Human Values, and the Jewish State*, edited by Eliezer Goldman
and translated by Eliezer Goldman, Yoram Navon, Zvi Jacobson, Gershon Levi,
and Raphael Levy (Cambridge, MA: Harvard University Press, 1992), 214–20.

THE RELIGIOUS SIGNIFICANCE
OF THE STATE OF ISRAEL (1975)

I wish to introduce myself at the outset as one who hasn't been at all disap-
pointed by the State of Israel. . . . Zionism meant for me the endeavor to liberate
Jews from being ruled by the Gentiles. The State of Israel completely satisfies
the demand for freedom from domination by others. To that extent that I am
able to recall my opinions of fifty years ago, I believe that it never occurred to
me to assign to the state—any state, including Israel—the function of realizing
values, whether educational, cultural or moral; certainly not the religious values
of Torah and Mitzvoth.

. . . The struggle to realize these values is the problem of the Jewish people,
not the State of Israel. . . . It seems to me . . . that the discussion that took place
here . . . suffered for lack of a clear distinction between two things: between the

Jewish people as the bearer of Judaism and the sovereign state instituted by this people as its instrument. The crucial religious problem of the Jewish people, the continued historic existence of which has become questionable ever since the identification of the Jewish people with Judaism ceased to be axiomatic. . . .

The problem of the religious significance of the State of Israel is, in one respect, a theological-political problem. In another, it is a problem of the psychology of faith. . . . I believe that no state whatsoever, in the past, present, or any foreseeable future, in any society, in any era, in any culture, including the Jewish culture, ever was or will be anything but a secular institution. The function of the state is essentially secular. It is not service to God. . . . Religion, that is, man's recognition of his duty to serve God, cannot be integrated with the machinery of government. . . . The calamity of religious Jewry in this state consists in its voluntary dependence upon the political organization—a dependence which spells its doom. . . .

There is the additional problem of the Halakhah. We have established our independent state, and in so doing have raised questions that were not issues and could not be issues in the Halakhah as crystallized in recent times. From the halakhic point of view, the renewal of the independence of Israel is a veritable catastrophe. . . . To reiterate things that I have written repeatedly, the presupposition underlying the crystallization of the Halakhah over hundreds of years has been the fact—the empirical datum—that the Jewish people was independent and was bereft of any functions in the spheres of statehood, politics, security, diplomacy, and so on. . . . [F]rom the standpoint of faith the great question . . . can be phrased in one sentence: do we conceive the essence of our Judaism to be the service of God, or do we conceive it as the fulfillment of the interests and needs of the people of Israel?

Born in Romania, Berkovits (1908–92) was educated in Pressburg and Berlin, where he received rabbinical ordination and a doctorate in philosophy. He served as a rabbi in England, Australia, and the United States, where he also held an academic position. He lived in Israel for the last seventeen years of his life. In the selection included here, Berkovits offers a succinct definition of Jewish law, which he describes as a means for realizing the moral and social ideals of the Torah in reality. He follows Naḥmanides in arguing that the specific rules of Jewish law are guided by principles to achieve this result. Following Moshe Shemuel Glasner, who was an influence on him, Berkovits also reflects on the effects of exile (*Galut*) on the development of Jewish law. He argues that the historical codification of Jewish law was a result of the defensive and narrow conception of Judaism that resulted from Jews' having to live under the control of non-Jewish authorities. Berkovits urges those committed to the observance of Jewish law to recognize that with the establishment of the State of Israel, Jewish law needs to and can return to its natural, holistic form. In particular, Berkovits stresses that such Jews need to concern themselves with matters of law related to social justice and morality in Jewish law.

Eliezer Berkovits, *Not in Heaven: The Nature and Function of Halakhah*
(New York: J. Ktav, 1983), 71–73 and 85–91.

WHAT IS HALAKHAH?

. . . Halakhah is the wisdom of the application of the written word of the Torah to the life and history of the Jewish people. However, this wisdom and its implementation cannot be contained in any book. No written word can deal in advance with the innumerable situations, changes of circumstances, and new developments that normally occur in the history of men and nations. The eternal word of the Torah required a time-related teaching in order to become effective in the life of the Jewish people. This was the tradition passed on by the living word from generation to generation, . . . the Oral Torah beside the . . . Written Torah. The need for it has been clearly described by philosophical as well as halakhic authorities. . . .

. . . While these considerations apply to the entire ambit of human reality, other commentators emphasized the specifically ethical aspects of the problem and its solution. Thus, Nachmanides, commenting on the verse "thou shalt do the right and the good in the eyes of God,"[84] has the following to say:

> . . . [ellipsis in original] at first the Torah said, "thou shalt keep His statutes and His testimonies which He has commanded thee"; now it adds: but also in matters about which He did not command you, set your mind to it to do what is good and right in the eyes of God, for He loves the good and the right. This is very important. It is impossible to mention in the Torah the entirety of (what should be) human conduct with neighbors and friends, in all business activities and all the improvement of society and of the state. But after a great many of them (instances of what should be the right conduct in particular) are mentioned . . . [ellipsis in original] the Torah states generally that one should do the good and the right.

Using these remarks of Nachmanides somewhat differently from the context for which he intended them, one might say that even the "particulars" like "thou shalt not be a talebearer," "thou shalt not stand idly by the blood of thy neighbor," etc.,[85] are generalities that require some understanding of realization in the numerous different life situations. Commenting on the biblical words used by Nachmanides, one of the great commentators on the halakhic work of Maimonides explains:

> The meaning is that one should conduct oneself right and with goodness toward one's fellow men. It would not be correct (for the Torah [author's insertion]) to command in these matters in detail. The Torah was given for all periods and for all times and concerning all subjects—and that was necessary. But human qualities and conduct change with the times and the people. So our sages made a record of some helpful (decisions regarding [author's insertion]) details that they derived from the general principles, some of them as binding laws, others to be done (but without consequences if not done [author's insertion]) or recommended as pious deeds.[86]

84. Deut. 6:18.
85. Leviticus 19:6.
86. Cf. *Maggid Mishneh* [(Second announcement), by Vidal of Tolosa, first published 1509] on [*Mishneh Torah*, "Laws of Neighbors,"] 14:5.

All these ... authors in a way make clear the need for the Oral Torah to accompany the Written Word on its journey through the history of the Jewish people. The crystallization of the Oral Torah into a system of teachings and norms for human conduct is the Halakhah.

By some of the words in our last quotation one may be guided to an appreciation of another problem present in the application of the Torah to the human condition in its daily reality. In a sense, every system of an established law has to cope with a problem that derives from its generality. The Jew has to formulate general principles; but life situations are always particulars, there is something unique about each of them. In this sense, every law is to some extent "inhuman." The problem is much more serious when the basis of the law is the revealed Word of God, which by its very nature is timeless. How can an eternal truth and command take notice of the forever-changing needs of the fleetingly uncertain human condition? ...

The problem is further complicated by the fact that the process of the application of the Torah to life all through the history of the Jewish people had to be entrusted to man. It had to be because "the Torah was not given to God's ministering angels,"[87] but to mere man. Once the Torah was revealed to the children of Israel, its realization on earth became their responsibility, to be shouldered by human ability and human insight. That is, we suggest, the ultimate meaning of Rabbi Y'hoshua's bold stand: "The Torah is no longer in heaven!"[88] One pays no attention to the voice from heaven in matters of Torah-realization on earth. So is it intended and explicitly stated in the Torah itself: It could not be otherwise. The divine truth had to be poured into human vessels; it had to be "humanized." Having left its heavenly abode, it had to be accommodated in the modest cottages of human uncertainty and inadequacy. This, in essence, is the task of the Halakhah....

HALAKHAH IN OUR TIME

With the destruction of the Second Temple and collapse of the Jewish commonwealth, both the Jewish people and their entire spiritual world went into exile. The [Oral Torah] and the Halakhah lost their natural habitat. Judaism was meant to be the total way of life of the Jewish people. It comprehends the entire

87. [See, for example, b. Berakhot 25b; b. Yoma 30a; b. Kiddushin 53b.]
88. [b. Bava Metzia 59b.]

manifestation of a national existence, its political and economic structure, its social-ethical goals, its spiritual vision, and its cultural strivings. Judaism is not a religion but a comprehensive religious civilization. . . .

Since Halakhah is the wisdom of application of the words of the Torah, its teachings and commandments, to the real-life situation of the Jewish people, the field of application narrows to the extent to which control over their lives falls from the hands of the people. . . .

. . . In the *Galut* [exile], Halakhah is confronted with the problems, needs, and demands of non-Jewish realities forced upon a people scattered into communities in the midst of cultures and civilizations alien to the spirit and ideals of Judaism.

. . . In the *Galut* the encounter between Torah and reality is a confrontation; in an autonomous Jewish civilization, it is a challenge. In the situation of confrontation, the task of Halakhah is preservation: how to preserve the life of the people and its Jewish character in the midst of a politically mostly inimical and spiritually and morally alien world. Halakhah in Exile is essentially protective Halakhah, often on the defensive. . . .

. . . Unfortunately, as the result of the destruction of the Second Jewish Commonwealth and the dispersion of the Jewish people from its homeland, the situation changed radically. Because of external necessity, a process of solidification of the Oral Torah set in. It became increasingly difficult to entrust the entire accumulated oral teaching to memory. The problem was aggravated out of all proportion as the result of the political upheavals and the uncertain conditions. . . .

The very idea of codification violates the essence of the [Oral Torah]. According to one formulation in the Talmud, those who write down [rules] are like people who burn the Torah.[89] "These as well as those are the words of the living God"[90] would be an intellectual and moral monstrosity within a code of law. But again conditions detrimental to the preservation of the tradition seem to have been the determining factor in this new phase. The process of codification reached its most authoritative forms in the code of Maimonides, the *Tur* by Rabbi Ya'akob the son of Rabbi Asher,[91] and the *Shulḥan Arukh* by Rabbi Yosef Karo. . . .

. . . The twofold *Galut* of Halakhah—its exile from reality and its exile into literature and codification—forced it into a straitjacket as we face the challenges of

89. [b. Temurah 14b.]
90. [b. Eruvin 13b.]
91. [1270–c.1340, author of the *Tur (Arba'ah Turim)*.]

our time. Nowhere is this more seriously felt than in the modern State of Israel. After almost two millennia of *Galut*, Halakhah has been given back its authentic partner, the daily reality of the life of a Jewish people living in its own land. . . .

Halakhah has once again a comprehensive form of Jewish reality to work with, a wide field of Torah application to life—political, economic, social, ethical. Once again, Torah may move from the private congregational domain to which the *Galut* had limited it into the public domain of a nation. Halakhah, which in the *Galut* had to be on the defensive, building fences around communal islands, ought to resume now its classical function and originate new forms of relevant Torah realization in the State of Israel. It should concern itself with questions of social justice, of economic honesty and fairness, with problems of labor relations and of the work ethos, with the social gap [between rich and poor], with ethics and morality in public life, even with such matters as traffic laws in the cities and on the highways. . . .

Shaul Yisraeli (1909–95) was born in Belarus. With the help of Abraham Isaac Kook, Yisraeli immigrated to Palestine in 1934, where he studied with Kook at his yeshiva, Merkaz Harav. When Kook died the following year, Yisraeli was appointed joint head of the yeshiva. In 1965 Yisraeli became a judge of the Supreme Rabbinical Court in Jerusalem. He founded and edited the journal *Ha-Torah ve-ha-Medinah* (Torah and the state). In the selection included here, Yisraeli first argues for the political and institutional Jewish legal authority of the Chief Rabbinate beyond the individual authority of its incumbent. Then he weighs the advantages and disadvantages of voting for a law that would shut down public transportation on Shabbat for most of the country except Haifa. This is an example of Yisraeli attempting to apply Jewish law to coalition politics within the context of a state that is not governed by Jewish law. Yisraeli's realist position with regard to Israeli political reality may be helpfully compared to the more idealist perspective of Eliezer Waldenberg in the following selection.

Shaul Yisraeli, *Amud ha-Yemini* [Pillar of the right] (Jerusalem: Eretz Ḥemdah, 1991), 30–34 and 78–80 (translated by Shlomo Zuckier).

SECTION 6: ON CLARIFYING THE JEWISH LEGAL (HA-HILKHATIT) AUTHORITY OF THE CHIEF RABBINATE OF ISRAEL

On occasion of several decisions (piskei) of the Chief Rabbinate of [the State of] Israel with which some Torah scholar disagreed, there has been perplexity within society and also among Torah scholars as to the authority of the Chief Rabbinate regarding establishing the rule (halakhah) and to the extent this decision obligates the community. I saw someone who wrote that the authority of the chief rabbis (and of the Council of the Chief Rabbis) is not changed at all from what it had been prior to their election to this role. This is based on the simple and correct (in itself) statement that the Torah with all its details and fine points and explanations is from heaven and that its explanation was transmitted as the Oral Torah, which we possess today and which is integrated into the Talmud and early and later decisors [poskim rishonim ve-aḥronim]. And since this is the case, the Rabbinate cannot change the law (din) in any matter. However, there are several other points that need clarification, from which we can understand the power to decide [the law] possessed by those who were chosen to stand at the head of the holy people. . . .

Behold, the Chief Rabbinate was accepted upon itself by the majority of the community in Israel in the capacity of being its rabbis. And even the local rabbis are only accepted with the approval of the Chief Rabbinate. Thus, the national rabbinate has the authority (*tokef*) of the master of the place (*mara de-atra*) for all places in Israel, because even local rabbis only work as its representative. . . . One may not rule against a decision of [the Chief Rabbinate], and one cannot publicize as a practical rule (*le-halakhah le-ma'aseh*) an opinion that is opposed to its determination of the rule (pesak halakhah), so long as [the determination] is not based on an error in a basic matter, but rather an error in decision and judgment. This [applies to the Chief Rabbinate] even when it rules leniently, and even when it concerns a biblical prohibition. [This applies to the Chief Rabbinate] as well before it decides and certainly after it decides. [To such a case] applies the decision of [Rabbi Moshe Isserles], that even when a scholar who rules to permit [something], a second scholar cannot prohibit [it], which is . . . unanimously held, according to Rabbi Akiva Eiger.[92] At least *ab initio*, one should refrain from ruling out of honor to the first rabbi. In our case, even if the second [scholar] violated and ruled [against the first scholar], his ruling is not a [valid] ruling as regards this community, since its members accepted the Chief Rabbinate as their rabbis, as described above.

If, indeed, one considers that for the members of the community who never accepted the Chief Rabbinate originally, one can rule that they do not have the prohibition of "Do not create factions."[93] . . . However, [for] this community, whose members are the majority of the settlers in the Land of Israel, [and] who chose the Chief Rabbinate and sees it as their rabbis, both for them and for the rabbis who serve in the various communities by dint of the appointment and agreement of the chief rabbi, [the Chief Rabbinate] certainly possesses the status of the master of the place, whose rulings are laws and whose decisions are binding (*dinam din u-pesakam pesak*), even for issues that relate to questions of biblical prohibitions, so long as no error in a basic matter is ever revealed, God forbid.

From thence, my announcement: [Concerning,] all those decisions of the

92. [Poland, 1761–1837.]

93. [See Deut. 14:1, as interpreted at b. Yebamot 13b.]

Chief Rabbinate that were published after analysis and discussion as is proper (*ki-halakhah*), even though there are scholars who oppose them, there is no room to view [their opposition] except as a dispute in judgment, and in such a case the decision of the master of the place is certainly valid without any doubt. . . .

. . . .

SECTION 11: LAWS OF THE COALITION

. . . .

IV. The Proposed Shabbat Law: Choosing the Lesser Evil

The proposed law, according to which public transportation on Shabbat and festivals will be stopped for the vast majority of the State [of Israel], and similarly work in the factories will be restricted on Shabbat and festivals, [includes] on the other hand, that there will remain a type of enclave of the city of Haifa, in which no transportation limitations will take effect. Similarly, the suggested law does not include limitations on individual transportation or taxi service. We will clarify the positive and negative aspects in this [law] and weigh its gains and losses. . . .

These are the points that seem to have to be dealt with:

A. The benefit of the law from a practical perspective in terms of minimizing Shabbat desecration

B. The benefit of the law from the perspective of Jewish Law (ha-halakhah) in terms of limiting public Shabbat desecration

C. Leaving behind a minority of the community for the sake of the rectification of (*takkanat*) another part, namely the majority

D. Strengthening sinners through raising this law in the Knesset and supporting it

E. Desecration of God's Name in supporting this law

A. THE BENEFIT OF THE LAW FROM A PRACTICAL PERSPECTIVE

. . . [T]he very fact that there is no organized mass transportation in operation causes the creation of a spirit of Shabbat in the community. . . .

However, some claim that . . . by legislating a Shabbat law for the State but leaving Haifa outside of it, there is the perpetuation of the situation of breach [of the commandments] that has ruled in this city for a sustained period of time. . . .

. . . It is a fact that over the years since the founding of the State, we have not merited to see an improvement of the situation [of religious observance], not even to see an awakening of the religious sector to strengthen its organization and to increase the makeup of its representation in the Knesset to pass more preferable laws from the perspective of the Torah. This is nothing but the fostering of an illusion, [that is,] that soon we will merit seeing a strengthening of the measure of religious Judaism (*yahdut ha-datit*) to the point where it is possible to apply sufficient pressure to pass laws according to our will. . . .

. . . There is also the opposite reasoning; that improving the situation in the rest of Israel will also have a positive influence, at the end of the day, on Haifa itself. . . .

In any event, whatever our concerns regarding the influence of the law on the development of the matter in the future, we must act in accordance with the stated principle: An uncertainty does not override a certainty. And since the improvement is clear, and the concerns are only concerns, we must take into consideration the certainty and act in accordance with it.

B. THE VALUE OF THE LAW FROM THE PERSPECTIVE OF JEWISH LAW

. . . [I]n the opinion of Tosafot there is a commandment of saving an individual from committing a sin, even when that individual has the status of an apostate (*mumar*). However, in truth the overwhelming majority of the community caught up in desecration of Shabbat does this not because of a calculated, malicious intention; but rather, they are drawn into it by the atmosphere on the street, the example that they see in front of them, and the existence of lines of transportation that operate in an organized manner, which are like a breach calling for a robber. So, too, some who desecrate Shabbat at work in various factories do this out of fear for loss of their job and due to pressure on them. . . . The enactment of a law that will stop this to a large measure qualifies both as a great commandment and a commandment of the many simultaneously. . . .

C. LEAVING BEHIND A MINORITY OF THE COMMUNITY FOR THE SAKE OF THE MAJORITY

. . . [T]he entire purpose of legislating this law, which will restrict desecration of Shabbat in the rest of the country, does not come from the initiative of those interested in desecrating Shabbat. On the contrary, they wish to entrench themselves, as it were, in one place while as regards the rest [of the country] they agree because they have no choice. From their perspective, they would certainly prefer the present situation, in which there is no [national] law in any place and to the extent that there is a local law, it is not effective. If so, this is not like a case of idolaters who use the threat of killing everyone as a form of pressure [on the community to force them] to hand over an individual to be killed, where their entire purpose is that the Jews themselves will hand over one of their own to be killed.

D. STRENGTHENING SINNERS

It is obvious that even though this proposed law is brought with the language described above before the Knesset by religious members of the Knesset, and even though they vote for it, there is no problem of supporting sinners. . . .

But even if there were [an issue of] supporting [sinners] in this . . . , there is the principle that in such a case we say to someone, "Sin so that your fellow can receive merit," and "Better to desecrate one Shabbat so that one may observe many Shabbats" (b. Yoma 85b). . . .

E. DESECRATION OF GOD'S NAME

. . . There is a difference between one who supports a transgressor in his carrying out of the transgression and one who supports him by encouraging it and agreeing with it, for thereby he appears to identify with the transgressor. The mere act of supporting his action without encouragement is only a rabbinic prohibition, and there is no issue of desecrating God's Name. If so, in our case described above, bringing the law to the Knesset and voting for it will certainly not be accompanied by the religious members of the Knesset encouraging sinners, but—to the contrary!—by their remorse and expression of pain that it is not in their power to offer a proper law in accordance with their preferences. There is [thus] no element of the desecration of God's Name that can at times be entailed by the issue of supporting [sinners]. . . .

However, we should consider how much the desecration of God's Name will decrease due to this law, and how much public desecration of Shabbat will be prevented by this law. We should recall that even the best proposal [for a law] cannot fully control desecration of God's Name by individual [cars] and taxicabs. . . . This entire discussion is only about a partial restraint which, while not all-encompassing, still has some degree of improvement. If we weigh all of this with thoughtfulness and levelheadedness, without interest in altercation or any tangential thoughts in which the "not for the right reasons" (lo lishmah) overrides the "for the right reasons" (lishmah), we will then reach the conclusion that the acceptance of the Shabbat law, even in its limited form, should be seen as a great accomplishment for religious Judaism in the Land [of Israel]. It will be able to serve, God willing, as a cornerstone for the imposition (hashlatat) of the Torah on the public lives in the State of Israel.

Eliezer Waldenberg (1915–2006) was born and died in Jerusalem, where he served on the Supreme Rabbinical Court and was also the rabbi of Shaare Zedek Medical Center. Waldenberg is best known for his responsa on biomedical issues, such as abortion, in vitro fertilization and other fertility treatments, and euthanasia. In 1952, he published a comprehensive legal treatise on the relationship between Jewish law and the laws of the State of Israel. In contrast to the attempts at moderation by Shlomo Goren and Isaac Halevi Herzog in their conceptions of the relationship between Jewish law and the laws of the State of Israel, as well as in contrast to Yeshayahu Leibowitz's strict separation between halakhah and the laws of the state, Waldenberg argues that traditional Jewish law is sufficient for the governance of the modern Jewish state.

Eliezer Waldenberg, *Hilkhot Medinah* [Laws of the state] (Jerusalem: Mosad ha-Rav Kook, 1952), 5–26 (translated by Michael Schultz).

PREFACE

"My Lord let loose a word against Jacob and it fell upon Israel."[94] Great are God's kindnesses toward us, and after thousands of years of exile, He has given us the merit to be returned to our patrimony as at the beginning, to live the life of an autonomous people (*am atzma'ei*) in its own land—admittedly, still in only part of the Land [of Israel], and absent the crown of our glory, the sanctuary of the King, royal city with the mount of majesty toward which all mouths turn [in prayer]—.

. . . .

At the present moment, to our great sorrow we have not yet merited to rise up at this great hour, to all walk together in the light of God. Not only have we not cast off the idols of our wealth and the idols of our gold . . . [but w]e have even added further sin on transgression, abandoning the well of spring water that the chieftains dug, that the nobles of the people started with their maces, with their own staffs.[95] Instead we hewed out cisterns, broken cisterns, that cannot even

94. [Isa. 9:7.]
95. [See Num. 21:18.]

hold water,[96] imitating foreign laws or fabricating laws as the heart desires that are opposed to the eternal law. A divine voice cries softly like a dove and shouts like a crane,[97] "Ha! Those who write out evil writs and compose iniquitous documents" (Isaiah 10:1). I hoped for justice, but behold, injustice.[98] How has this come to be, to turn away from God, our Lord, to go and worship the nations' gods, where is the root, the source sprouting poison weed and wormwood?[99] "Be mindful of the Teaching (torat) of My servant Moses, whom I charged at Horeb with laws and rules for all Israel" (Malachi 3:22). Let it circumscribe your way of life, that everything will be encircled, from without and from within, with its ways, the ways of my God, my King, into the sanctuary.[100] For the Torah is eternal, and hidden and concealed within the treasury of its precious vessels is the instruction (torat) for the highest moral perfection, not for [God's] sake but for yours, that it be good for you for all days, for God will again delight in you, as He delighted in your ancestors.[101]

I am very zealous for the laws (mishpetei) of our living Torah, the Torah of Sinai, for the sake of His great Name, may He be blessed, which becomes greater and is sanctified through the performance of the Torah's righteous laws. For He is a King who loves righteousness and justice, as it says, "God of hosts is exalted by justice, the holy God is proved holy by righteousness" (Isaiah 5:16).[102] Therefore I have girded my loins like a man[103] and inspired my soul with courage[104] to set my face as flint[105] to approach and enter into the sanctuary; to compose a broad, comprehensive treatise on the rules of the doctrine of our Hebrew state (hilkhot torat medinateinu ha-ivrit), the state of God's people; and to display before the people and its officers, to the extent that my weak hands are capable [of doing so], that God's statutes and His Torah, written and oral—two that are one, along the lines of, "One thing God has spoken, two things I have heard, for might

96. [See Jer. 2:13.]
97. [See b. Berakhot 3a and b. Kiddushin 44a.]
98. [See Isa. 5:7.]
99. [See Deut. 29:17.]
100. [See Ps. 68:25.]
101. [See Deut. 30:9.]
102. [New Jewish Publication Society (NJPS) Tanakh translation, modified.]
103. [See Job 38:3.]
104. [See Ps. 138:3.]
105. [See Isa. 50:7.]

belongs to God" (Psalms 62:12)[106]—contain within them an entire, comprehensive view of life for a people thrust forth and away,[107] living autonomously in its precious Land [of Israel], strong enough to successfully solve all its problems of politics and of governing, to enlighten it, and to successfully establish its sovereignty. . . .

INTRODUCTION

I

. . . The purview of the law (halakhah) has newly expanded before us, and new tasks have been placed before us, spreading wide in dimension, to be deeply engaged in these fields of law, which for the last nearly two thousand years had only needed to be engaged inasmuch as any of the "rules for Messianic times (hilkhata le-misheḥa)." . . .

It is our duty to show the path and the way for a nation reborn, to explore the laws and statutes of the Torah, for by traversing its eternal ways you will achieve, "Do not read ways (halikhot) but rather rules (halakhot)"[108]—the clear recognition that only the ways of our holy Torah can provide a foundation, a precedent, and a continuous pipeline from which to draw for the laws of our state. It will bear us on its wings to a turning point, the unification of the entire people under a broad, comprehensive framework, held together from end to end by the linchpin of the statute of Hebrew law (ḥok ha-misphat ha-ivri) in its fullest sense. . . .

. . . The long history of our people has taught us clearly and determined unambiguously that the ultimate foundation and pillars of the state of the Jews are set on a layer of bricks—the book, our holy Torah, given to us beforehand so we could turn to it. . . . [A]nyone who comes to separate the Torah from the state imperils the life of the nation: . . . Thus, the location of the verse "The judgments of the Lord are true, altogether righteous,"[109] referring to the laws of the state of the Jews, is set in Jerusalem, the center of gravity of holiness of all worlds. . . .

106. [NJPS, modified.]
107. [See Isa. 18:2.]
108. [b. Niddah 53a.]
109. [Ps.19:10.]

II

This is eternal. It is a direction shown at the six days of Creation. Prior to the act [of Creation] a condition was set, that the continued existence of all that was created would always be dependent on [the fulfillment of] "keeping the way of the Lord by doing what is just and right."[110] For this reason, from the moment it was created, mankind was commanded to establish a legal system (*dinin*) (see b. Sanhedrin 56b . . .). . . .

. . . From the moment He [God] handed us the secrets of his mandates to the present day, it is as if a condition was made that the foundation of our stable existence depends at all times on the level of our ably observing and pledging allegiance to these statutes and laws. . . . [A]ny generation that tried to outsmart and circumvent this foundational condition, that became intransigent and estranged itself from the original Hebrew law (*mishpat ha-ivri*), and threw the yoke off its shoulders—sooner or later it drained the bowl, the cup of poison,[111] as various forces encompassed it round about and brought its rule to the brink of collapse. . . .

III

In saying to us, "Judgment is God's,"[112] the precise intention is without any distinction between judgments relating to God and judgments between people. . . .

The secret hidden in the mysteries of creation impatiently hopes and wishes for the revelation of this ultimate judgment, and for its recognition to penetrate decision makers across the face of the Earth. . . .

Upon delving deeper, one reaches the key point, that there is a great, chasmic difference between divine Torah law and human law, even in this area, the laws of society and state. . . .

IV

. . . The Jewish nation knows in no uncertain terms how to set [up] the mutual relationship between religion (*dat*) and state and how to define the boundaries of their mutual authority. For our nation's goal is not to aspire to momentary delights and base pleasures that pass from the world, vanishing as if they had never been. Rather, it turns to eternal aspirations, and it is oriented toward achieving

110. [Gen. 18:19; NJPS, modified.]
111. [See Isa. 51:17.]
112. [Deut. 1:17.]

supreme bliss in all its fullness, its divine mission. Thus, without the statutes of its Torah, its state would be like a body without a soul. For this nation, religion and state were said simultaneously[113] and by no means can they be separated, along the lines of "if you cut off its head, will it not die?"[114] ...

Any attempt to separate religion from state will lead the state to a terrible collapse, [and] who can see what will be its end?[115] ...

....

VI

The outlines of our legislative activity must be delineated by the frame of the statutes of the Torah, in which we have abiding faith that all of its laws are precisely those given to our rabbi Moses, peace be unto him, at Mount Sinai, in view of all Israel. And God will not alter or change His law (*dato*) for any other, ever.[116] ...

Listen, my nation, understand this. Walk in God's ways and His faithful laws, and He will subdue your enemies before you, and you will merit to dwell securely in your land, with nothing to terrify you. "You shall observe My laws and faithfully keep My rules, that you may live upon the land in security" (Lev. 25:18).

VII

When the State [of Israel] came into being, dread and horror gripped those who held themselves to be progressives at the fearful possibility that a miracle would happen and the state would be run according to the statutes of Moses's Torah. The term "theocratic state" was sounded in all directions, threatening the masses like some terrible monster looming over them, wishing to swallow them alive. ...

... They neither know nor understand[117] that not even the most advanced democratic rule can compare to divine rule, what they term "theocracy." They go about in darkness,[118] blind to the great light that shines through in every matter of statute and judgment flowing forth from the fountains of the great deep

113. [As is said regarding "Remember the Sabbath" and "Preserve the Sabbath" in the Ten Commandments.]

114. [This is a rabbinic principle for judging the permissibility of actions on Shabbat.]

115. [See Job 17:15.]

116. [From the daily morning prayers.]

117. [See Ps. 82:5.]

118. [Ibid.]

of the Torah of the supreme ruler of all. Missing out on "learn to do good" is what made them shortsighted and narrow in their horizons and brought them to their pointless panic in the face of the "devote yourselves to justice"[119] of the God of justice. It prevented them from seeing truly, that the goal of the divine law of justice is actually to provide the nation [with] good instruction for how to live its lives justly and uprightly, and to show it the path it should take—via the golden mean—and the ways it should act, to enjoy eternal bliss and live lives free from shame or disgrace.[120] "I gave them My statutes and taught them My laws, by the pursuit of which a man shall live" (Ezekiel 20:11).[121] . . .

Now comes one of the leading members of the Israeli intelligentsia of our time, Dr. A. H. Freimann, and here is what he suggests to them: . . .

> . . . Theocracy does not stand in opposition to the customary form of political rule exercised by the nations of the world. They expounded the verse well: "Then He became King in Jeshurun, when the heads of the people assembled, the tribes of Israel together."[122] No matter the form of rule and political governance in Israel, be it monarchy—the rule of one, the "king"; be it aristocracy—the rule of the "heads of the people"; or be it democracy—"the tribes of Israel together"; regardless, the foundational statute, the Israelite constitution, eternally remains "Moses charged us with the Torah, the heritage of the congregation of Jacob. [ellipsis in original] . . ."[123] . . . (Dr. A. H. Freimann, *Yavneh*, 1:2–3; Av 1950)

. . . [I]n truth the Torah has sufficient strength and might to resolve the questions of life, in all its wending paths and new developments, at all times. . . . Without any doubt, it can solve all the problems of the state and through the appropriate means can shape and fulfill the state's character. It depends only on us. . . .

Our state's foundational constitution was already given at Sinai and will never change. We did not grant it its authority, and in any event it is not in our hands to void it—even against our will it will remain. Therefore, to avoid putting our national existence in danger we must return the royal crown to our Torah by minting our way of life in its image and in its likeness. . . .

---

119. [Isa. 1:17.]
120. [A reference to the blessing of the new month.]
121. [NJPS, modified.]
122. [Deut. 33:5.]
123. [Ibid., 33:4; NJPS, modified.]

VIII

The masses in every rank and file are overcome with ravenous demands to establish [rabbinic] enactments (takanot) in every area of Israeli life. Everyone wielding a pen expresses his demands in writing, using all means of persuasion.

Those making demands can be divided into two [groups]: One group simply aims to deceive those upright people walking in the ways of God's Torah, obliquely unburdening the state of the yoke of the Torah and the commandments in their entirety. . . . The second group is drawn to this out of a foolish naiveté, as if the wise ones of Israel have the power and the ability to detract from or add to the essence of the Torah. . . .

As for the first group, we do not need to stand in their way beyond responding simply and clearly: Why veil yourselves? "Is it not enough for you to treat men as helpless that you also treat my God as helpless?" (Isa. 7:13). . . . Stop doing evil, return to the Rock from which you quarry and to His statutes that provide a stronghold, so that you may live.

And to those who walk in opposition in the second manner, we will respond and say: You are making a great mistake in thinking that we are able . . . to add to or detract from God's laws and His teachings. . . . [Yet] in every generation, from the time of Moses, our rabbi, until the completion of the Babylonian Talmud, and from the completion of the Babylonian Talmud to the present day, the sages of Israel have always been deciphering the hidden mysteries of the living God's Torah, whose measure is longer than the earth and broader than the sea.[124] They resolve the novel questions engendered by the age and innovate enactments as protective barriers, determining what the generation needs based on their judgment—the judgment of the Torah—and on what their eyes see, in keeping with the holy obligation thrust on them, to guard the walls of the Torah and the religion (ha-dat). . . .

There are even interpretations left alone by the heavens to be developed in each era, for everything has its season, and a time for every purpose.[125] . . . [This] is all the more clear in our days, when our autonomous state has been renewed, and the field of civil law has very greatly grown and expanded, as economic life has greatly developed. . . .

Know, however, that even when we have the authority to enact, still "the burden lies on whoever comes to suggest an enactment to demonstrate the reasons

124. [See Job 11:9.]
125. [See Eccl. 3:1.]

and rationale for why the enactments are necessary." And the rationale for these demands must derive from a holy source, founded on internal reasons and worthy intentions, to glorify and adorn our living home with the prestige of our holy Torah's crown of kingship. . . .

IX

They are fooled, those who think, whether willfully or ignorantly, that the leaders and stewards in each generation, whatever their communal status and spiritual outlook may be, have the authority to decree rules for the general good as they see fit in all areas of life. . . .

. . . [E]ven in those matters where authority has been given to promulgate enactments for the needs of the time or to set the religion (dat) in its place, as the leaders of the time see fit, where these matters relate to the laws and customs of the Torah, then such authority is granted only to the Torah sages of that time, who have a monument and a name[126] in understanding the words of the Torah. . . .

126. [See Isa. 56:5.]

34

Ovadiah Yosef, "Regarding Women's Recital of the Blessing over the Lulav and Other Time-Bound Positive Commandments"

Born in Baghdad, Iraq, Ovadiah Yosef (1920–2013) immigrated to Palestine at the age of four. In 1947, he moved to Cairo, Egypt, where he headed a rabbinical court and a yeshiva. He returned to Israel in 1950 and was appointed the chief Sephardic rabbi in 1973. Yosef energized the Jewish, working-class, Sephardic public during his tenure as chief rabbi and is often credited with the political success of the Israeli political party Shas, which claims to represent Israel's Sephardic citizens. In the selection included here, Yosef rules that women may not say a blessing before performing a commandment for which they are not obligated. In the process, he engages in a forceful polemic against Eliezer Waldenberg, who had argued that they could. Yosef maintains that European women may continue their practice of saying a blessing before performing such commandments, but in strident tones he asserts the legitimacy of the Sephardic halakhic tradition, following Yosef Karo in the *Shulḥan Arukh*. In general, this selection demonstrates four related features of Yosef's jurisprudence: first, the assertion of the equality, if not supremacy, of the Sephardic halakhic tradition to that of European Jews; second, the identification of that Sephardic tradition with the rulings of Karo in the *Shulḥan Arukh*, which suppresses the diversity of non-European halakhic traditions; third, his legal rationalism, expressed by his rejection of the prophetic responsa; and fourth, his encyclopedic use of precedent. Yosef gathers together many more sources than most other decisors do.[127]

---

127. Two studies have informed the choice of this selection and assessment of its significance: Benyamin Lau, *Me-Maran ad Maran: Mishnato ha-Hilkhatit shel ha-Rav Ovadiah Yosef* [From our master (Karo) to our master (Yosef): The halakhic doctrine of Rabbi Ovadiah Yosef] (Tel Aviv: Miskal, Yediot Aḥronot ve-Sefrei Ḥemed, 2005); and Ariel Picard, *Mishnato shel ha-Rav Ovadiah Yosef be-Eidan shel Temurot: Ḥeker ha-Halakhah ve-Bekoret Tarbut* [The doctrine of Rabbi Ovadiah Yosef in a period of change: Halakhic examination and cultural critique] (Ramat Gan, Israel: Bar Ilan University Press, 2007).

Ovadiah Yosef, *She'elot u-Teshuvot Yabi'a Omer* [Responsa It Utters Speech][128] (Jerusalem: Yeshiva Porat Yosef and Mosad ha-Rav Kook, 1968), 5:147–152 (translated by Michael Schultz).

Regarding Women's Recital of the Blessing over the *Lulav* and Other Time-Bound Positive Commandments

(1) I took note and set my mind to the matter that I raised previously (Responsa *Yabi'a Omer* Oraḥ Ḥayyim 1: no. 39ff) regarding women's recital of the blessing over the lulav[129] and other time-bound positive commandments[130]: that the opinion of our great rabbi Maimonides ([*Mishneh Torah*,] "Laws of Tzitzit," 3:9 and "Laws of Sukkah," 6:13) is that women may not recite a blessing over the performance of time-bound positive commandments that they perform. [*Maggid Mishneh*] (*ad loc.*) elucidates: "For how can they say [in the blessing prior to performance of the commandment], 'who has sanctified us through His commandments and has commanded us' since they are exempt?" . . .

. . . Maimonides' prohibition of women's reciting the blessing over time-bound positive commandments follows from his position that it is biblically prohibited to recite a blessing that is not mandated. A number of later authorities offered this same explanation for his position. . . .

. . . Our master [Yosef Karo] ruled this same way, in the *Beit Yosef*[131] and in the *Shulḥan Arukh* (sections 17 and 589), that women may not recite a blessing over time-bound positive commandments, for in case of doubt one should not recite a blessing. He ruled in keeping with his own position, for he ruled (section 215) that the prohibition of reciting a blessing that is not mandated is a biblical one. . . .

. . . Mahari Navon saw clearly when he wrote in his book, *Nehpah Bakesef*,[132] volume 1, page 181c):

In practice we follow the opinion of Maimonides and rule that women may not recite a blessing over time-bound positive commandments, for in case of

---

128. [The title of this book alludes to Ps. 19:3 "Day utters speech to day," in a context of all the works of creation glorifying God.]

129. [The lulav is a ritual object that consists of a palm frond bound together with branches of myrtle and willow. With the *etrog* (a citrus fruit), these are known as the four species used on the festival of Sukkot.]

130. [The time-bound positive commandments are those that must be performed at specific times. Traditionally, women are not required to perform these commandments.]

131. [Karo's commentary on *Araba'ah Turim*.]

132. [(Sheathed in silver), by Yonah ben Hanun Navon (Jerusalem, 1712–60).]

doubt one should not recite a blessing, as our master Beit Yosef [referring to Karo by the title of his work] wrote (section 17). . . . [T]he women's custom of reciting a blessing over the lulav is a mistaken one, especially where we are, in the holy city of Jerusalem, where the rulings of our master [Karo] were accepted. Anyone who endeavors to put an end to this custom, may he be blessed, for the rule is straightforward. . . . And our rabbi, Rabbi Moshe [Isserles] who wrote in his note that the custom is for women to bless, that is only in Ashkenaz, where they follow the teachings of Tosafot. But it would certainly not be appropriate for us to bless.

His [Mahari Navon's] student, Ḥida,[133] wrote in *Birkei Yosef* (section 554: 2): "As for the custom of some women in the land of Israel to recite a blessing over the lulav, I have been objecting to it for many years. They took this custom on by themselves, but we have accepted for ourselves the instruction of Maimonides and of our master [Karo], and they ruled against reciting the blessing. I asked the sages, the elders of our generation, and they responded that it is a mistaken custom that some of the women are following, unawares, and this custom should be ended. . . ." . . .

We find that all the great later authorities ruled like the instructions of our master, which we accepted for ourselves. The still-flowering custom of some women, to recite a blessing on time-bound positive commandments, has been publicly challenged by the geniuses of Jerusalem. They say that the women do so unawares, probably having observed this practice among the women who ascended to Israel from the lands of Ashkenaz, who would recite the blessings when they were covenanted [to those countries], when they lived outside of Israel. A woman's wisdom is only in women's work,[134] and they followed their neighbors, unawares, without realizing or understanding that we accepted for ourselves to follow our master [Karo]'s instruction, and he ruled not to recite the blessing. In his light we are enlightened. . . .

. . . However, the genius Ḥida, in his work *Birkei Yosef* (section 654) cited above, after writing all that we cited in the previous section, concluded his discussion by bringing the responsa of Mahari of Marvège.[135] He would direct dream inquiries to the heavens and would receive a response in a dream. In section 1 of that book, [Mahari] asked about this matter, and the heavens responded, "If women

133. [Ḥaim Yosef David Azulai ben Yitzḥak Zeraḥia (Jerusalem, 1724–1806).]
134. [b. Yoma 66b.]
135. [Ya'akov Halevi of Marvège (thirteenth century).]

wish to bless, they are free to do so." In [Ḥida's] responsa, *Yosef Ometz* (no. 82), he raised this [issue] once more:

> Ever since I, the inadequate, saw what the heavens responded to Rabbi Yaakov of Marvège, I customarily tell women to recite the blessing over the lulav, as was the women's custom in Jerusalem, may it be built and firmly established. Even though our master [Karo] ruled in the *Shulḥan Arukh* that they should not recite a blessing, it seems certain that if his holiness had laid his masterful eyes on the responsa of Mahari of Marvège, that the heavens empower women to recite the blessing, he would certainly have ruled and instructed in that way. In such a case, since many decisors think that they should recite a blessing, we do not say "it is not in the heavens," rather the divine assistance we enjoy here enables us to rule following those decisors.

> . . . .

> In my work, responsa *Yabi'a Omer* volume 1 (no. 41), I considered at length the matter of whether we should rule (*le-fsok halakhah*) based on the heavenly responsa of Mahari of Marvège, may his memory be for a blessing. I ultimately ruled that in rendering practical rulings we do not rely on the opinion of Mahari of Marvège when doing so would violate the principles for making rulings, namely that we follow the opinion of Maimonides and our master [Karo] and the other decisors whose rulings we customarily follow. Even when there is a dispute among decisors, we do not rely on Mahari of Marvège's rulings, for "it is not in the heavens,"[136] as Maimonides explicates ([*Mishneh Torah*], "Laws of the Foundations of the Torah," 9). . . .

> And "go out and see" that the Ḥida's assertion, that if our master [Karo] had seen the words of Mahari of Marvège he would certainly have ruled and instructed in that way, is not at all correct, may his honorable Torah eminence forgive me. For our master of blessed memory has strength and resourcefulness, and will not retreat from his approach of ruling like Maimonides and those in line with him just because of some dream inquiry. . . .

> . . . I needed to explain all this—and it is harder to remember something old than something new—because I saw what our friend, the genius Rabbi Eliezer Y. Waldenberg,[137] . . . wrote . . .:

---

136. [See Deut. 30:12 and b. Bava Metzia 59b.]

137. [This passage is a mixture of direct quotation from Waldenberg's book and a summary of it. It is preserved as a quotation since that is how Yosef presented it.]

. . . .

Many have asked if we should be concerned that of late a few scholars and Torah-learned people have risen up to object in all cases to the women's custom of reciting blessings on time-bound positive commandments, and they are publicly expounding on and teaching this message . . . [ellipsis in original].

. . . [O]ur rabbi Ḥatam Sofer[138] previously wrote (Yoreh Deʿah section 19) that one should not rush to create a new prohibition, for the custom of Israel constitutes Torah. . . .

. . . [M]y renown and my glory consist in not venturing even a hairsbreadth beyond the bounds set by Rema [Rabbi Moshe Isserles] (to paraphrase the Ḥatam Sofer's words in [his responsa] Even Ha-Ezer section 151), and our rabbi Rema ruled that they [women] recite a blessing . . . [ellipsis in original]. . . . Even regarding our brothers, the Sephardim, though Beit Yosef ruled in the Shulḥan Arukh that they should not recite a blessing, note that in Birkei Yosef, after going against the elders [by saying that they should not recite the blessing, Ḥida] brings a lasting edifice for the custom of reciting a blessing over the lulav from the Responsa from the Heavens . . . [ellipsis in original]. So, too, [Ḥida] ruled explicitly in his work, Yosef Ometz. . . .

. . . [A] doctrine (torah) emerges that the custom of women to recite a blessing over time-bound positive commandments, in particular over the lulav, follows the will of the sages, even among our brothers the Sephardim. And acceptance and custom are the pillars of instruction. . . .

. . . Of course, his whole responsa comes to challenge what I brought to light with the help of the heavens, words that were justified from every direction, words of good sense and knowledge. . . .

Regarding what he wrote, that his renown and his glory are in not venturing even a hairsbreadth beyond the bounds set by Rema. Behold, one who examines . . . what I wrote in my book, Yabiʿa Omer volume 1 (nos. 39: 7 and 40: 13) will see that in fact the genius Ḥakham Tzvi[139] . . . would regularly instruct women not to recite a blessing on time-bound positive commandments. . . . Behold, some of the geniuses of Ashkenaz saw fit to put an end to this practice, even though it had already spread throughout their countries for generations. In any event, we have not gone so far as to call on Ashkenazic women to stop reciting a bless-

138. [See part 3, especially the selections from Moshe Sofer.]

139. [Tzvi Hirsch ben Yaʿakov Ashkenazi (active in Salonika, Constantinople, Germany, Amsterdam, England, Poland; 1656–1718).]

ing over the lulav. Our sole purpose is to silence those few [Sephardic] women who on their own began reciting a blessing, in opposition to the ruling of Maimonides and of our master [Karo]. And even though the practice of reciting a blessing has now spread robustly, following the opinion of the Ḥida, we must restore the former glory (le-haḥzir atara le-yoshnah) and follow Maimonides and our master, whose instruction we have accepted for ourselves....

Thus, our purpose is not to instruct Ashkenazic women to do the opposite of what Rema instructed, such that [Rabbi Waldenberg] would need to write, "his renown and his glory are in not venturing beyond the bounds set by the Rema." Our purpose is to instruct Sephardic women (who, as attested to by the elder sages of the Ḥida's time, did so unknowingly) to once more follow the teaching of Maimonides and of our master [Karo], and not recite blessings in vain in opposition to Maimonides and to our master whose rulings we have accepted for ourselves. And from my elders I have gained understanding that this is not the custom as established by the sages and rabbis of Jerusalem, [God's] beautiful city, and they are not acting in keeping with the wishes of the sages....

(In truth, it is quite possible that even those Ashkenazic geniuses who uphold the practice of the Rema only do so in their own cities and in the public places of their communities, for they must follow the master of the place (mara de-atra). But this is not the case for Ashkenazic women who come to settle in the Land of Israel, which is considered the place of Maimonides and of our master [Karo] because here [the people] have accepted [the] instruction [of these authorities] for themselves. One could suggest that the women must abandon their custom and refrain from reciting a blessing on time-bound positive commandments. For according to the opinion of our rabbis, who in Israel have the status of the master of the place, this would be a blessing recited in vain.... It could be that even Ḥatam Sofer, who does not stray at all from the path of Rema, would acknowledge that in the Land of Israel women must follow our master, who is the master of the place....)

On the contrary, one should turn his argument on its head [literally, "toward the tail"] and question our friend the rabbi, may he be distinguished with a long, good life, how could he provide instruction (le-horot halakhah) to Sephardic women that runs counter to the opinion of Maimonides and of our master [Karo], instructing them to recite what would be blessings made in vain.... [I]n the responsa of Mahari Faraji[140] (no. 59, page 54a) he wrote that in our region,

---

140. [Ya'akov al-Faraji (Alexandria, seventeenth century).]

where we follow the rulings of our master, who is the master of the place, his teachings are established like an undisputed law taught to Moses at Sinai, even if many dispute his ruling [in a particular instance]. And anyone who diverges from his teachings, even from a lenient ruling to a strict one, it is considered like diverging from the laws of the Torah and he has degraded his rabbi's honor. . . .

This being the case, why does the fact that they are publicly advocating to restore the former glory displease [Waldenberg] . . . , is it out of bias? Especially regarding the prohibition to recite a blessing in vain, which is so serious that we even override our master [Karo] and rule not to recite a blessing in case of doubt, how could these women recite a blessing in vain contrary to the rulings of Maimonides and of our master, whose words we have accepted as if they were law taught to Moses at Sinai? "Does he mean to ravish the queen in my own palace?"[141] And note that regarding what our friend the rabbi prides himself on, namely that he does not venture even a hairsbreadth beyond the bounds set by the Rema, he is not speaking precisely, may his honorable Torah eminence forgive me. For behold, Rema in *Darkhei Moshe* (section 589: 2) wrote, "although we do not object when women recite a blessing over a time-bound positive commandment, still it would be better for them not to recite a blessing," as Tur wrote in section 17, that it is better for them not to recite a blessing. . . .

 . . . [Waldenberg's] further argument, following the opinion of the Ḥatam Sofer, that "one should not rush to create a new prohibition, for the custom of Israel constitutes Torah," is very puzzling. Should a law explicitly found in Maimonides and the decisors and ruled by our master [Karo] in the *Shulḥan Arukh* be categorized as creating a new prohibition? That is very strange. Regarding his comment that "the custom of Israel constitutes Torah" (referring to Tosafot [on] b. Menaḥot 20b), the genius the author of *Ḥikrei Lev*[142] wrote in his responsa *Smikha le-Ḥayyim* (Yoreh De'ah no. 4, page 23a): "It seems to me that custom is of no use in resolving a dispute between the decisors. Only customs that are known to have spread from the days of the rabbis of old have the power to resolve a dispute among the early authorities. But in our generation, with the diminution of our hearts, we do not have the power to resolve disputes other than by deciding the rule according to the majority. . . ."

 . . . .

As for me, I will stand on my watch, to affirm the words of our master [Karo],

141. [Esth 7:8.]
142. [Rabbi Yosef Rafael ben Ḥayyim Ḥazzan (born in Izmir, 1741–1819).]

whose instruction we have accepted for ourselves. For anyone who dissociates [himself] from him, it is as if he is dissociating [himself] from life. As Rema wrote about him in his responsa (no. 48), "anyone who disputes him, it is as if he disputes the Heavenly Presence." . . . Whoever puts an end to the practice of women reciting a blessing over the lulav, may the blessing of the genius, author of *Nehpah Bakesef*, be fulfilled through him. . . .

Ovadiah Yosef
A pure Sephardi

V | Jewish Feminist Views of Law

In her 1982 essay, "The Right Question is Theological," the Jewish feminist theologian Judith Plaskow (b. 1947) urged her readers to move away from discrete questions about the compatibility of Jewish law and feminism and to turn instead to the theological premises of Jewish law as such. According to Plaskow, "women's Otherness is far more basic than the laws in which it [this otherness] finds expression."[1] Plaskow's essay spurred feminist Jewish thinkers to raise anew the question of what Jewish law is. And in doing so, those thinkers—Liberal and Orthodox alike—reconsider a number of the strategies for describing the nature of Jewish law found in the first four parts of this volume.

Not all of the thinkers included in this part agree with Plaskow that the right question is theological per se, though they all agree that the difficulties of reconciling aspects of gender egalitarianism with Jewish law are rooted in ideology. In different ways, the selections that constitute this part all reject the broad claim, made by some Ultra-Orthodox and religious Zionist thinkers included in parts 3 and 4, that specific changes to Jewish law ought to be adjudicated according to the perceived corrosive effects of secular values on an otherwise pure Jewish legal system. Three of the four feminist thinkers included in part 5 (Rachel Adler, Tamar Ross, and Ronit Irshai) also oppose, though at times for different reasons, two widespread—at times overlapping and at other times competing—modern claims about the nature of Jewish law: first, that it should be described in positivist terms (that is, as a realm wholly distinct from politics, morality, and theology), and second, that the dynamics of Jewish law are best portrayed in formalist terms (that is, in terms of an internally coherent and self-generating system). In contrast, Tova Hartman, while sharing Adler's, Ross's, and Irshai's rejection of what all four argue

---

1. Judith Plaskow, "The Right Question Is Theological," in *On Being a Jewish Feminist: A Reader*, edited by Susannah Heschel (New York: Schocken, 1983), 224.

is ideologically based opposition to egalitarianism by various members of the rabbinic establishment, describes Jewish law in positivist terms.

While the four feminist thinkers differ in some of their assumptions and conclusions, they all emphasize the stories or narratives that underlie and constitute legal systems. The late American legal theorist Robert Cover's seminal essay "Nomos and Narrative," an excerpt of which is included in part 1, has provided an important conceptual framework and starting point for Jewish feminist philosophers of law as well as for thinking about gender and sexuality more generally in Jewish law.[2]

2. Robert Cover, "Nomos and Narrative," *Harvard Law Review* 97, no. 4 (1983): 4–68. On the use of Cover's framework in contemporary Jewish arguments about gender and sexuality, see Gordon Tucker's 2006 dissent from the Conservative Movement's Committee on Jewish Law and Standards ("*Derosh ve-Kabel Sekhar*: Halakhic and Metahalakhic Arguments Concerning Judaism and Homosexuality," accessed January 23, 2017, www .rabbinicalassembly.org/sites/default/files/public/halakhah/teshuvot/20052010/tucker _homosexuality.pdf). For recent work that contextualizes the thinkers included in this section, see Yonatan Y. Brafman, "New Developments in Modern Jewish Thought: From Theology to Law and Back Again," in *The Cambridge Companion to Judaism and Law*, edited by Christine Hayes (New York: Cambridge University Press, 2017); David Ellenson, "To Reshape the World: Interpretation, Renewal, and Feminist Approaches to Jewish Law and Legal Ruling in America and Israel," *Journal of Religious Ethics* 2, no. 2 (2016): 38–63.

35

Rachel Adler, *Engendering Judaism:*
An Inclusive Theology and Ethics

Rachel Adler (b. 1943) has long been associated with the Reform movement's Los Angeles campus of the Hebrew Union College–Jewish Institute of Religion. She argues that liberal Jews need Jewish law and that Jewish law, far from being the sole possession of Orthodoxy, needs liberal Jews to reimagine it. In describing her proactive, liberal, and feminist approach, Adler criticizes classical Jewish law and previous liberal attempts to reform it. In their place she maintains that halakhah as such is not mere rules and procedures but a comprehensive life world. Drawing on Robert Cover's conception of the dynamic tension between what he calls law's twin imperialistic and paidaic, or jurisgenerative, functions, Adler stresses the latter function and argues that new narratives create new norms. In this context, she suggests that liberal Jewish communities, in imagining new Jewish worlds, can and should be halakhic communities. As such, they might even act as an impetus for more traditionalist forms of Judaism to reimagine themselves.

Rachel Adler, *Engendering Judaism: An Inclusive Theology and Ethics*
(Boston: Beacon, 1999), 21–22, 25–30, 34–35, 38–39, and 46–48.

. . . Halakhah comes from the root HLKh, to walk or to go. Halakhah is the act of going forward, of making one's way. A halakhah, a path making, translates the stories, and values of Judaism into ongoing action. That makes it an integral component, not merely of Orthodoxy, but of any kind of Judaism. Such a definition of halakhah breaks the traditionalist monopoly on the word halakhah. . . .

. . . To determine where we ought to go, we must reflect on where we have been. We do this best by storytelling. As individuals, we continually rework and relate our life stories to ourselves and to others and project ourselves into possible futures through dreams and fantasies. We also lay claim as members of groups to the collective memories of the group. Transmitted from generation to generation, they help to constitute our sense of who we are and to shape our future actions. . . .

Halakhah belongs to liberal Jews no less than to Orthodox Jews because the stories of Judaism belong to us all. A halakhah is a communal praxis grounded in Jewish stories. . . .

A praxis is more than the sum of the various practices that constitute it. A praxis *is a Judaic embodiment in action at a particular time of the values and commitments inherent to a particular story.* Orthodoxy cannot have a monopoly on halakhah, because no form of Judaism can endure without one; there would be no way to live it out.

What happened to Judaism in modernity was that its praxis became both impoverished and fragmented. . . .

A contemporary Jewish praxis would reduce our sense of fragmentation. If we had a praxis rather than a grab bag of practices, we would experience making love, making *kiddush*,[3] recycling paper used at our workplace, cooking a pot of soup for a person with AIDS, dancing at a wedding, and making medical treatment decisions for a dying loved one as integrated parts of the same project: the holy transformation of our everyday reality. . . .

We cannot simply resurrect the old premodern praxis, because it no longer fits us in the world we now inhabit. Some of its elements are fundamentally incompatible with participation in postindustrial, democratic societies. . . .

The secular values of equal respect, inclusivity, diversity, and pluralism obligate citizens to recognize and protect one another's integrity and well-being. Jews have obvious cause to espouse these values. At the same time, classical halakhah is committed to the subordination and exclusion of women in communal life. The inability of classical halakhah to resolve this dissonance is the paradigmatic example of its inadequacy as a praxis for Jews in modernity. . . .

. . . The feminist critique of them [halakhic practices and categories] is restated as "women's desire for equal access or equal obligation" and pasted onto a basically intact halakhic system, like a Band-Aid covering a superficial cut. . . .

The problems actually raised in the feminist critique, however, are *systemic* wounds too deep for liberal Band-Aids. . . .

. . . To argue that the system requires no systemic critique, a liberal halakhist must ignore or discount [the facts] that halakhic rules, categories, and precedents were constructed and applied without the participation of women, that they reflect perceptions of women as a commodified subclass, and that they are often inadequate or inimical to concerns that women themselves possibly would raise if they were legal subjects rather than legal objects. . . .

. . . The two philosophies of jurisprudence that liberal halakhists have adopted as theoretical grounding for this project are legal formalism and legal realism.

3. [The blessing over wine to sanctify the day on Shabbat and the festivals.]

Legal formalism asserts that what is definitive about law is its form. A legal outcome is valid if the system's rules and categories are correctly applied. Because the rules and categories that constitute the law's form are taken as givens about which there can be no argument, a formalist approach makes an end-run around questions about the sociohistorical contexts these forms may reflect. The only possible arguments concern whether the formal applications are valid or invalid. . . .

Legal realism, a theory of jurisprudence influential during the first half of the twentieth century, maintains that law is determined not by the language of legal texts and enactments but rather by the discretionary power of judges. This power, the legal realists have argued, is appropriately employed to shape social policy. The judge's decisions are "realistic" because they adopt the law to address social realities. The problem with legal realism is its tendency to reinforce the power of the already powerful. If the wording or intent of legal texts or the existence of legal precedents does not present curbs or boundaries for judicial decisions, the discretionary power of judges will be unrestrained. Given that [rabbinic] decisors are chosen by the dominant group, who is likely to be selected to wield power, and whose social investments do such persons protect?

Versions of liberal halakhah attempt to synthesize these apparently antithetical theories, one radically atemporal and the other radically context-dependent, because both are essential to the liberal project. What the theories have in common is that each offers a means of overriding the component of jurisprudence that is most resistant to change: the power of precedent. In tandem, the two theories serve to authorize and to derive changes that run counter to all legal precedent. Legal realism allows the decisor to predetermine the outcomes he or she deems most appropriate to the time and place. Legal formalism provides the means to validate those outcomes as long as the categories are tenably applied. . . .

. . . The place to begin is not with the principles we need to preserve or the content we may need to adapt but with what we mean by halakhah altogether. An understanding of law that lends itself to such a project can be found in the work of an American legal theorist, Robert Cover . . . [, who] offers a basis upon which feminist hermeneutics, praxis, and commitments can make defensible claims to authenticity.

Law is not reducible to formal lawmaking, Cover maintains, because it is generated by a *nomos*, a universe of meanings, values, and rules, embedded in stories.[4] A nomos is not a body of data to master and adapt, but a world to inhabit. Knowing how to live in a nomic world means being able to envision the possibilities implicit in its stories and norms and being willing to live some of them out in praxis.

Cover characterizes the genesis and the maintenance of law as two distinct elements in legal development. He calls these the *paidaic* or world-creating mode and the *imperial* or world-maintaining mode. Paidaic activity effects *jurisgenesis*, the creation of a nomos, a universe of meaning, out of a shared body of precepts and narratives that individuals in [a] community commit themselves to learn and to interpret. This generative mode is unstable and impermanent, but without its creative and revitalizing force, societies could not sustain the sense of meaning and shared purpose essential to social survival.

The paidaic mode can create worlds, but it cannot maintain them. Inevitably, the single unified vision that all social actors share in a paidaic period splinters into multiple nomic worlds holding differing interpretations. To coordinate and maintain these diverse worlds within a coexistent whole, there is a need to enforce standard social practices among them. The imperial mode universalizes the norms created by jurisgenesis and empowers institutions to reinforce them by coercion, if necessary. However, institutionalization and coercion are not the only means by which the imperial mode maintains the stability of law. Because the imperial world view does not strive for unanimity, but harmonious coordination of its differing parts, it can admit as an adaptive mechanism some tolerance for pluralism, a value foreign to the paidaic ethos. Cover imagines these two legal moments, the paidaic and the imperial, coexisting in dynamic equilibrium....

...Ultimately, law is maintained or remade not by orthodoxies or visions but by commitments of communities either to obey the law as it stands or to resist and reject it in order to live out some alternative legal vision....

...Feminist scholars of law and philosophy have pioneered in using narrative both as a method of vision and as a tool of legal and philosophical critique....

...Because narratives testify so powerfully to the impact of context, they are capable of reflecting the context-bound nature of human existence more accurately than abstract theories that claim to express truths unrestricted by time and place.

Contexts narrow the range of possibilities in narratives and provide bound-

4. [See the selection by Cover in part 1.]

aries for both history and fiction. At the same time, because contexts are conditional rather than inevitable, there is always a possibility of bursting their boundaries, of breaking and remaking contexts. The mutability of contexts is related to the capacity for change in human beings themselves. Human beings in their contexts create the need and the potential for structural transformations....

"Perhaps what distinguishes feminist Judaism from traditional rabbinic Judaism," [Judith] Plaskow concludes, "is not so much the absence of law in the former as a conception of rule making as a shared communal process."[5] All that Plaskow lacks is a frame of reference in which she can identify this feminist lawmaking as the inception of a legitimate and authoritative halakhic process. This is where the work of Robert Cover is so helpful. Not only for feminists, but for all moderns who cherish democratic values, lawmaking requires a communal component. Cover reminds us that all law, including rabbinic law itself, originates in a paidaic community. Its understandings as embodied and institutionalized in the law are revised and revitalized when they are challenged by interpretive communities claiming a place in it....

... [U]sing Cover's framework, so-called nonhalakhic groups are more properly identified as incipient paidaic communities attempting to establish differing nomic visions. The norms they establish for living out the implications of the poems and stories they create will be a halakhah.

... [T]he fears feminist theologians express about the dangerous precedents for oppression in halakhah seem to be counterbalanced by an acknowledgment that halakhah also cannot be easily dismissed. Any authentic modern Jewish theology has to account for the norms and praxis of Judaism. Our task, then, is to engender a Jewish tradition for modernity that would inform and be informed by a diverse but unified communal praxis and an inclusive, pluralistic communal discourse rooted in Jewish narratives.

5. Judith Plaskow, *Standing Again at Sinai* (New York: HarperOne, 1990), 71.

After a long and distinguished career, Tamar Ross (b. 1938) retired from Bar Ilan University's Department of Philosophy, but she continues to teach at religious institutions in Israel. Along with her interest in Jewish feminist theology, Ross is committed to a theology of ongoing revelation for which she draws inspiration largely from the thought of Abraham Isaac Kook. In the selection included here, Ross argues that the dynamism of narrative should always be balanced by the constraints and cohesion reflected in a commitment to divine transcendence, the consensus of Jewish legal decisors, and the Orthodox community's commitment to Jewish law. Ross turns to Hans-Georg Gadamer's hermeneutics of tradition, which she argues appropriately describes the simultaneously dynamic yet conserving dimensions of life committed to Jewish law. Because Modern Orthodox women participate in the language game of Jewish law and tradition, they are, Ross avers, best situated to develop a Judaism that integrates feminism and Jewish law.

Tamar Ross, *Expanding the Palace of Torah: Orthodoxy and Feminism* (Waltham, MA: Brandeis University Press, 2004), 155–58, 160–1, 167, 169–70, and 174.

. . . [Rachel] Adler's plan for concentrating upon community as a primary source of halakhic development has promise. But . . . it is not enough for would-be reformers simply to invoke a new redemptive vision via an alternative reading of canonized texts, and then hope it will be accepted if they live it out in practice. Adler's rejection of positivism and its assumption of law's determinate meaning fails to take into account that complete interpretive freedom is never available. For one thing, there are certain inherent constraints that are built into any legal system as such. . . . [I]f a new narrative is to have any effect on the larger community of the halakhically committed, it must be capable of engaging with the sensibilities and interpretive traditions of the chief players within the system. The moderating influence of these factors is especially powerful in the case of legal systems, such as the halakhah, that also bear religious claims. . . .

Any interpretation must contend with certain existing frames of reference in order to qualify as relevant and worthy of consideration in the eyes of the traditionalist. Irrespective of more specific and substantive considerations of content, three elements are indispensable: appeal to the consensus of experts, solidarity with the larger community in which the transformative narrative is to be played out, and acknowledgment of the law's claims to transcendence....

...Aside from his greater proficiency, such a scholar [a rabbinic decisor] has a global view of the system, enabling him to make sure that his decision will cohere holistically and "fit" according to some conception of the law. The component of piety (*yirat shamayim*) that has been traditionally regarded as a necessary attribute of the halakhic decisor lends an added dimension of religious weight and earnestness to halakhic deliberation that distinguishes it from ordinary legal discussion. This added weight is another reason that those who seek to observe the law in a religious context often prefer to turn to an authority figure in order to ensure that their final decisions are free from illegitimate forms of self-interest....

...[W]hile Adler's narrative relates in richly imaginative ways to the sacred texts..., [h]er project's most glaring flaw is its lack of appeal to transcendence as a source of legitimacy for its new interpretation....

...Community (unlike God) does not demand total devotion....

...[H]alakhically committed Jews stand in desperate need of a contemporary understanding of revelation that will accommodate the following two requisites: (1) ability to acknowledge with a maximum of intellectual integrity the degree to which the Torah is formulated in a time- and culture-bound social mold; and (2) the ability to assert that this same Torah is nevertheless the voice of God speaking to us, with every word of that voice equally holy and indispensable, even finding theological meaning in the fact that our sacred and revered texts have been bound to androcentric premises....

...[M]ore substance is required to fill in the gaps that Adler leaves between real and ideal. Her attempt to affect authentic halakhic change is stymied by the lack of a method that could enable her external criticism to be assimilated in terms of the halakhah's own internal language, standards, and procedures....

What emerges from [Hans-Georg] Gadamer's insights is that admitting to the role of subjectivity in interpretation does not mean that the reader is free to interpret the text however he likes.[6] Rather, he already finds himself in the

6. [In her discussion of Gadamer, Ross refers throughout to Hans-Georg Gadamer, *Truth and Method*, translated by Garrett Barden and John. Cumming (New York: Seabury, 1975).]

beliefs and opinions that enable discovery of a text's meaning as something that derives necessarily from the general sociopolitical context in which he and the words take part. Because it is impossible to separate the broader cultural baggage the individual reader brings to reading the text and his own understanding, he is never entirely free to "impose" meaning upon the text in a manner that ignores the burden of his interpretive tradition. This limitation derives necessarily from the general sociopolitical context in which he and the words take part. Interpreters always "see" from within their context because no other way of seeing exists. This explains why certain interpretations in certain periods and circumstances appear perfectly plausible, yet are utterly implausible in another setting. Thus the hermeneutic process, according to Gadamer, is neither objective nor subjective. It is rather the combined product of the reader, the tradition of established conventions that he brings with him to the text, and the power of the text to delimit and guide his interpretive quest. . . .

. . . This appreciation for the constraining influences of interpretive traditions sits well with the classic ideal of the Torah student who, although not a passive recipient, both molds and is molded by the divine word and its multi-layered interpretive tradition. It also comports with the weightier attitude of respect for all opinions that is fostered by the rabbinic notion of the divine word's all-inclusiveness, as opposed to the random and free-wheeling choices of postmodernism. It is the Torah that must absorb the world rather than the world the Torah, and it is the skill of its adherents in doing so, in a manner that is coherent in their eyes with its existing network of beliefs and practices, that constitutes its vitality. Tradition must function as the ever-present lens through which halakhah views the contingencies of contemporary experiences as they arise rather than seeing them as an object of inquiry whose religiously significant or literal meaning is located in some fixed and objective standard either within or outside itself. . . .

. . . When Orthodox women speak to the existing establishment from within a specified set of common interests and concerns, they would like to assume that the halakhic establishment will hear their words. They profess a common language due to a manifest level of formal agreement regarding the authority of individual rules and values and the procedures for applying them. Employing this level of discourse, women attempt to "demonstrate" or "prove" that certain strategies of interpretation are acceptable and halakhic solutions possible. . . .

Men interacting with women living out an alternative narrative are forced to experience the same sense of dissonance that the women themselves feel when they encounter equality of opportunity and status in the everyday secular sphere and discrimination in the synagogue and other communal religious institutions. It is this anomaly that creates the environment for the "correctness" of a different reading of the legal sources. On this level of influence, the power of Orthodox women is not in constituting an external force that influences the religious establishment or the community at large simply by appealing to its authoritative bodies or engaging them on their terms. Rather, it lies in the fact that such women situate the interpretation of halakhah in a particular context by living out their new vision while still remaining part of the community. In this way they play an instrumental role in determining how interpretation will go. . . .

A specialist in gender studies, religion, and psychology, Tova Hartman (b. 1957) taught at Bar Ilan University before joining the law faculty of Kiryat Ono Academic College, in Jerusalem. In the selections included here, Hartman provides a gender-critical reading of a number of twentieth-century rabbinic responsa to women's efforts to attain equality within Jewish law, including Abraham Isaac Kook's responsum concerning women's voting. She detects an eschewal of "halakhic" arguments for "meta-halakhic" arguments that share in the rhetoric of patriarchical backlash against the articulation by women of their own needs and desires. In contrast to both Rachel Adler and Tamar Ross, Hartman is thus committed to the claim that it is both possible and necessary to distinguish halakhah, which she regards as legitimate in adjudicating questions of egalitarianism, from nonhalakhic or meta-halakhic arguments, which she regards as illegitimate in these debates.

Tova Hartman, *Feminism Encounters Traditional Judaism: Resistance and Accommodation* (Waltham, MA: Brandeis University Press, 2007), 101–2, 106–15, and 118.

In the early twentieth century, as liberal democracies throughout the world faced the issue of women's suffrage, the Jews of pre-state Israel were engaged in this conversation in their own localized terms: their debate included the question of whether women could hold public office.[7] ...

... Rav [Abraham Isaac] Kook categorizes women's suffrage as something foreign to Jewish tradition and the values it represents, locating it definitively "outside."[8] ...

It is this broad societal concern that preoccupies Rav Kook most deeply ...

[Kook] implicitly—but very clearly—casts as collaborators and accomplices to these enemies [of the Jewish people] any and all who might support, even unintentionally, their insidious agenda. Those promoting greater participation for women in public life—those claiming that women should be able to vote,

7. [For some of these arguments, see part 4.]
8. [See the selection by Kook in part 4.]

and/or hold public office—fall in perforce with this unsavory crew, standing in brazen opposition not only to Israel's covenantal past but to its existential present and national future. . . .

In the late 1970s, a group of women defining themselves as "Modern Orthodox" took the then-radical step of establishing all-women's prayer groups. Two prominent rabbis, Meir Twersky and Moshe Meiselman, responded with a litany of objections.[9] . . . As with Rav Kook, the halakhic discussion is a jumping-off point for an intriguing, complex discourse treating the cultural ideology of these authority figures vis-à-vis religious women's appropriate, sanctioned roles and the necessity of maintaining them. The proposed change is delegitimized and deemed dangerous to communal continuity, its proponents' motivations are called into question, and they themselves demonized by comparison with well-known upstarts (idolators, Eve)—all exclusively metahalakhic arguments. . . .

. . . Invoking the extrahalakhic principle of building legal fences to mitigate against possible *eventual* violation of the law, [Twersky] invokes the ominous and necessarily vague discourse of the "slippery slope." The danger of greater women's participation in this instance is no halakhic violation per se, but rather its potential to form a link in a causal chain leading to un-halakhic behavior at some unspecified future point—a chain of events whose culmination is nothing short of catastrophic. . . .

R[abbi] Meiselman . . . arrives at the same conclusion as Twersky via a different, even opposite, tack. Women's prayer groups, he claims, have no clear halakhic status and as such are spiritually meaningless. . . . Meiselman's line of argument commits him to a view of prayer that runs counter to a long tradition of contemplative and ecstatic Jewish practitioners whose prayer is offered outside of the sanctioned minyan.[10] . . . Even on its surface, it is a strange argument: if women's prayer groups have no halakhic significance, then why should its [sic] performance be considered a halakhic issue? What threat can an act of no significance pose? . . .

The last few years have witnessed other examples of Orthodox women's increased participation in public life . . . [such as] the centuries-old custom of

9. [Hartman refers to Mayer Twersky, "Halakhic Values and Halakhic Decisions: Rav Soloveitchik's *Pesak* Regarding Women's Prayer Groups," *Tradition* 32, no. 3 (1998): 5–18; Moshe Meiselman, "The Rav, Feminism and Public Policy: An Insider's Overview," *Tradition* 33, no. 1 (1998): 5–30.]

10. [A minyan is a group of ten (traditionally male) Jews that make up a quorum for certain ritual purposes.]

publicly reading the wedding contract (*ketubah*), an ancient Aramaic document. ... Orthodox women, seeking areas in which to increase participation without violating Halakhah, have begun to read the *ketubah*. ...

... [Rabbi Hershel] Schachter ... makes a rhetorical move that he repeats several times: "Yes, even if a *parrot or monkey* would read the *ketubah*, the marriage would be one hundred percent valid."[11] Schachter's invocation of parrots and monkeys—natural mimics that imitate human speech and activity without any consciousness of what they are doing—is ostensibly technical. ...

Notwithstanding the ritual's irrelevance, Schachter goes on to develop a comprehensive and insistent metahalakhic argument for why women should refrain from reading the *ketubah* under the wedding canopy. In order to do this, he draws Jewish tradition down a single, simple axis:

> All people were created [in the image of God], and the Torah has instructed each of us to preserve his [Godly image] [bracketed text in original]. One aspect of [Godliness] [bracketed text in original] is the fact that God is a "Hidden God," He always prefers to hide (in private). Therefore, we assume that part of our mitzvah of preserving our (Godly image) is for all of us to lead private lives.[12]

Based on this speculative, contingent principle regarding the importance of leading "private lives"—no more than an assumption, and only "part" of the much larger (by definition infinite) endeavor of *Imitatio Dei*—Schachter draws sweeping conclusions about ritual life and women's place in it (and, primarily, out of it). He does not acknowledge any inconsistency between the blanket inclusiveness of his verdict—to say nothing of its binding force—and his own admission regarding the highly provisional character of his claim. ...

Taken broadly, the discourse of backlash can be reduced to an exhortation for women to remain in the private sphere. ... Collectively, the array of rhetorical strategies these rabbis employ—defining the desire for anything beyond the status quo as foreign and dangerous to tradition, attacking the motivations of those petitioning for such change, associating them with classic cultural villains, and defining them as enemies of Jewish stability and continuity—all point to one cultural fact: the only way for the community to survive is for women's roles not to change. ...

11. [Hartman refers to Herschel Schachter's 2004 "Can Women Be Rabbis?" (accessed January 23, 2017, www.torahweb.org/torah/2004/parsha/rsch_dvorim2.html).]

12. [See ibid.]

. . . If these traditional roles are viewed as indispensable to maintaining cultural stability, political viability, and the word of God, then any change, however seemingly innocuous, is every bit as radical and threatening as the rabbis claim. The need to articulate this threat, and to do so as stridently and compellingly as possible only arises from the need to squelch it; that the threat has arisen already bespeaks a destabilization of the status quo.

Ronit Irshai, "Toward a Gender Critical Approach to the Philosophy of Jewish Law (Halakhah)"

A student of Tamar Ross, Ronit Irshai (b. 1965) teaches gender studies and Jewish law at Bar Ilan and the Hebrew Universities. Building on while also moving beyond the work of Rachel Adler, Ross, Tova Hartman, and Robert Cover, Irshai rejects the notion that Jewish law is a closed system that must rely on its internal rules and processes. To make this case, she proposes looking to the values that underlie Jewish law. She suggests that instead of moving only from the direction of narrative to nomos, Jewish feminists must also move from nomos to narrative. In particular, Irshai considers what she calls the "pronatalist" tendency of rabbinic discourse and asks how this tendency can be balanced with a more egalitarian approach to individual autonomy, which is a value that is strongly endorsed in other Modern Orthodox debates about Jewish law.

Ronit Irshai, "Toward a Gender Critical Approach to the Philosophy of Jewish Law (Halakhah)," *Feminist Studies in Religion* 26, no. 2 (2010): 61–62, 67–72, and 75–76.

. . . I do not disagree with [Rachel] Adler, [Tamar] Ross, or [Tova] Hartman in finding that the halakhic problem is firmly rooted in more deep-seated theological or ideological concepts, but I believe that Judaism's legalistic character suggests a "reversal of course." Yes, let us work with the "narrative," which can generate a new nomos, and let us carry on a theological or ideological analysis of the feasibility of introducing feminist concepts into Jewish thought; but let us also work with the nomos itself in order to create, within the religious world, a new narrative. Given that Jewish norms shape Jewish theology more than the converse, I believe it is direct engagement with halakhah, rather than engagement with theology, that can exert the greater influence on normative views of the world. In the spirit of Robert Cover, we can say that nomos and narrative are inseparably interdependent, but nomos should be seen not only as grounded in narrative but also as creating and influencing narrative. . . .

An important way in which women situated simultaneously inside and outside the system can promote the development of a gender critical approach to the philosophy of halakhah is by creating "alternative halakhic stories." By that I do not mean the proposing of local halakhic solutions to one or another problem that women face. I am not seeking the halakhic tools that can be used to effectuate desired change in a specific halakhic matter (though I of course do not deny the importance of such local solutions). An "alternative halakhic story" is much wider and comprises two elements:

1. Creating a halakhic genealogy with the goal of uncovering the hidden values or moral paradigms on which halakhic rulings related to women rely and the exegetical tactics and the rhetoric that have been used to generate the prevailing hegemonic story. Doing so would pave the way to creating a different halakhic genealogy, based on the same sources but with different predispositions.

2. Proposing a preference for halakhic principles that can overcome halakhic rules that fail to produce gender justice for women.

. . . [H]alakhic genealogy unfolds the legal background of the hegemonic halakhic story and provides examples of how certain links in the chain have been forgotten, how the genealogical continuity presented by the hegemonic story is not necessarily the only one possible. It therefore has a liberating effect and therapeutic value as well, freeing us in particular from the illusion of necessity, that is, from the view that no other verdict could possibly have been formulated.

To illustrate, let us consider contemporary halakhic rulings concerning fertility issues. If we examine trends within those rulings in light of halakhic genealogy, we find something quite interesting: in all matters related to abortion and contraception, the signal tendency is one of stringency, while in matters related to modern artificial fertility, the decisions tend to be extremely lenient. In other words, sex without procreation is treated strictly; procreation without sex is treated leniently, on the premise that reproduction at almost any cost is the preferred value. What can account for this pronatalist tendency? Multiple explanations have been offered, but I believe they must be supplemented by an understanding of the gender-related issues that underlie the ideology reflected in the decisions. In my judgment, a latent concept of gender that defines women and femininity with reference to women's biological functions constitutes a necessary (though not sufficient) condition for this trend. This concept does not regard woman as an "end in itself" (in the Kantian sense); rather, it sees her primarily in her reproductive role—as a means.

. . . Is it possible to create an "alternative halakhic story" that will enable women to realize themselves as human beings with roles beyond the reproductive, even though the only justifications advanced in classical halakhah for limiting procreation were factors that took account of the interests of men, not of women?

The halakhic genealogy of this subject suggests, I believe, that the foregoing questions can be answered affirmatively. For example, we can see that the ongoing tension between a man's duty to fulfill the commandment to procreate and his duty to study Torah was almost always resolved in favor of Torah study. Moreover, the need to make a living was considered, over the generations, to be a relevant and legitimate reason for limiting childbearing, even though today's hegemonic halakhic rhetoric rejects economic considerations as totally irrelevant and even disparages them as indicating a lack of faith in God. This tendency, of course, is harmful primarily to women, who are required to undergo frequent pregnancies and invest all their energies in childrearing, but it is far from being a necessary implication of halakhic sources, even though it is presented as such. . . .

Such a process will encounter resistance, given the clear and obvious "danger" that it might bring about radical changes in the structure of religious life. Indeed, we can already identify a typical sort of response, a tactic used effectively against efforts such as those I am proposing; and it seems to me that part of the critical project of the alternative halakhic story is to expose that tactic and publicly show it for what it is. I call this form of response "formalistic reductionism," by which I mean that whenever one identifies an effort to uncover the morally problematic value system implicit in halakhic rulings with respect to women, the conservative counterattack goes something like this: "You misunderstand entirely; it's entirely a formalistic matter, and questions of values, if one is concerned about them, are situated totally elsewhere." . . .

What this suggests is that the weapon of formalistic reduction does more than offer those who wield it theological benefits, allowing a return to the safe harbor of neutral objectivity without confronting disturbing moral issues and perhaps the need for change. In addition, it devalues women's efforts in the area at issue. If women want to worship in the masculine "style," that style becomes, on purely formalistic grounds, simultaneously unchangeable and less important (at least rhetorically: it is merely a halakhic requirement, not an expression of value).

It is clear as well that moving the focus of discussion to halakhic formalism closes the door to analysis and ultimately divests the halakhah of all moral significance. . . . [U]ncovering "formalistic reductionism" directs the community back to fundamental questions regarding the moral concepts that shape its religious world. Is the community prepared to accept this formalism as its overall religious philosophy? If not—and I assume that answer will be the one most often given—why accept it only as part of the counterattack against feminism? . . .

. . . [U]ncovering the problematic moral consciousness on which many halakhic rules rely will likely force the Modern Orthodox community to confront the question of why it continues to cooperate with that consciousness, even though it has managed, in certain areas, to find halakhic solutions that enable it to overcome similarly problematic situations. For example, the halakhic principle of "acting in the interests of peace" overcomes the arguably racist halakhic rule—a rule not applied—that forbids violating the Sabbath in order to care for a sick gentile. (There was no question that a sick Jew may be cared for.) In other words, Modern Orthodox society will have to account in a meaningful way for its inconsistencies: Why, when it is the dignity of women that is at stake, does it fail to apply halakhic principles that would allow for reasonable solutions? . . .

. . . [T]he success of the Orthodox feminist project depends in great measure on attaining that basic agreement on fundamental principles or moral values. And here I come full circle, returning to the alternative halakhic story I proposed earlier. The main goal of an alternative halakhic story is to present the moral values regarding women and gender justice on which there is a consensus within the Modern Orthodox community. By presenting the halakhic paradigms that are hidden beneath the surface of final halakhic rulings, we can impel many Modern Orthodox Jews to confront the basic premises they are unwittingly buying into when they accept those rulings—premises at odds with their shared values and that, as a practical matter, they likely reject in most areas of their lives. If we can show that there is no divide in the values, and that the distinction between how they are applied in the religious and secular dimensions of life is artificial, then the task will be made easier, for it will widen the circle of people within the halakhic community who will express their dissatisfaction with the status quo or will, at least, be troubled by it.

Index

piety, 241

pikuaḥ nefesh (principle of saving a life), 9, 88–90

Plaskow, Judith, 233, 239

political theology, xxx

politics, xxiv–xxv, xxvii–xxviii, 180–83

polygamy, 18

positive commandments, women's recitation of blessings over, 225–31

Positive-Historical Judaism, 24

Posthumous Writings (Geiger), 15–19

praxis, halakhah as, 235–36

prayer rites, changes to, 97–100

precedence, 121, 237. *See also* rabbinical courts

premodern era, Jewish legal theory in, xxiv–xxviii

priests (kohanim), 89, 110

Pri Ḥadash (New fruit, Hezekiah da Silva), 79, 100

prohibitions, 72–73, 80–81, 82

public transportation, on Sabbath, 213–15

Pufendorf, Samuel, xx, xxi

Ra'ah (Aharon ben Yosef of Barcelona), 151

Raavad (Abraham ben David of Posquières), 101, 193

Rabbinical Council of America, on military chaplaincies, 87

Rabbinical Court of Hamburg, 97–103

rabbinical courts, 99–101, 120–21, 171–74

rabbinic authority, as expertise, 140, 141

Ran (Nissim ben Reuven of Girona), 78, 135, 181, 188, 190

rape, 153

Rashba (Shlomo ben Aderet), 186n53, 188, 189

Rashi (Shlomo Yitzḥaki), 120, 138, 141, 147–48, 153, 166, 188

Rav (Abba Akiva), 142

Rava (Rabbi Abba ben Joseph ben Ḥama), 136, 148, 149

"Regarding Women's Recital of the Blessing over the Lulav . . ." (Yosef), 224–31

religion: as faith in the spiritual, 58–60; laws, relationship to, 33–34; religious subjectivity, 85–86; states and, 175–76. *See also* Judaism; Muslims

Religion of Reason out of the Sources of Judaism (Cohen), 29, 33–34

religious law: Spinoza's views of, xxvi. *See also* halakhah; Jewish law; Torah

"The Religious Significance of the State of Israel" (Leibowitz), 204–5

Rema. *See* Isserles, Moshe

resident aliens, 134–35, 190–94

Responsa of Maimonides (Maimonides), 105

revelation, xv, 20–21

"The Right Question is Theological" (Plaskow), 233

rights, as contracts, 31–32

rishonim (early authorities), 47, 50, 79, 149n128, 154, 166n11, 181

Roman law, 24–25

Ross, Tamar, 233, 240–43, 244, 248

Rousseau, Jean-Jacques, 30

sabbatical years, 161, 163, 164–71

Salanter, Yisrael (Lipkin), 44, 65–68

Samuel ben Meir (Rashbam), 17

Sanhedrin, 99, 100n20, 132, 163

Satmar Hasidism, 146

Savigny, Friedrich Carl von, xxii, xxiii, 24, 31n45, 58, 62–63n55

Schachter, Hershel, 246

Schlesinger, Akiva Yosef, 93, 108–15

Schmitt, Carl, xxx–xxxi

scientific theory of law (legal science), xxii–xxiii

Sefer Dor Revi'i (Fourth Generation, Glasner), 118–24

Sefer ha-Mizvot (Book of the Commandments, Maimonides), 16, 133

Sefer Ḥazon Ish: Zera'im (Karelitz), 133–39

Sefer Malki ba-Kodesh (My king, in the Sanctuary, Hirschensohn), 179, 182

self-consciousness, 30–32